To my dear friend

Anne

GRAMSCI AND CONTEMPORARY POLITICS

Beyond pessimism of the intellect

Can politics be both radical and realistic? This book is a collection of Anne Showstack Sassoon's writing which spans the major transitions from Thatcher and Reagan to Clinton and Blair; the collapse of communism to the regeneration of social democracy. Looking at the role of intellectuals in 'rethinking' politics, she argues that drawing from the past and broadening contemporary sources of political and academic knowledge can contribute to a grounded, radical hegemonic politics which can shape change.

Applying original interpretations of Antonio Gramsci's ideas on intellectuals, political language, civil society and political leadership, Anne Showstack Sassoon goes well beyond his framework to examine key contemporary political issues including citizenship, modernising the welfare state, and the relationship between parents and teachers. Informed by feminist debates, and reflecting on women's changing socio-economic roles, she argues that, particularly in periods of rapid change, the inconsistencies and contradictions of social change can produce valuable theoretical, and practical, insights.

Engaging with the radical claims of centre-left politics, this book brings together theoretical discussion with empirical and personal examples to suggest how to negotiate the difficult line between wishful thinking and weary fatalism in order to create the basis for widespread consent for political and social reforms. *Gramsci and Contemporary Politics: Beyond Pessimism of the Intellect* is aimed at students of politics, political and social theory, gender studies, and sociology.

Anne Showstack Sassoon's publications include *Gramsci's Politics,* and *Women and the State: The Shifting Boundaries of Public and Private.* She is Professor of Politics at Kingston University, UK.

ROUTLEDGE INNOVATIONS
IN POLITICAL THEORY

GRAMSCI AND CONTEMPORARY POLITICS

Beyond pessimism of the intellect

Anne Showstack Sassoon

London and New York

First published 2000
by Routledge
11 New Fetter Lane, London EC4P 4EE

Simultaneously published in the USA and Canada
by Routledge
29 West 35th Street, New York, NY 10001

Routledge is an imprint of the Taylor & Francis Group

© 2000 Anne Showstack Sassoon

Typeset in Times by
Exe Valley Dataset Ltd, Exeter, Devon

Printed and bound in Great Britain by
MPG Books Ltd, Bodmin

British Library Cataloguing in Publication Data
A catalogue record for this book is available from the British Library

Library of Congress Cataloging in Publication Data
Sassoon, Anne Showstack
Gramsci and contemporary politics: beyond pessimism of the
intellect / Anne Showstack Sassoon.
p.   cm. — (Routledge innovations in political theory: 4)
Includes bibliographical references (p.   ) and index.
1.   Gramsci, Antonio, 1891–1937 — Contributions in political
science.   2.   Political science — History — 20th century.   I.   Title.
II.   Series.
JC265.G68S26   1999
320.53'2'092 – – dc21   99–37055
                                                                 CIP

ISBN 0–415–16214–9

FOR MY FATHER,
NATHANIEL SHOWSTACK MD,
FOR HIS SENSE OF WONDER.

To see a World in a Grain of Sand,
And a Heaven in a Wild Flower,
Hold Infinity in the palm of your hand,
And Eternity in an hour.

From: 'Auguries of Innocence'
William Blake (1757–1827)

CONTENTS

1

FACING THE FUTURE, EVALUATING THE PAST

A collection of essays provides the occasion to revisit an intellectual and personal itinerary. Changes in political, social and economic contexts, and implicitly or explicitly the author's own growth and development, all come into play. These pieces were written during major transitions spanning the Thatcher and Reagan governments, the collapse of communist regimes in Central and Eastern Europe, attempts to regenerate social democracy, and the election of centre-left governments throughout Western Europe and in North America. They reflect my continuing interest in the work of the Italian Marxist Antonio Gramsci (1891–1937), in women's changing socio-economic roles, and in projects to refashion left politics to take account of major socio-economic change, and are accompanied by a desire to demystify academic practices. Theoretical discussion is joined to political and personal reflection. The majority of the essays have been substantially revised for this book. All are explorations of themes of continuing contemporary relevance. They do not pretend to be definitive. They are often tentative and suggestive. The intention is to open up discussion rather than close it down.

THEMES AND CONJECTURES

As political and intellectual signposts change so dramatically, a rush to judgment is to be resisted. The dynamic of the tennis match of many academic and political debates, which simply bounce arguments back and forth, can detract from the need to confront significant questions. Above all, polarised positions often mean that the inconsistent and contradictory nature of social development is either considered a problem to be eliminated or becomes a rationale for abstaining from engagement. It is striking how rare it is to find work which draws out what could be useful from what appear to be otherwise contradictory positions, or, indeed, which makes an analysis that searches for the contradictions and inconsistencies in social development in order to learn from them. The definition of being analytical and critical is too often reduced to describing the negative aspects of reality

1

and the limits of social thought and political practice, rather than trying constructively to draw on what is potentially positive and useful. At the same time, social analysts have the right to 'de-construct' earlier traditions of ideas as they seek answers to today's questions without endorsing them in their entirety or reducing their importance to their contemporary relevance.[1]

Participating in an open-ended process implies recognising a continuous need to change and to grow. Such a need is too rarely acknowledged. The absence from most academic or political debate of explicit self-interrogation is not surprising given the vulnerability which this can expose. The strange pretence that we – authors, readers, collective agents – have always been what we are now provides a defensive shield. In order to be convincing and authoritative, it is assumed that intellectual and political argument, whatever the content and whatever the gender or provenance of the author, must don the cloak of infallibility. By convention academic and political legitimacy and authority are rooted in certainty, which is required both of those in leading roles, and, it is expected, of those who accept such leadership. All too often a parent–child relationship is constructed in which little if any change and development is expected on the part of either.

Reflective modes of intellectual and political conduct run the risk, of course, of self-indulgent narcissism which is neither interesting nor productive. Nonetheless both political processes and intellectual engagement have much to gain from thoughtful reflection, even if the manner in which academic careers or political power and influence are achieved hardly encourages it. Tracing personal trajectories can offer an additional, even if small, contribution to producing some of the questions which can inform wider discussions. Individual biographies are not representative or even pre-figurative of wider truths, but they can provide insights into more general phenomena. And in a book which weaves together a variety of themes, discussion of the different influences on the writer may help to guide the reader.

Gramsci's ideas, feminist debates, empirical work on women's changing socio-economic roles, discussion about the futures of welfare states, and reflection on professional practice and personal experience all inform these essays. The topics covered range from Gramsci's ideas on the intellectuals and his use of language, to citizenship and the concept of civil society, contemporary left politics, the relationship between parents and teachers, and ways of working in the social sciences. The essays are linked by a number of themes, above all, the idea that political projects to change society for the better need to avoid both passive, fatalistic resignation to seemingly overwhelming historical trends and schemes which have little basis in reality and therefore little chance of success because they are unlikely to win widespread consent. This is encapsulated in the phrase, 'pessimism of the intellect, optimism of the will'. Indeed, the subtitle of the book, *Beyond Pessimism of the Intellect*, links a current concern, the politically debilitating effects of cynicism about the possibility that reform programmes can make a positive difference to society, with the major intellectual influence in the essays, the work of Antonio Gramsci.[2]

INFLUENCES FROM THE PAST

Yet my encounter with Gramsci's ideas was almost accidental. Although at that time few people outside of Italy had heard of Gramsci, he was suggested as a research topic by one of my teachers during my final year at the University of California, Berkeley where I had returned after a year at the University of Padua. When I took up this challenge, I had no idea how the decision would shape what was to come. The complexity of Gramsci's writing and the specificities of his context forced me to learn about theoretical and political debates and political and social history far from my previous education or background. But over many years his writing has served as a foundation to tackle a range of other topics well beyond his own concerns. His analysis of changes in the role of the state and the transformation of the meaning of politics from the end of the nineteenth century, his sensitivity to what was new in social development in all its contradictions, and his insistence on taking the reactions and activities of the mass of society as an essential point of departure even, or especially, when confronted by political defeat from a prison cell, have all contributed to lateral thinking.

A major political defeat, the triumph of fascism in Italy in the 1920s, propelled Gramsci's politics. He challenged models and preconceptions which inhibited the rethinking essential to the construction of a progressive politics which could provide an alternative both to fascism and to the mistakes of the left which had contributed to its own defeat. Having set himself an ambitious programme of study,[3] Gramsci was seriously constrained by prison conditions and restrictions on what he could read and write. Yet his curiosity about what might now appear the minutiae of contemporary debates was not simply the result of his confinement. He was in fact predisposed to a method which seizes on the smallest detail, particular instance, or intriguing episode to open up important wider questions which might not otherwise be posed. He refused to cast such elements aside, to explain them as mistakes, for example, support amongst sectors of the population which had been marginalised and disaffected the Italian fascist regime. Nor did he try to fit his observations into a preconceived model or theoretical framework.[4]

On the contrary, the pieces which did not fit theoretical or political preconceptions served as clues to insights into the mystery and puzzles and potential of wider social development and indicated new questions demanding novel answers.[5] Moreover, an underlying assumption in his work in prison was that no historical development could be understood as wholly negative or wholly positive. Each had to be analysed in its complexity and

3

contradictions and, most importantly, grounded in historical and cultural specificities.[6] This was the only way to begin to grasp the new problems and the new possibilities presented by historical transitions and to map the political terrain on which they would be addressed.

The novel features of contemporary society could, of course, only partly be understood through existing concepts. Gramsci recognised the continuing influence of old institutions, processes, and ideas. But while acknowledging the weight of history, he derived a theoretical and political agenda from the problems and possibilities of the present and future rather than from a programme of the past. Inspired by Machiavelli as well as by Marx, Gramsci confronted the potential and the limits of political creativity with openness and courage in facing the most unfavourable realities. In his attempt to contribute to a renewal of left thinking from a prison cell in the 1930s, Gramsci managed to combine intellectual rigour and political commitment. In so doing, he provides a role model for other, far more modest, efforts.

The simplest, indeed the most simplistic, relationship to thinking from a different period is either to embrace or to reject a thinker. But the tendency towards 'all or nothing' polemic runs the risk of losing the very insights which earlier writers offer if we could only develop a mature, secular approach to their ideas. That is, we need to avoid reducing them to crude and partial representations as a reaction to the unfounded expectation that any one thinker can provide all of today's requirements. Critical adaptation of what is still useful and the need to undertake creative, imaginative new thinking remains *our* responsibility.

THEORETICAL FOUNDATIONS

The first section of the book provides a substantial part of the theoretical foundation for subsequently addressing a number of important issues in the second and third parts which, however, go well beyond both Gramsci's time and framework. Re-reading the *Prison Notebooks* in order to prepare a paper about his ideas on education lead me to a re-interpretation of his concepts of traditional and organic intellectuals and to what is still a novel interpretation of Gramsci's work on intellectuals as specialists in a complex historical and social division of intellectual labour. The first two essays place these ideas in the context of the debates in the 1920s in the Soviet Union and in fascist Italy about the political role of intellectuals. It is argued that Gramsci's work was generated by urgent and concrete political questions, including the challenge of what he called Americanism and Fordism, and led him to focus on the role of technical, organisational and political expertise in a period of transition.

Themes which are discussed include aspects of educational theory, the problem of bureaucracy, and the pre-conditions of expanding democracy. A critical assessment is made of Gramsci's argument that, while not everyone automatically and unproblematically has the capacity to rule, everyone potentially has abilities which can and must be developed further for a meaningful democracy. In challenging Lenin's rhetoric, Gramsci puts the problem of creating the conditions for the expansion of democracy firmly on the socialist agenda, and confronts head on some of the enormous obstacles to the realisation of such an objective. A close analysis of the notes shows that he is not a populist but an 'intellectual democrat'.

Although Gramsci was writing in a very different period, the interpretations of Gramsci's work on intellectuals in these essays provide a link to contemporary problems. The transformations in Central and Eastern Europe and in South Africa which require new political institutions and legal frameworks, and major changes in old administrative structures, the economy and society more generally demonstrate the enormous difficulties to be faced during major historical transitions. Indeed, any project for substantial change, large or small, confronts pre-existing mentalities and structures and practices of power. Gramsci's ideas help us to think about these and other issues such as the relationship between professionals like doctors or social workers or teachers and the public at large and the possibility of more active and meaningful citizenship.

A puzzle leads to the next essay, on the subversion of the language of politics. This piece examines the way in which Gramsci stretches the meaning of terms like 'intellectual', 'hegemony', or 'state' almost to the point of absurdity at the same time as he also uses them in traditional ways. It is intriguing how Gramsci uses 'hegemony' to indicate consent, when its usual meaning in international relations, and indeed its use by fellow marxists like Lenin or Mao, was so different – as domination over a system of alliances. Curiosity lead me to try to 'make sense' of what might otherwise appear simply contradictory[7] by examining 'clues' to a deeper understanding not only of Gramsci but of our own use of language.[8]

What might appear a minor point, Gramsci's frequent use of inverted commas to warn the reader that the meaning of a word should not be taken for granted, became a 'lead' in an investigation which concluded that the reason for this caution with language went well beyond the usual explanation that he had to hide from the censors to encompass profound aspects of his thought and of his politics.[9] To invent new terminology in an ahistorical way would have run the risk of losing touch with 'normal' political language, with those who use it, and also with that part of reality which still corresponds to the old meaning. Gramsci therefore retains common political terminology but stretches it to refer both to the new and to the traditional. For example, there is still a sense in which the state is government, or law and policy making and enforcement, but it is not only that. The state in this sense has power but not a monopoly of power.

Gramsci's use of terms has a 'dialectical' intent; that is, he wants to indicate past, present and potential future meanings all contained within the same word. His perspective also implies that some aspects of reality are ahead of our ideas and our language, which have roots in the past, because traditional ways of being and thinking are embedded in institutions and practices which are still influential even when they are being undermined by socio-economic change. This poses the problem of how to relate in language and in concepts to a complex past, present and future.

POLITICAL INTERVENTIONS

The first part of the book engages directly with Gramsci's ideas. The next section addresses a range of topics of contemporary political relevance which go well beyond his framework and reflects other influences: empirical work on women's socio-economic roles, feminist debates in Britain, Italy, the Nordic countries, the US, and elsewhere, and attempts to re-think social provision in the light of changing socio-economic conditions, in particular changes in the roles of women and men over the life cycle. 'Equality and difference: the emergence of a new concept of citizenship' is an exploratory essay which draws on work done on the implications of women's changing socio-economic roles.[10] The methodology examined in 'Gramsci's subversion of the language of politics' is here applied to citizenship. I suggest that at the same time as traditional meanings continue to be significant, there has been a de facto transformation of the meaning of citizenship.

Both the theory and practice of citizenship have changed as a result of the development of the welfare state and the highly diverse and changing relationships that individuals have with it at any one time and over the life cycle. New kinds of differences are therefore inscribed in the relationship between individual and state. The fight for equality of opportunity and equal protection of the law is nonetheless as important as ever. There is a parallel discussion of the meaning of the abstract individual. For all that its pretence of universality is undermined when we understand how the concept is gendered,[11] such a notion, linked to constitutional guarantees of the rule of law, still represented an advance over attributions of legal identity which depended on social status. Rather than a polarised discussion of equality versus difference, I argue that taking account of diversity while providing guarantees of equitable treatment requires complex perspectives derived from the revision of conceptual frameworks in the light of socio-economic change.[12] In this and other essays in the book I attempt to move from theory to empirical reality and back again, paralleling Gramsci's own methodology. This process reflects the argument running through the book that because of changing reality it is necessary both to go beyond and to learn from earlier traditions of political thought, be they liberal or marxist.

The need to contextualise ideas and thinkers and to relate concepts to a changing reality also applies to contemporary debates on civil society. The rise of neo-liberalism, the collapse of communism, and the consequent undermining of traditional left assumptions about the state were the context in which debates about citizenship and the renewal of civil society became widespread. Yet these debates have often remained at an abstract level or taken the form of political rebuttal without making connections with the analysis of wider social change which is itself necessitating new thinking. 'Back to the future: the resurrection of civil society' examines the split between theoretical and empirical or historical discussions in the literature in English which this debate has generated. Evaluating Gramsci's own contribution in the light of factors which he could not fully take into account, such as the growth in the voluntary sector, or which he ignored, such as the relationship between family, civil society, and state, the question is posed whether he is of use for the contemporary thinking necessary to understand recent developments in civil society. The essay examines Gramsci's argument that the Catholic Church's claim to represent the whole of civil society in Italy after Italian unification was unfounded and his criticism of Italian fascism's professed aim to subsume civil society into a political project, and implicitly also the parallel attempt in the Soviet Union. I suggest that Gramsci's argument that only a full flourishing of civil society makes it conceivable to think about the state receding from dominating society distinguishes him from a long and highly problematic socialist tradition.

Contemporary centre-left attempts to formulate political strategies which can gain widespread consent because they are rooted in the needs of a society very different from that of fifty years ago provided the occasion to reflect on the difficulties faced in constructing a progressive politics which avoids weary cynicism and fatalism on the one hand and wishful thinking on the other. 'Beyond pessimism of the intellect: agendas for social justice and change' examines the reaction to a watershed in re-thinking the welfare state in Britain, the report of the Commission on Social Justice.[13] It is useful to remind ourselves that centre-left attempts to lay a new basis for social justice began in discussions by policy experts and politicians in the 1980s when it seemed a Herculean task to win the consent of the majority of the population to a programme of radical social, political, and economic reform as new right governments continued to receive electoral approval despite major socio-economic problems.[14] Such consent can only be won and maintained if political parties keep in touch with social change. This is no more true than with regard to major changes in women's and men's roles, in their identities, and in family patterns which have been as much a challenge to left political thinking as that of the new right and neo-liberal govern-ments. Evidence that the significance of these changes was at long last being recognised was the main reason why I was so favourably impressed with this major attempt to recast social provision, hand in hand with a more active and positive labour market policy, to provide the conditions to guarantee social justice in a world so changed from when Beveridge was writing. Indeed, the Social Justice Report placed overcoming the lack of fit between women's and men's changed roles at the very heart of a strategy to tackle social exclusion and poverty.

Recognition that change is unavoidable can as easily feed anxiety and fear as provide a platform for constructing a progressive alternative. Rethinking left politics as old models prove inadequate has been painful for many people as the claims of centre-left radical alternatives are posed in very different terms than traditional left approaches, and as the habits of opposition die hard. 'From realism to creativity: Gramsci, Blair and us' aims to be a careful investigation of whether Gramsci's ideas of political leadership and the art of politics have anything to offer contemporary politics, without any presumption that his ideas have anything but the most tangential bearing on the New Labour leadership.[15] The New Labour project is analysed with reference to a number of Gramscian categories such as hegemony, passive revolution, and the creation of a new collective will, and parallels are drawn between contemporary and earlier attempts at political renewal in the context of what can seem overwhelming odds. Earning the consent of a diverse population to a programme of reform, which is conceptualised as open-ended rather than finite, necessitates taking on the challenge of building co-operation between diverse talents in order to link the needs of those who are now excluded, marginalised, and poor to the majority of the population, all of whom depend on public services.[16] The essay suggests that the type of leadership appropriate to such a project resembles the conductor of an orchestra rather than a commander in an army.[17]

REFLECTIONS AND EXPLORATIONS

The concluding part of the book derives from the attempt to use subjectivity as a resource to consider the process of rethinking left politics, the relationship between parents and teachers, and the ways in which intellectuals and academics work. This reflects three dimensions of my own identity. 'Rethinking socialism: new processes, new insights' draws together strands from several of the other essays. It examines Gramsci's suggestion that 'the popular element "feels" but does not always know or understand; the intellectual element "knows" but does not always understand and in particular does not always feel . . .'.[18] I suggest that the intellectual and political courage with which Gramsci dealt with change and political and socio-economic turmoil in the 1920s and 1930s furnishes one useful model for confronting contemporary challenges. Rather than impose abstract schema on historical development, least of all a reductive marxism, he refused to take for granted the questions to be posed as he sought to understand what was new and different in historical development. Furthermore, he was open to insights from a wide variety of sources, from Sorel to Croce to Italian fascism, however great his political opposition to their aims or the limitations and mistakes in their perspectives. The essay therefore applies lessons drawn from the ways in which Gramsci faced the political catastrophes of the interwar period to the question of how to rethink socialism given the collapse of communism and other dramatic changes in recent years.

Going beyond Gramsci's example, the essay argues that intellectual attitudes have to change to expand our ways of seeing, hearing, and understanding the political. The split between what people say and their own experiences, common to intellectuals as much as to anyone else, is examined. I discuss the need to reflect and to avoid overly hasty diagnosis and suggest that feelings can be a resource for thinking about politics but that it is necessary to go beyond a naive belief in their obviousness. The possibility of comprehending changing reality and of creating really useful knowledge on the basis of which to rethink politics will improve if intellectual analysis reflects on daily experience. These 'reality checks' serve both as yardsticks of the veracity of theory and as raw material for further creative thinking. Examples from personal experience illustrate the argument that we need to hear and to work with messages coming from a variety of sources, including literature and film.

Such reflections on personal experience are the source of the essay, 'Dear parent . . .'. Although criticism of state provision has mostly been identified with the new right, it would be a mistake to ignore the basis in popular experience for the acceptance of much of that critique. The essay was a modest attempt to move beyond taken for granted left thinking in the Thatcher years which informed so many battles to defend the welfare state and educational provision. It is a down to earth application of Gramsci's notion that everyone is an intellectual although not everyone performs the social role of an intellectual. I consider the relationship between parents, who know something about teaching, even if it is only to do with tying a shoe lace, and teachers, who are specialised in teaching. The essay relates these reflections to debates about the role of parents in education, which are still relevant, and more generally to questions of who has what kind of knowledge and how practices of the welfare state in the broad sense do or do not harness the skills of the public.[19]

Reflections on professional practice, on the other hand, are the basis for the final essay, 'Subjective authenticity, cultural specificity, individual and collective projects'. This piece examines further the usefulness of subjectivity as an intellectual resource and considers the specificity of the individual intellectual and the national and international dimensions of knowledge, that is, how it is necessarily situated. Whatever its 'scientific' pretences, social science, I argue, inevitably reflects an individual, concrete, and ultimately subjective mode of work. The work of any individual is at the same time inevitably part of a collective project because it is inserted into one debate or another. A greater sensitivity to how debates vary depending on their spatial locality, different national traditions, and linguistic accessibility renders the notion of 'mastering *the* literature' highly problematic. Based on the experience of international conferences and seminars as well as 'conversations in kitchens' about women and the welfare state, the essay uses a variety of material to examine the 'voice' in which academic work is written and to speculate on the historical context of 'the repression of the author' of social science writing. I argue that openness to different sources of insights and modes of working would enrich our understanding of the world by making it more authentic and rooted, at the same time as we also need to aim for more general conclusions which cannot simply reflect limited circumstances.

AN INVITATION TO A CONVERSATION

Unspoken assumptions influence the work of social analysts with different national, intellectual, and institutional histories and cultures. These assumptions can have an impact on even the most theoretical and therefore presumably universal work and on the reception in different habitats of sets of ideas. The usefulness of comparative perspectives only partly derives from the need to widen horizons by learning about other societies and cultures. As important, they are a pre-requisite for acquiring an appreciation of the specificities of any single society and for denaturalising what appears unproblematically 'normal' or 'natural'. Cross-cultural points of reference are not just necessary to appreciate the perspectives of 'others' and their contribution to multi-cultural societies, but are essential to achieve an awareness of the particularities of what might be called 'ethnic majorities'. Recognising the real difficulty in avoiding the dual problems of regarding the object of study as 'other' or presuming to speak for others does not diminish the desire for more grounded and authentic academic work.[20]

Theoretical discussions and academic debates which are implicitly or explicitly concerned with social, political, and economic issues require more than the cut and thrust of academic life if they are to provide really useful knowledge, that is, if they are to be relevant. Hard-headed analysis must not shirk from speaking rigorously about harsh realities and political failures without fear or favour. But as citizens with specialist professional expertise, an honourable goal for academics and other social analysts is to engage with and contribute to the political as well as the policy process. Pessimism of the intellect is only constructive if, while remaining sceptical in best Enlightenment fashion, it avoids the cynicism which undermines optimism of the will and consequently the possibility of contributing to change for the better.

Social creativity can both be constrained and facilitated by government policy. It resides in actors well beyond the academy, think tanks, civil service, or government. Renewing academic and intellectual life requires new and different intellectual exchanges and conversations between those in these institutions and people in a myriad of organisations and places in society.

Essays which reflect in part a personal political and intellectual itinerary can but offer the basis for a wider conversation. If broadening the sources of insights and making use of earlier thinkers for inspiration to develop something new and better suited to a later age are accepted as ways to contribute to political and intellectual debate, then the fact that any book is inevitably an open text is not only to be recognised but to be welcomed. The need for rigour and analytical clarity invites critique but disposing of what needs discarding should not obliterate the possibility of making use of that which is still useful for the creative thinking of others. Readers are invited to read these essays in whatever order they like and to discard or to use whatever they feel appropriate.

ACKNOWLEDGEMENTS

Many people over many years have helped me with these essays. Anne Coddington has been invaluable in reading them all to help to improve both form and content. Wendy Stokes has offered intellectual and linguistic support. They and other friends and colleagues have supplied ideas, information, arguments, sounding boards, editing skills, feedback and encouragement. They are not, however, responsible for any mistakes. So thanks to Geoff Andrews, Anneli Antonen, Judith Astelarra, Paul Auerbach, Lesley Cauldwell; Ellie Fishman, Nina Fishman, Harriet Friedman, Vera Gáthy, Marja Keränen, Juha Koivisto, Anne Jamieson, Jane Lewis, James McCormick, Alan MacDougall, Nancy Mackenzie, Kate Moorse, Beryl Nicholson, Mark Perryman, Liisa Rantalaiho, Anne-Birte Ravn, Tanya Sassoon, Ann Sedley, Jon Showstack, Richard Showstack, Birte Siim, Gareth Smyth, Ken Spours, Zsuzsa Széman, Colleen Williams, Stuart Wilks, Michael Young; to the Institute of Political Economy, Carleton University; the Post-16 Centre, the Institute of Education, University of London; and the Feminist Research Centre in Aalborg (Freia), Aalborg University which have offered me periods in which to work and to reflect; to the faculty of Human Sciences, Kingston University which has granted me periods of study leave; and to Macmillan for permission to publish an amended version of 'Equality and difference: the emergence of a new concept of citizenship' which first appeared in David McLellan and Sean Sayers, eds, *Democracy and Socialism*, London: Macmillan, 1991.

Part 1

THEORETICAL FOUNDATIONS

2

THE CHALLENGE TO
TRADITIONAL INTELLECTUALS

Specialisation, organisation, leadership

POSSIBILITIES AND PARADOXES

Studies of popular culture, ideology and the intellectuals from a marxist perspective often acknowledge a debt to Antonio Gramsci. He has undoubtedly helped to put these topics on both the academic and political agenda. Yet there is more than one irony in the way his ideas have frequently been absorbed into a framework which endorses popular culture as the alternative to a set of ruling ideas, norms, and practices which are at the same time given the attributes of an all powerful social control. A close reading of his work reveals, in fact, what seems to be a series of paradoxes.

He insists that popular culture must be the starting point for both advanced intellectual work and an alternative hegemony by the working class, but he is harshly critical of its forms and most of its content. He considers ideas to have an historical force and yet says that they usually lag behind both the everyday experience of millions of people and of material conditions in general. In both his *Ordine Nuovo* articles and in prison he places great emphasis on the possibilities for an intellectual advance of the mass of society stemming from advances in the area of production. Yet in his notes on Americanism and Fordism he clearly recognises the brutalising effects of those very changes in production which he claims will dominate an entire historical epoch. Finally while the precondition for a socialist transformation of society is the creation of a new set of organic intellectuals and a new hegemony in society, which is now possible, Gramsci emphasises the immensity of the task.

These tensions in his writings are not accidental. They stem from the contradictory nature of society itself. In the 1930s capitalism was in crisis but had not collapsed. The Russian Revolution marked an historical watershed, but the possibility of an expansion of democratic control remained unfulfilled. The changing role of intellectuals and the development of the intellectual capacities of the population at large, both highly problematic, provide the key, according to Gramsci, to creating the conditions for a real rather than a demagogic development of democracy. From an Italian fascist prison, Gramsci goes back to Marx to help him to develop an original and creative body of work.

In engaging with the challenges presented by the re-organisation of capitalism, when nonetheless the basis for socialism, he maintains, is also being built, Gramsci is neither a populist nor an idealist nor a utopian, but a Marxist whose work is based on certain

> fundamental principles of political science: 1. that no social form-
> ation disappears as long as the productive forces which have
> developed within it still find room for further forward movement;
> 2. that a society does not set itself tasks for whose solution the
> necessary conditions have not already been incubated, etc.[1]

These two principles depict the possibilities and the paradoxes which provide the frame for his work in prison and the foundation on which he tries to develop a marxist political science based on the primordial fact 'that there really do exist rulers and ruled, leaders and led'. The fundamental question is whether it is

> the intention that there should always be rulers and ruled, or is it the
> objective to create the conditions in which this division is no longer
> necessary? In other words, is the initial premise the perpetual
> division of the human race, or the belief that this division is only an
> historical fact, corresponding to certain conditions?[2]

Gramsci analyses both those developments which make the task of over-coming this division possible and those which are allowing the productive forces to find room for manoeuvre and which are helping to maintain the split between leaders and led. In this sense the transition to socialism is on the historical agenda. Gramsci's project is to investigate all the dimensions of this transition: from the latest developments within capitalism, including fascism, to the dramatic, concrete problems posed by the Russian Revolution and the Soviet Union. Central to this project is the political question of the intellectuals.[3]

When Gramsci writes that, 'All men are intellectuals . . ., but not all men have in society the function of intellectuals', he illustrates his point with the following example: 'Thus, because it can happen that everyone at some time fries a couple of eggs or sews up a tear in a jacket, we do not necessarily say that everyone is a cook or a tailor.'[4] This neglected down to earth reference was not accidental. Lenin's populist slogan that 'every cook should be able to rule', which was current in the Soviet Union until the early 1990s,[5] goes back to the period immediately after the revolution. Far from simply endorsing Lenin's approach, having been in the Soviet Union in the early 1920s when the immense difficulties of building a new society were all too evident, Gramsci takes as his starting point the goal of expanding real democratic control, the defining feature of communism for him, to go on to investigate the conditions which might in fact make such an expansion possible.

Unlike Lenin's slogan, Gramsci's illustration emphasises specialisation and division of labour, the relationship between the skills possessed by millions of people and those of élites of specialists. These themes are the threads on which he weaves his writings. But why are the intellectuals so important for him? After all, in his notes he is most scathing about rationalistic projects woven by intellectuals out of thin air. His own feelings of isolation are manifest in his fear of being cut off from reality.

If the project he sets himself in prison takes a particular form, this form derives, I will argue, from his particular form of marxism which, by going both back to and beyond Marx and existing in critical tension with the limits of Lenin, validates the significance of ideas, culture, and intellectual skills in a much more radical way than is usually understood. As he writes the *Prison Notebooks*, he investigates the contradictory and at times surprising nature of concrete historical development and the problems and possibilities which it produces. Changes in the organisation of capitalism and problems in the construction of socialism *require* him to redefine the very meaning of the word 'intellectual' and to place the relationship between intellectuals and people at the centre of his work in prison. He is forced to define 'intellectual' in terms of the 'organizational and connective'[6] function, rather than the skill of thinking, in order to understand reality.

Intellectuals were such a significant theme for Gramsci because long-term economic, social, and political trends in capitalist society placed the question of the intellectuals at the centre of politics. These trends entailed an increase in the number of people with advanced intellectual and organisational skills, higher levels of education extended throughout the population, and new divisions of mental and physical labour. Both placed the question of the intellectuals or the experts and the organisers at the centre of politics.

This made a new, more democratic relationship between intellectuals and people conceivable. Gramsci arrived at this conclusion from an analysis of the increasing *organisation* of capitalist society from the 1870s onward. The transformation of the economic sphere into organised capitalism with the increasing dominance of trusts, cartels and limited companies was but one aspect of the increasing complexity of the social and political fabric as mass political parties, trade unions and pressure groups developed. These developments brought with them an increase in the number of people who needed organisational skills from managers to trade union, party, and pressure group leaders.

Above all else, the relationship between state and society changed. The role of the state expanded dramatically. Its impact on society increased and came to influence even those spheres where it did not intervene directly. The expansion of the suffrage, the introduction of a number of social reforms, the increase in state regulation were a response to political and economic pressures. They were implemented by governments of different political hues from Bismarck to Disraeli, from Theodore Roosevelt to Giolitti and Lloyd George. In the epoch of imperialism governments undertook new tasks abroad in the name of national economic interests, while the First World War and then the economic crisis of 1929–30 led to a range of interventionist policies. New Deal America, fascist Italy or Nazi Germany (and in a different way the Soviet Union) were but the latest manifestations of a long-term, irreversible decline in the non-interventionist liberal state. The number of civil servants and policy experts, educationalists and social workers, engineers and scientists, urban planners and architects all increased.[7]

Gramsci 'reads' this story of reformism and the decline of the liberal state, with its restricted role in society, as a dimension of the long-term, organic crisis of capitalism. According to him these changes indicate the increasing importance of the masses in politics as they become organised whether in trade unions, parties of left and right, or peasant or other movements – when what they do and what they think matters – as a sign of the actuality of the socialist project. Capitalism is forced then to embark upon different forms of what Gramsci calls passive revolution; to try to manage change and maintain control of economic and political power through compromises with different social interests and political forces within limits which neutralise anything which presents a serious threat.[8] The state undertakes new tasks in order to maintain a social basis of consent and to guarantee the conditions for an expansion of the forces of production. The full arc of this process is traced by studying the intellectuals.

THE IVORY TOWER BECOMES
AN HISTORICAL RELIC

The political function of the intellectuals was a result of what Gramsci considered the irreversible decline of that limited liberal state so highly constrained in its sphere of activities that it could be compared to a nightwatchman, a precondition of which was also highly limited political participation. The growth in state activities from the end of the last century was in part a response to the expansion of democratic rights and wider political organisation. The traditional role of an intellectual élite now existed in a new context. The concept of free floating intellectuals, whose roles and functions appeared to have little directly to do with the productive sphere, state policy, or political activity, was a myth. The idea of thinkers above the fray was an ideology which had important effects in maintaining a corporate esprit de corps amongst some groups of intellectuals, but which was ideological in the sense that it could not adequately describe reality.[9] Yet it continued to be influential.

When Benedetto Croce, philosopher and one-time Minister of Education in the fascist regime, sought to answer a public declaration of support for the regime, the Manifesto of Fascist Intellectuals, with a counter-manifesto, he argued that intellectuals could participate in politics as *citizens* but as *intellectuals* they had to serve a disinterested scientific function.

> . . . intellectuals, that is, the practitioners of science and art, if they join and faithfully serve a party, exercise their rights and fulfil their duties as citizens. However, as intellectuals their sole duty is to raise to a high spiritual level through scholarship, criticism and artistic creation all men and parties equally so that they can fight the necessary struggles with increasingly beneficial effects. To go beyond the role assigned to them, to mix up politics and literature, politics and science is an error. . . .[10]

According to Gramsci, this position was anachronistic. It reflected Croce's inability to comprehend the changed role of the state, the new historical role of the working class, and wider social change.[11]

The irony was that the manifesto organised by Croce, the ex-Minister of Education, proclaiming that intellectuals were above politics was itself a political act. Even he was forced to leave his mythical ivory tower

> to plunge into practical life, to become an organizer of the practical aspects of culture, if he wants to continue to lead; he has to democratize himself, to become more contemporary: Renaissance man is no longer possible in the modern world when enormous human masses participate actively and directly in history.[12]

If traditional intellectuals wanted to maintain their influence, they had to change their way of working and become organisers, that is, undertake cultural activity in a modern form appropriate to advanced capitalism. Moreover, traditional intellectuals like Croce and others came to perform a function organic to the maintenance of what Gramsci calls the historic bloc of social and political forces by providing an ideology to unify the ruling groups and to limit the revolutionary potential of the masses. Despite maintaining a traditional view of their role, they perform a function organic to Italian capitalism. They are 'assimilated' into the capitalist project as their old role becomes anachronistic. They, too, become organic intellectuals despite themselves. He and Gramsci are in fact talking two different languages when they use the word 'intellectual'.

19

AN OLD WORD ACQUIRES NEW MEANINGS

Gramsci is forced to develop a new language (as he does with the word state) because it is the pre-requisite for acquiring the analytical tools necessary to understand changes in capitalist society.[13] Gramsci applies 'intellectual' to 'a whole series of jobs of a manual and instrumental character' which do not even have 'directional or organizational'[14] attributes, which he recognises is unusual. He uses 'intellectual' in this broad way, rather than using 'petty bourgeoisie' or 'declassé', because it is necessary to go beyond both the liberal and the socialist traditions. The difficulty presented to anyone reading Gramsci is to fill the concept in the same way he does. To the extent that we fill it in fact only with 'creators of the various sciences, philosophy, art, etc.' and neglect 'the most humble administrators and divulgators of pre-existing traditional, accumulated intellectual wealth',[15] if we do not 'think . . . the entire social stratum which exercises an organizational function in the wide sense – whether in the field of production, or in that of culture, or in that of political administration',[16] the word intellectual will function ideologically rather than analytically, and we will not 'reach a concrete approximation of reality'.[17] What Croce and we miss by using an historically outmoded concept of intellectual is the way in which politics and state policy plus the organisation of the productive sphere define the work of intellectuals, their specialisms, their 'job specifications'.

Gramsci, then, tries to map the changes in the mode of existence of intellectuals and in the organisation of knowledge which are a manifestation of changes in the organisation of society as a whole. Above all, the number of intellectual jobs, the institutions to fill them, and the number of intellectuals in the state bureaucracy, in the productive sphere, in institutions which produce the skills needed by the development of capitalist society, and in the institutions of mass culture have vastly increased. This 'massification' and organisation of intellectuals are a measure of the complexity of capitalist society and have a multitude of effects.

Intellectuals are 'standardised', they organise in professional associations, and while enjoying and defending relative privileges, they face unemployment. Yet this does not mean they are being 'proletarianised' or that they will automatically acquire a particular political identification as a consequence of their changing function in society. The question of the intellectuals is not sociological but political. Gramsci argues that it is necessary to undertake an historical analysis of the different kinds of intellectuals, different grades of intellectual activity and the organisation of culture in each country to comprehend the concrete dimensions of what is an overall trend of capitalist societies. Although the pattern of specialisms will be influenced by technical needs and the social division of labour, the forms intellectual functions take – in particular their ways of relating to the rest of the population – are historically and politically determined.

The increase in the numbers of those with specialised skills who have the social function of intellectual reflect what for Gramsci are two intimately related phenomena: first, the vast increase in advanced knowledge and the need for specialisation which this produces (and the specialised web of educational structures to produce both knowledge and specialists), and second, the huge increase in knowledge and skills in the population as a whole. Specialisation goes hand in hand with socialisation and organisation. Specialisation is a manifestation of that increasingly complex division of labour which is the mark of an advanced society. It is reflected in the increase in the number of specialised educational institutions which, Gramsci writes, is an indication of the general cultural level of a country, just as the complexity of the machine tool industry is indicative of the technological level.[18] Gramsci's continual use of terms like specialisation, specialist, division of labour, skill, apprenticeship has the effect of demystifying the intellectual function as he tries to grasp changes in the mode of intellectual work.

His approach is in stark contrast to the traditional liberal view of the production of advanced knowledge. Gramsci argues that although Croce might believe that intellectual achievement depends on the genial creations of brilliant minds, advanced discoveries only have permanent, effective historical significance in relation to a structure of knowledge and learning: a web of institutions and the level and complexity of education, knowledge and culture in society at large. The great breakthroughs are in a sense but the tip of an intellectual iceberg. Gramsci never reduces the intrinsic differences between skills.[19] Rather, he places them within a structured division of labour which rests upon the foundation of skills possessed by millions of people. The organisation of this structure of specialisms, specialists, and skills is constantly changing. Gramsci is convinced that a division of labour reflects historical advance.

The question is not whether a division of labour is necessary but which division of labour exists and for which reasons. He continually emphasises the necessity of a technical division of labour, that is, according to skill rather than a division based on class. Class indicates a permanent structural division such as that defined, in Marx's terms, by relationship to the means of production. Gramsci uses the term élite polemically and contrasts it to class.[20] Skills can be learnt, they change, they relate to the knowledge and rational capabilities of everyone. Position in a hierarchy and authority and discipline based on the recognition of skill (Gramsci's example is that of the leader of an orchestra)[21] are defined democratically, and those with more advanced skills can be considered representative of the people, if the conditions are being created for an organic exchange between specialists and people, leaders and led, if the traditional division between those with power and the rest of society is being overcome, class divisions are being eliminated, politics as control by the few over the many is being socialised and therefore transformed.

This creation of the preconditions of expanding democracy is in fact Gramsci's way of describing the socialist project. If modernising regimes like the Soviet Union and fascist Italy which depended so heavily on the skills of intellectuals showed that defining such a goal in terms of a new relationship between intellectuals and people was highly problematic, Gramsci thinks that capitalism is creating the foundations for fulfilling it.

INTELLECTUAL DEMOCRACY RATHER THAN DEMAGOGIC POPULISM

Gramsci differs from both Lenin and Mussolini when he addresses the question of creating a democratic, organic relationship between intellectuals and people. What is striking about Gramsci's approach is his constant reference to hierarchy and mediation as an aspect of the division of labour. The relationship between, say, the woman or man in the street and the advanced specialist must be a mediated one in which there are different levels or grades which can be achieved and a web of intermediate intellectuals who link top to bottom in a series of democratic, representative relationships.

But democratic and representative in what sense? Here Gramsci is trying to examine the conditions necessary for fulfilling the promise of democracy embedded in a formal, legal concept of democratic rights. Democracy is functional, organic and necessary to the organisation of a society in which intellectuals (specialists and political leaders) conceive of their skills as part of a hierarchical structure resting on the skills of the majority of the population who set the problems to be resolved. These problems are constantly redefined in the process. The functions of intellectuals are defined in terms of the increasing skills, autonomy and therefore power of the population.

What is necessary from the outset is a moral and intellectual reform in which intellectuals 'feel' in order to 'know' and the people are equipped to 'know' as well as 'feel'.[22] The precise structure of skills, the kinds of division of labour which are developed, and the organisation of the hierarchy will depend on the specific terms of the political project which can only be articulated on the basis of the needs of the population. For example, as demands by ethnic minorities or women to break down crystallised divisions based around race or gender come to be embedded in the socialist project, institutions and practices have to be created which will ensure that the divisions of labour which exist are no longer based on differences of skin colour or sex.

The needs of society are represented and democratic practices ensured not by formal legal guarantees, which are a *necessary* but not a *sufficient* condition for a democratically functioning society, but by creating the concrete conditions which will make democracy a reality. Gramsci refers

22

constantly to a hierarchy and to a division of labour because it reflects the historical development of organised capitalism. The classical liberal schema of an unmediated relationship between citizen and state, where the rational, isolated individual makes choices between alternatives and elects representatives who determine policy in the interests of the whole had been made anachronistic by history. The individual has the most impact in modern mass politics if a member of an organisation, and increasingly interests, even of those who are not members, are represented by organisations. Consequently s/he is represented both by representatives elected to legislatures and by a variety of groups.

The institutions of representative democracy now exist in the context of other forms of representation, not just the corporations of business and labour but mass political parties and all the other groups in which the people organise themselves. The relationship between individual and state therefore is mediated by a web of relationships not least through state institutions themselves as state services expand. This is another expression of the decline of the liberal state.

EXPERTS, NOT JUST IDEOLOGUES

Fascism welcomed the ideological support of intellectuals, but it also gave them an important practical role in its project of reconstructing the Italian state and Italian society. In a speech to university students in December 1923, a little more than a year after taking power, Mussolini explained the importance of educational reform.

> The fascist government needs a ruling class [*classe dirigente*]. . . . I cannot create functionaries for the State administration from nothing: the universities must gradually produce them for me. . . . It is precisely because we are backward and latecomers that we must powerfully fortify our intelligentsia. . . . These are the profound reasons for the Gentile [Educational] Reform.[23]

In addition to training the new specialists needed by the regime, Mussolini sought to win over a wide range of experts by giving them a role in modernising Italy: to reclaim land and to build modernist cities, to create institutions of mass culture like radio and cinema, to organise intellectuals in associations, institutes and academies.[24] Fascism's agenda for the intellectuals stemmed from a recognition that intellectuals, both as experts and as cultural practitioners, had acquired a political function, whatever their idea of themselves and whether they were enthusiasts for fascism or not. While attacking the demagogy of the populist rhetoric of Mussolini or Gentile, Gramsci recognised the modernity of the way fascism connected the intellectuals to wider society and to social and political projects. Indeed, fascism's very populism was a sign that social conditions and the needs of the wider population had to be *addressed* in modern politics.

Fascism recognised the crisis of the liberal state and corporatism was in part an attempt to reorganise political relationships to take account of changes in capitalist society while maintaining the structure of capitalist economic relations. After having destroyed autonomous organisations, fascism filled the vacuum and organised women, youth, intellectuals, workers, etc. Yet the relationship between individual and leader, individual and intellectual was *mediated* through organisations in a bureaucratic rather than democratic way, an example of what Gramsci called organic central-ism,[25] because there was no attempt to ensure that elements from the rank and file or the base were trained to assume positions of power or to control those who do. The claims by Mussolini and Hitler on the one hand and fascist intellectuals on the other to be authentic representatives of the people, to have a direct relationship with them were demagogic because of the absence of a democratic exchange between leaders and led and because they justified their positions of power on the basis of their exceptional qualities, their genius.

The Bolshevik project was very different from that of the fascists: its declared aim was to build a new society on the basis of the political protagonism of the masses. After the Russian Revolution the question of creating a new type of state based on a democratic relationship between intellectuals and people became concrete. The problem of the relationship between the intellectuals – be they army generals or bureaucrats, agrono-mists or Bolshevik cadres – and the people was posed in dramatic terms. It derived from the need to defend the Russian Revolution from invasion and counter-revolution, to rebuild the economy and create a new political system, to create a new socialist culture, to organise consent, to increase literacy, and to lay the foundations for industrialisation. If fascism rein-forced Gramsci's conviction that the question of the intellectuals was relevant, the experience of the Soviet Union could only have convinced him of the enormous difficulties of creating a new democratic relationship between the population and political power. Skills and knowledge were required which went well beyond ideological adherence.

His analysis of a mediated relationship between masses and state, between people and intellectuals differs not only from Mussolini but from Lenin. Lenin assigned an important political role to intellectuals, to the ideological struggle and to theory. Yet he had a traditional, narrow concept of intellectual – borrowed from Kautsky – as the science carriers of the bourgeoisie. Whereas the socialist movement had often simply dismissed intellectuals as bourgeois or sought to ally with them as declassés or white collar wage earners who were being proletarianised, Lenin argued that the working class needed their theoretical skills to develop a political strategy based on a scientific understanding of historical laws and a scientific analysis of the concrete situation.[26]

Lenin emphasised the *difference* between these theoretical skills and the skills of the mass of the population. Intellectuals who are separate and different from the working class could be joined to it by making a personal, political choice: to become professional revolutionaries. As revolutionary cadres their way of living as intellectuals changed and became different from others of their background and from the mass of society. The political party was the organisational form which would provide the link between intellectuals and people, transforming theory into revolutionary science as it intervened in the class struggle. As for the technical experts, the agronomists, economists or engineers, Lenin's perspective is that skills are neutral.

> the development of capitalism . . . itself creates the premises that really *enable* all to take part in the administration of the state. . . . [It] is quite possible, after the overthrow of the capitalists and bureaucrats to proceed immediately, overnight, to supersede them in the control of production and distribution, in the work of *keeping account* of labour and products. . . . (The question of control and accounting must not be confused with the question of the scientifically trained staff of engineers, agronomists, and so on. These gentlemen are working today and obey the capitalists; they will work even better tomorrow and obey the armed workers.)[27]

The workers will give them orders while the need for bureaucrats is supposed to wither away as administrative functions are simplified and the people perform them directly without need of intermediaries.

What is presented is a direct, unmediated relationship between people and specialised intellectuals. The relation between both revolutionary intellectuals and experts and the political objective of socialism is defined in terms of the application of skills to a different project, as one ruling class is substituted for another. They work towards the creation of a different society but there is no indication that they will need to transform the way they learn about reality; they work, they acquire skills.

What is missing in Lenin's perspective is an examination of the *problem* of transforming the mode of existence of intellectuals or of preparing the majority of the population for the task ahead. These changes were left to the period after the revolutionary break and viewed as deriving from rather than being a precondition of the socialisation of the means of production.[28] There is no analysis of different levels of intellectual specialisation or of the relationship between different types and grades of advanced skills and the varied skills of the population or of a network of organisations linking people and state. Lenin did not ask *how* the cook would acquire the skills needed to govern a modern society, or how the experts would reflect wider social needs, other than through party allegiance.

Within Lenin's perspective, the party retains a monopoly over setting the political agenda, possessing advanced theoretical tools. Even after being won over to a different political project, intellectuals learn and perform the way they always have, using their individual skills and applying them to the problem in hand. The irony is that, while Gramsci admires the Russian national-popular tradition, Lenin in breaking with populism and attacking economism stopped asking the question 'what can be learnt from the people?' because he could only conceptualise it in conditions of backwardness. The question had to be reformulated in the context of an organised, complex civil society which was precisely what Russia lacked and which, according to Gramsci, had to be constructed.[29]

The modern web of institutions, relationships, and divisions of labour did not simply reflect advanced capitalism but, according to Gramsci, were a mark of *any* advanced historical development. Yet Russian backwardness meant that they had to be created in the Soviet Union contemporaneously with socialism. If Lenin's concept of the relationship between state or experts and people is a direct rather than a mediated one, it reflects the 'primordial' state of Russian civil society[30] with its historically backward division of labour. Lenin does not analyse the vast expansion of the intellectuals nor pose the problem of how the mode of existence of intellectuals is to be transformed as control over politics and production is democratised. He was influenced by the heritage of the utopian socialist St Simon, who, writing almost 100 years earlier, inspired the aspiration that state administration could become ever more simplified, and by the brief experience of the Paris Commune almost fifty years earlier which Marx argued prefigured direct control over politics by the people. Moreover, he confronted a backward Russian civil society. These factors inhibited Lenin from thinking about key issues presented by the project of building a modern socialist state.

Gramsci's writings reflect on the challenge to traditional intellectuals constituted by socio-economic change in advanced capitalism. A new type of intellectual who belongs to a new political project which is rooted in more democratic relationships between those who have specialised knowledge and the rest of the population, with their own skills and intellectual potential, has become possible, but only if the concept and practice of being an intellectual changes dramatically.

3

THE POLITICS OF THE ORGANIC INTELLECTUALS

Passion, understanding, knowledge

Suspicion of a political role for intellectuals is understandable. Populist demagogy and ideological distortions of intellectual enquiry accompanied by repressive measures against independent thinkers have been attributes of a wide range of authoritarian regimes. Post-modernist critiques of so-called grand narratives and Foucault's analysis of the repressive effects of professional discourses are in part a reflection on the failures – and worse – of modernising projects this century. Although framed very differently, the arguments of Karl Popper and other critics of the instrumentalisation of Enlightenment reason to legitimate the activities of a paternalistic and at times a highly repressive state challenge the idea that state intervention directed by an élite of intellectuals results in providing beneficiently for the universal general interest. Whether as described in the writings of Hegel or followers like Croce, or in those of John Stuart Mill and the Fabians, or expressed in the policies of Roosevelt's New Deal and Scandinavian and other post-Second World War reformist projects, an ethical, modernising role for the state and public policy influenced by the knowledge of experts is widely questioned at the end of the century. From another perspective, feminist criticism of the gendered nature of an historically constituted opposition between feelings and reason has also contributed to a re-examination of the bases of different fields of knowledge and policy.

When Gramsci was writing in prison in the 1930s many of these questions were already contentious. The relationship between the achievement of political objectives and analytical clarity about the world was at the heart of the marxist tradition. It also appeared in a particularly Italian guise in a contemporary debate about Machiavelli in the light of Mussolini's claim to be his heir and the incarnation of the Prince.[1] The concept and practice of political leadership was widely discussed. Gramsci extends the debate substantially by investigating the link between intellectuals and people, and between political goals and popular desires, through a discussion of the relationship between feelings, understanding, and knowledge.

> The popular element 'feels' but does not always know or understand; the intellectual element 'knows' but does not always understand and in particular does not always feel. . . . The intellectual's error consists in believing that one can know without understanding and even more without feeling and being impassioned . . . that the intellectual can be an intellectual (and not a pure pedant) if distinct and separate from the people-nation, that is, without feeling the elementary passions of the people, understanding them and . . . connecting them . . . to a superior conception of the world, scientifically and coherently elaborated – i.e. knowledge. One cannot make politics – history without this passion, without this sentimental connection between intellectuals and people-nation. In the absence of such a nexus the relations between the intellectuals and the people-nation are, or are reduced to, relations of a purely bureaucratic and formal order; the intellectuals become a caste, or a priesthood (so-called organic centralism).
> If the relationship between intellectuals and people-nation, between the leaders and led, the rulers and ruled, is provided by an organic cohesion in which feeling-passion becomes understanding and thence knowledge . . . then and only then is the relationship one of representation. Only then can there take place an exchange of individual elements between the rulers and ruled, leaders and led. . . .[2]

The pre-requisite for developing the capacities of the population at large and for retraining intellectuals which will provide the possibility for such an exchange is a fundamental reform of a wide range of institutions.

EDUCATION AND THE CREATION
OF INTELLECTUALS

Two kinds of institutions appear in Gramsci's notes on the intellectuals which are particularly revealing about the relationship between people, intellectuals, and specialised knowledge: the party and the educational system. The internal organisation of the party and the way different levels of intellectuals relate to each other and the way the party relates to society are, for good or ill, indicative of forms of political relationships in society at large.[3] The vast expansion and organisation of education, Gramsci says, indicates 'the importance assumed in the modern world by intellectual functions and categories'[4] and is a symptom of transferring functions from the private to the public sphere.[5] It reflects two trends simultaneously.

'Parallel with the attempt to deepen and broaden the "intellectuality" of each individual, there has also been the attempt to multiply and narrow the various specializations.'[6] The precise forms of organisation of education, 'the number and gradation of specialized schools', the number of '"vertical levels" of schooling' as well as the breadth of the '"area" covered'[7] indicates the complexity of a society's intellectual and cultural organisations, that is, the divisions of labour which have been achieved and the forms of hierarchy which are consequently produced.

Here we encounter a problem in reading Gramsci; a certain 'blur' appears and forces the reader to ask: 'Is he analysing things as they *are* under capitalism or as they *might be* under socialism?' This derives from the very nature of his project: to differentiate between those developments which allow 'the productive forces to find room for further forward movement',[8] and which reproduce the division between leaders and led, and those which are creating the conditions in embryo for a new organisation of society. When in his notes on the organisation of education he begins by saying that a process of specialisation and the creation of specialised educational institutions at various levels to train specialist intellectuals are the mark of 'modern civilization',[9] he means that this will continue to be the case under socialism.

Education is in crisis, he writes, because the predominance of the old humanistic school[10] has been challenged as the growth of modern industry has required a new type of intellectual and an expansion of technical education. The 'previously unquestioned prestige'[11] of a disinterested, generalist, humanistic culture which had dominated the formation of intellectuals is undermined as a new kind of society emerges based on a new productive system bringing with it an increase in the number of intellectuals, higher degrees of specialisation and greater differentiation between types of intellectuals. This 'crisis of the curriculum and organisation of the schools, i.e. of the overall framework of a policy for forming intellectual cadres' is a manifestation of 'the more general comprehensive and general organic crisis', an aspect of the crisis of hegemony. It 'rages' out of control because of the chaotic, unplanned 'process of differentiation and particularization' taking place.[12]

Given that specialisation, related to the development of modern industry, is a mark of historical advance, the solution is not simply to eliminate it. A new balance is needed between the creation of specialists and the provision of a general, 'humanistic' education which is reformulated[13] so that now the mass of society rather than only a restricted élite is made capable of 'thinking, studying, and ruling – or controlling those who rule'.[14] Counterposed to the possibilities inherent in this crisis is 'the tendency today', i.e. the Gentile Reform, the fascist education policy which was the regime's response to social and economic changes, to limit traditional, humanistic education to a small élite and to push the vast majority into 'specialized vocational schools, in which the pupil's destiny and future activity are determined in advance'.[15] The consequence was to reproduce the division of labour and the relations of domination and subordination which maintain the lack of democratic control of capitalist society. Although the Gentile Reform was portrayed as democratic by the fascist regime,[16] it created a new type of school which was 'destined not merely to perpetuate social differences but to crystallize them in Chinese complexities'.[17]

The reform was a response to the demand for new skills and new special-isation, so that what was crystallised were the *differences* between social groups not the skills themselves. It was not an attempt to defend the status quo or to turn the clock back. Moreover, the democratic ideology it used to gain acceptance was not simply pretence. The increase in types of vocational school encouraged higher levels of specialisation *within* social groups, allowing individuals to better themselves so that as Gramsci writes 'the labourer can become a skilled worker . . . [or] the peasant a surveyor or petty agronomist'.[18] It thus provided the material conditions for achieving a basis of consent lending credence to the ideological representation of the reform as democratic. It was an example of what Gramsci called a passive revolution, of improving the opportunities of sections of the population and managing change without broadening the effective exercise of power.

A truly democratic reform would challenge the division between a traditional humanistic education for the few who will rule and a vocational training for the subordinate masses. Gramsci argued that

> democracy . . . cannot mean that an unskilled worker can be skilled. It must mean that every 'citizen' can 'govern' and that society places him, even if only abstractly, in a general condition to achieve this, . . . ensuring for each non-ruler a free training in the skills and general technical preparation necessary to that end.[19]

This goal is not mere idealism, utopianism, or populism because, according to Gramsci, historical developments have made it possible to extend the aims of the old élite education (to prepare those who will rule)[20] to the mass of society, but only on condition that the curriculum is transformed. The common, basic education, which will enable children to become people 'capable of thinking, studying, and ruling – or controlling those who rule' must 'strike the right balance between development of the *capacity* for working manually (technically, industrially) and development of the *capacities* for intellectual work'.[21] A rational (i.e. historically progressive) solution of the crisis in education must thus go well beyond giving individuals more technical skills.

The foundation must be created on which to build 'new relations between intellectual and industrial work, not only in the school but in the whole of social life'.[22] This is the only way to ensure that, within a perspective of even greater specialisation and of specialist education, the difference between intellectual and technical work and the divisions of labour which develop are not crystallised into different social groups. The answer to the problems posed by capitalist development is articulated by Gramsci in the same terms as he uses to describe the creation of 'a new stratum of intellectuals'[23] organic to the project of building socialism.

Thus an important manifestation of the long-term organic crisis of capitalism requires a socialist answer, but it is by no means inevitable that it will be found. Quite the opposite. In Italy Gramsci feared that society was returning to 'juridically fixed and crystallized estates rather than moving towards the transcendence of class divisions'.[24] If Gramsci's direct target is the Gentile Reform, there is also a lesson for the Soviet Union and indeed for other reformist projects. Democracy, and socialism, are not just a matter of educating more people in specialist skills or of increasing skills in society as a whole but of creating institutions which are organized to ensure that the new divisions of labour which develop do not simply reproduce the split between leaders and led.

Moreover, the creation of 'a new stratum of intellectuals' depends on a mass intellectual advance in which there is 'the critical elaboration of the intellectual activity that exists in everyone'.[25] The development of the skills and talents of the population at large was the precondition for producing a new kind of intellectual, organic to a new kind of society. Gramsci's concept of organic intellectual is rich and complex and cannot be reduced to party cadres. When he emphasises the special role of the party for 'some groups' in elaborating 'organic intellectuals directly in the political and philosophical field',[26] he is talking about the political organisation which is a precondition for the working class and others to count in politics. But this does not exhaust the matter. He sets it within the context of the wider organisation of education and culture and a process which is a part of a long-term project in which the transformation of schooling and a new organisation of knowledge in the productive sphere are necessary to prevent a chasm developing between what goes on in the party and the state and what takes place in society. Whereas at the moment the organic intellectuals of the working class 'are formed in this way and cannot indeed be formed in any other way, given the general character and conditions of formation, life and development of the social group',[27] the implication is that as these conditions change and as education and culture are transformed the special role of the party will wither away.

But we must constantly return to the *problem* Gramsci is investigating: how to ensure that the conditions are created for an expansion of democratic control. Although modern industry and the general expansion and complex organisation of educational institutions provide the premise for such a revolutionary project, his notes on Americanism and Fordism make it clear that a democratic division of labour is not a *reflection* of technological advance or the specialisation of skills accompanying industrialisation. It is by no means automatically produced by modernisation and the elimination of backwardness. It will only be created through a conscious intervention on the basis of what is possible.

Yet if the goal is something new, it will have to be built on the old. The realism of Gramsci's project stems from the effort to place problems on the political agenda rather than avoid them. The question is always: 'what organisation and which pedagogy will both achieve a mass intellectual advance and produce scholars of the highest quality which are necessary to *every* civilization?'[28] Quantity *and* quality.

For Gramsci, studying itself is an acquired skill and the precondition for developing the capabilities in each of us to increase our control over nature and over our social and political circumstances.[29] Any techniques which imply that the educational process is natural or spontaneous will reinforce cultural and social divisions, and reproduce those divisions of labour and hierarchies which allow a few to rule and keep the vast majority subordinate. There is a difference between advanced specialists and 'the simple'.[30] At the same time, the gap is bridgeable, mass education is *possible*. The responsibility extends beyond schooling to a much wider transformation. 'The passage from knowing to understanding to feeling and vice versa from feeling to understanding to knowing', the only basis, according to Gramsci, for 'organic cohesion' between rulers and ruled, implies change in both intellectuals and in the wider population.[31]

Gramsci's language is significant. He writes of studying as a 'job', an 'apprenticeship', a training involving muscles and nerves. Just as anyone can become a skilled mechanic or plumber, albeit starting with different aptitudes, so anyone can acquire advanced intellectual skills. His language has a double function. It demystifies the process so that academic achievement does not appear as a trick, magic, out of our control, or a 'gift of God'. At the same time it stresses the labour involved for most people. By talking about studying as hard work Gramsci emphasises what it has in common with manual labour as well as authenticating the experience of those who find it difficult. It is hard but possible. To pretend that it is easy is to endorse that ease with which a minority succeed because they obtain from their social background those skills and values which most people must struggle to develop.[32] It leads to collusion in the continuation of a rigid division of labour between a caste-like intellectual élite and those whose potential for understanding and knowledge remains unfulfilled, and a democratic relationship between specialist intellectuals and people – between rulers and ruled – continues to prove elusive.[33]

THE PROBLEM OF BUREAUCRACY

Here we turn to an important distinction between political and technical specialisation that runs throughout his notes. The goal is to enable everyone to control those who rule. Yet Gramsci clearly recognises that the very expansion of knowledge, advances in technology and changes in the productive system and the growth of mass organisations, all of which, he argues, have made increased democratic control conceivable, have already produced serious problems for parliamentary regimes. Bureaucracy has expanded and grown in power along with the role of the state as politicians make decisions which are dependent on the advice of experts. Moreover, experts from industry and finance, even more removed from parliamentary control, are gaining increasing influence. The 'personnel specialized in the technique of politics' are being integrated 'with personnel specialized in the concrete problems of administering the essential practical activities of the great and complex societies of today'.[34] The threat to parliamentary regimes and democratic control was well recognised in the period, but could not be eliminated by 'moralistic sermons and rhetorical lamentations'.[35]

Gramsci's comments are still relevant. We can draw the conclusion that the trend cannot be reversed simply by appeals for greater legislative control or by condemning the bureaucracy and the experts or by attacking outside interests. It is impossible to limit the power of experts and restore parliamentary democracy to some earlier, simpler 'golden age'. Nor is direct democracy the answer. When Lenin criticised parliamentarism in which the legislature was a mere talking shop, he attacked but a manifestation of a long-term historical trend which could not be overturned through a simplification of procedures and direct, unmediated democratic control. The limited example of the Paris Commune, referred to by Marx, Engels, and Lenin, was of little use for confronting the complexities of modern politics.

What is necessary, according to Gramsci, are new kinds of organic intellectuals formed according to a *different* division of labour. On the one hand 'the training of technical-political personnel' must be modified so that political leaders have 'that minimum of general technical culture which will permit [them], if not to "create" autonomously the correct solution, at least to know how to abjudicate between the solutions put forward by the experts'. At the same time, 'specialized functionaries of a new kind' are needed 'who . . . will complement [the] deliberative activity' of elected politicians.[36]

A NEW STRATUM OF INTELLECTUALS

In what sense are intellectuals organic? Although they are not defined in relation to the means of production in the same way as the capitalist class or the working class,[37] the functions they fulfil are justified either by 'the political necessities of the dominant fundamental group' or 'by the social necessities of production'.[38] In this sense their specialisations reflect a social division of labour in the productive sphere and in society and their functions reveal a complex web of relations which mediate between rulers and ruled. The question of developing a new kind of organic intellectual of the working class can only be posed as it was for capitalism: in relation to the transformation of the productive sphere and the construction of a new state.[39]

When Gramsci writes that

> [e]*very social group*, coming into existence on the original terrain of an essential function in the world of production, creates *together with itself*, organically one or more strata of intellectuals which give it homogeneity and an awareness of its own function not only in the economic but also in the social and political fields,[40]

he is describing a *process* in which a class eventually develops a new mode of production and a new society.

> the organic intellectuals which *every* new class creates alongside itself and elaborates in *the course of its development*, are for the most part 'specializations' of partial aspects of the primitive activity of the *new social type* which the new class has brought into prominence.[41]

The examples of these 'specializations' which he gives for capitalism are 'the industrial technician, the specialist in political economy, the organizers of a new culture, of a new legal system, etc.', while he points out that the entrepreneur must also have the 'technical i.e. intellectual capacity . . . [to] be an organizer of masses of men . . . of the "confidence" of investors in his business, of the customers for his product, etc'.[42] At least an élite of entrepreneurs (or their 'deputies' or 'specialised employees') must be able to organise 'society in general, right up to the state organism' that is, 'the general system of relationships external to the business itself'.[43] The relationship between intellectuals and the needs of the economy is not direct but is '"mediated" by the whole fabric of society'.[44]

Moreover their social origins, their specialisations and the kind of training they receive, their status and the way they view their roles, and their attitudes to other groups in society and their relation to the state and to politics are historical rather than theoretical questions. They vary over time and according to different national traditions.[45] Organic intellectuals, Gramsci writes, are formed by all social groups although 'they undergo more extensive and complex elaboration in connection with the dominant social group'.[46] They are not 'givens'; their attributes are not predetermined by the economic structures in any abstract sense but will be affected by tradition, cultural practices, political decisions, and public policy.

Of major importance to the working class are those intellectuals who now perform functions which are organic to capitalism. From the point of view of the new historical project of socialism, and of expanded democracy, their way of working is 'traditional' – as out of date as the ivory tower, Crocean intellectual is to advanced capitalism – yet they will have to be assimilated and conquered 'ideologically' to put their services at the disposal of a new historical project.[47] This process will be facilitated by the development of new groups of organic intellectuals, including from social strata whose intellectual capacities have not traditionally developed, and a new conception of the world. Yet the goal of making 'politically possible the intellectual progress of the mass and not only of small intellectual groups'[48] requires both a criticism of common sense and of traditional philosophy.[49]

This is the precondition for a new hegemony.

> Critical self-consciousness means, historically and politically, the creation of an *élite* of intellectuals. A human mass does not 'distinguish' itself, does not become independent in its own right without, in the widest sense, organizing itself and there is no organization without intellectuals, that is, without organizers and leaders. [50]

When Gramsci goes on to define these leaders as 'a group of people "specialized" in conceptual and philosophical elaboration of ideas', we might have returned to Lenin's formula except that his attention is firmly focused on the people. The process of developing intellectuals he writes,

> is tied to a dialectic between the intellectuals and the masses. The intellectual stratum develops both quantitatively and qualitatively, but every leap forward towards a new breadth and complexity of the intellectual stratum is tied to an analogous movement on the part of the mass of the 'simple' . . .[51]

Yet this is a far from straightforward process. Great difficulties are encountered in developing intellectuals adequate to the historical task of the working class which is to create the conditions for the full democratic protagonism of the masses.

> the process of creating intellectuals is long, difficult, full of contradictions, advances and retreats, dispersals and re-groupings, in which the loyalty of the masses is often sorely tried. (And one must not forget that at this early stage loyalty and discipline are the ways in which the masses participate and collaborate in the development of the cultural movement as a whole.)[52]

Intellectuals might wish, as Brecht later commented ironically, to abolish the people and elect a new one, when in fact it is the people who are forced to be patient with wayward intellectuals. Any party or organisation which continues to depend on the generic loyalty and discipline of the population and fails to raise their political-intellectual level and to create a qualitatively new, democratic link with the people remains trapped within a low, economic-corporative level of specialisation. The mode of being of these intellectuals and these organisations retains the paternalistic, instrumental attitude towards the masses which is a mark of intellectuals in capitalist society because they are not an organic expression of them.[53]

The problems which beset the process of developing intellectuals organic to a democratic, socialist project stem from such deep-seated historical trends that they will not automatically be overcome. That is, contrary to Lenin's argument in *State and Revolution*, extended democracy is a project which can only be brought to fruition by confronting the enormous problems attached to it.[54] The forms of intellectual specialisation and the web of social relations that intellectuals 'weave' which are organic to a democratic socialism may or may not develop fully as a new mode of production is created and will determine whether a new democratic state is built.

In the course of a democratic, socialist transformation of society intellectuals may fail to construct a democratic relationship with 'the simple' so that socialism itself remains 'primitive', trapped within the limits of economic-corporatism, (a type of passive revolution),[55] unable to expand consent and become fully hegemonic. At times, despite the fears of prison censorship, the reference to the USSR becomes transparent. In the context of discussing the dialectic between intellectuals and masses during the frequent moments when 'a gap develops between the mass and the intellectuals', when there is 'a loss of contact' and theory becomes separated from practice and appears subordinate. Gramsci writes that this signifies

> that one is going through a relatively primitive historical phase, one which is still economic-corporate, in which the general 'structural' framework is being quantitatively transformed and the appropriate quality-superstructure is in the process of emerging but is not yet organically formed.[56]

The question, then, of developing intellectuals organic to the project of building a socialist society begins under capitalism and concerns, in the first instance, the development of political leaders and organisers. Yet in fact it is a measure of much more. It indicates the degree to which the working class is able to transform the productive sphere. The building of a new kind of state and an expansion and transformation of the forces and relations of production depend on the creation of new organic intellectuals as the division of labour becomes more complex.

TRANSFORMATION OF THE
PRODUCTIVE SPHERE

For Gramsci both these questions were already posed under capitalism. The decline of the limited, liberal state and the new relationship between state and society which was developing meant that the role of the state was changing but, without a hegemonic intervention of the working class, various forms of passive revolution maintained the dominance of capital, and the rule of the few over the many. The challenge also existed at the level of production itself. In Gramsci's articles in Turin in 1919–20, he argued that changes in the organisation of production and the relationship between the state and the economy were providing the conditions in which workers could transform their identity from wage earners divided according to skills to producers conscious of their role in a complex, economic, political and social system able to direct a complex productive process.[57]

A defect of Gramsci's *Ordine Nuovo* articles is that they tend to use the organisation of production in the factory under capitalism as a model for the new society.[58] But in the *Prison Notebooks* his study of the intellectuals and his notes on Americanism and Fordism manifest a much more critical and complex view. The increasing socialisation of production under capitalism now appears more clearly as an aspect of the long-term organic crisis to which it is forced to respond. Its answer is to reorganise the productive process as new technology is developed and applied. Frederick Taylor's scientific management and assembly line production signified a long-term trend which had to be examined at its most advanced stage of development: in an international situation composed of highly differentiated national realities which have to respond to the challenge of changes in the American productive system.[59] This is the specific reason for Gramsci's intervention in the debate which was widespread in Italy about the American 'model' when modern assembly lines hardly existed in Italy at that time.[60]

The notes on Americanism and Fordism show that Gramsci is under no illusions about the brutalising effects of an application of the new technology and new organisation of production under the hegemony of the present ruling class. He observes both the failure of a struggle by American trade unions based on pure and simple opposition to the new developments and resistance in Europe to American culture. Any understanding of what is happening must be based on an 'extremely important' criterion

> that both the intellectual and moral reactions against . . . the new methods of analysis and the superficial praises of Americanism, are due to the remains of the old, disintegrating strata, and not to groups whose destiny is linked to the development of the new method.[61]

The working class could neither simply condemn nor uncritically accept the new technology and organisation of production. Here Gramsci both breaks with the productivism of his earlier writings and demarcates himself from Bolshevik productivism.[62] According to Gramsci, what was needed was a novel response. The future of the working class, and of socialism, depends on transforming the relationship between the mass of the population and technical and scientific knowledge.[63] The question which is being posed is 'whether we are undergoing a transformation of the material bases of European civilization which in the long run . . . will bring about the over-throw of the existing forms of civilization and the forced birth of a new'.[64] Socio-economic structures are changing, and at a pace influenced by the power of the United States, so that Europe's 'excessively antiquated economic and social base'[65] is being undermined and elicits criticism from those strata who will be crushed by a new order.

But, Gramsci argues, a truly ' "new culture" and "new way of life" ' are represented neither by 'Americanism' nor by the attempt by fascism to modernise and 'rationalise' Italy. For a new order and a new material basis on which to build it can only come from another direction.

> it is not from the social groups 'condemned' by the new order that reconstruction is to be expected, but from those on whom is imposed the burden of creating with their own suffering the material bases of the new order. It is they who 'must' find for themselves an 'original', and not Americanised system of living, to turn into 'freedom' what today is 'necessity'.[66]

The working class 'must' come up with a solution to the new problems posed by the development of capitalism because it cannot avoid them. Yet if the possibilities presented by technological advance are to result in an expansion of 'freedom' instead of being dictated by 'necessity', what is required is a changed relationship between the working class and the process of production and re-production. The condition which is necessary to allow the working class to be hegemonic in the process of technical progress is the creation of new groups of organic intellectuals and a new organisation of scientific knowledge.[67]

We thus arrive at a series of questions which were being posed in different ways both by the development of advanced capitalism and by the first attempt to construct socialism. American methods of production and the dynamism and modernity of American society, with its technocratic faith and emphasis on efficiency, held great fascination in the Soviet Union in the years after the revolution and were influential in the communist movement in the period.[68] It was assumed that technology was neutral and could simply be applied for different political purposes in a different context.

The implication we can draw from Gramsci is that this position is theoretically and politically backward. In the course of industrialisation, as 'the general "structural" framework is being quantitatively transformed and the appropriate quality-superstructure is in the process of emerging but is not yet organically formed',[69] what predominates is an application of scientific knowledge and technology under conditions of 'necessity', in which the gap between people and intellectuals is filled by a tie based on discipline and loyalty. An answer adequate both to the latest developments of capitalism and the construction of democratic socialism must be pitched at a much more advanced level: the creation of organic intellectuals related to each other and to the world of production in a division of labour and an organisation of knowledge which is able to break the historical link between 'the needs of technical development [and] the needs of the dominant class'.[70] That is, for knowledge to be used to transform society in a democratic way, intellectuals, experts, or specialists must change their view of themselves and their skills as part of the process in which the potential of the vast majority of the population is being developed. But this is far from simple.

Gramsci argues that while the process of deskilling depreciates the work of an individual worker, so that it then appears easy to substitute it and to identify technical advance with the interests of the ruling class, the social-isation of production made it possible for workers to conceive of themselves as part of a complex productive process, as a 'collective worker'. The present link between the dominance of capital and 'the needs of technology' could be demystified so that it no longer appeared 'objective' or natural but specific to an historical phase and thus temporary. Gramsci argues that, to the extent that the working class becomes aware that the link can be broken, that a new 'synthesis' between technology and its class interests is historically possible, it is no longer subaltern, and technology and science can become part of a subjective transformation of the world.[71]

THE TRANSITION TO SOCIALISM REFORMULATED

The historical task of the working class in all its aspects, from its political constitution as a class to its ability to build a new state to the transformation of the productive sphere, requires 'the creation of a new stratum of intellectuals'.[72] Although rooted in the work of the *Ordine Nuovo* 'to develop certain forms of new intellectualism and to determine its new concepts [which] corresponded to latent aspirations and confirmed to the development of the real forms of life',[73] once Gramsci is in prison, the political question of the intellectuals is intertwined with the whole process of the transition to socialism. 'The mode of being of the new intellectual,' he writes, 'can no longer consist in eloquence . . ., but in active participation in

39

practical life, as constructor, organiser, "permanent persuader" and not just as simple orator.'[74]

Intellectuals and forms of intellectualism that are practical and go beyond the abstract, rationalistic schemes which Gramsci so often attacked as cut off from real life could only be developed through a new organisation of knowledge rooted in the practical activities of the people. The aim was a new balance between intellectual and manual work in which the intellectual capacities of the population are developed and 'practical activity' becomes the basis of a new conception of the world.[75]

Technology and the skills of individual workers which are now instrumentalised by capital in conditions of necessity, can become the foundation of a new freedom, providing the basis for a new rational, social control implying a new unity between the specialised skills which we each have and the task of the political direction of society.[76] What begins to emerge from Gramsci's work is the *possibility* imbedded in ongoing trends of overcoming a series of divisions in which differences do not disappear but are negotiated in new ways: between leaders and led, between mental and manual labour, between politics and society, between philosophy and science.

The expansion of knowledge with its corresponding complexity and the consequent necessity of specialisation – which mirrors an increasing social complexity and differentiation – challenges, however, the very possibility of generalisation and with it the traditional role of the philosopher, that is, of those who specialise in generalisation or the attempt to comprehend the whole, indeed, of any philosophical system to comprehend society. The long-term organic crisis which Gramsci says is undermining traditional humanistic education also sets enormous problems for *any* generalising philosophy, including marxism and challenges those claiming to be organic philosophers of the working class. These are problems which will *increase* rather than diminish in the transition to socialism. Lenin's concept of revolutionary intellectual is anachronistic. Technocratic solutions of any sort which are 'the result of a rationalistic, deductive abstract process – i.e. one typical of pure intellectuals (or pure asses)'[77] are bound to be inadequate before the enormously complex needs of society. The only way to 'know' reality involves understanding popular feelings.[78] The educators *need* to be educated.

Yet so, too, do the people. If Gramsci continuously stresses that the conception of the world which the majority of the population now have must be a starting point for the organic intellectuals of the working class, it is because the effect of its fragmentation, of its incoherence, of a whole list of negative characteristics, is to maintain the 'simple' in their subordinate position and to protect the dominance of the present ruling groups who have a hegemonic world view. This ideology is not accepted wholesale but is filtered down from on high through intermediaries to combine with a variety of elements to make up a common sense which holds the potential of the population in check. Thus the function of the present hegemony is to keep the 'simple' ignorant of their historical role, to maintain the split between leaders and led.

Overcoming this split means creating a new hegemony. It is an historically unprecedented task which will only be accomplished as the 'simple' are themselves transformed as their intellectual capacities are developed.[79] Moreover, there are contradictions between the conception of themselves and the world which most people have and their daily practical activities. Gramsci validates the importance of people's ideas for their identities, their activities, and as the starting point for political strategy, but he also argues that these ideas always lag behind material conditions.[80] He carefully specifies that intellectuals must learn about the common sense of the people *in order to criticise* it. This is the first, essential step in transforming backward ideas.

Rather than a populist glorification of the ideas of the people, Gramsci argues that it is in their practical activities and their feelings that the population provides *problems* for organic intellectuals to study and resolve. But these specialist intellectuals will only be able to undertake this task successfully if two things happen concurrently: the popular conception of the world becomes more coherent and more unified with people's practical activities, and their rationality and intelligence – their intellectual activities – are given greater weight in their 'professional' roles. This is not a question of unskilled workers individually acquiring more skills. It can only be conceptualised as a transfer and re-definition of the most advanced skills which are put at the disposition of the 'collective worker' who is no longer subjected to the imposition of science and technology but who appropriates and transforms this knowledge.

HISTORY PROVIDES NO GUARANTEES

The dangers in the Soviet Union of coercion dictating politics rather than consent were obvious to Gramsci before he was arrested[81] and continued to preoccupy him in prison. Historical development was providing the conditions which could allow for the creation of a democratic exchange between leaders and led, intellectuals and people. But history held no guarantees.[82] This relationship may remain bureaucratic, the intellectuals resemble 'a caste, or a priesthood',[83] and the 'simple' continue in their subaltern condition. Successful opposition to such outcomes depends on developing democratic alternatives which go beyond hollow rhetoric by being rooted in the capacities of the population as a whole. History may carry no guarantees, but nor, according to Gramsci, was there anything inevitable about the reproduction of old relations of dominance and subordination.

4

GRAMSCI'S SUBVERSION
OF THE LANGUAGE
OF POLITICS

Over the years an extensive literature has built up on Gramsci and language. These studies usually concentrate on his writings on linguistics, which he studied at university in Turin, and connect his notes on language to his concept of the national-popular, his critique of the cosmopolitanism of Italian intellectuals, and his centring of the significance of popular culture both as a field of study and as a starting point for political strategy. Language is, thus, a fundamental theme, it is argued, which not only illuminates other vital ideas such as hegemony or the intellectuals but is the very foundation stone for those concepts.[1] In Italy, as in many other countries, language has been important politically and historically in the context of nation-building and with regard to the relationship between intellectuals and people. A significant aspect of the widespread disaffection from the national project, a key theme investigated by Gramsci, is the fact that only a tiny minority of the population used Italian as its daily language at the beginning of the century, and the majority not until the 1950s, preferring to speak a dialect.[2] To this day written Italian is much more distant from the spoken language than is the case, for example, with English, and 'intellectual' and 'political' Italian often only communicates between a self-selected few, even more so than in English.

Beyond Italy, Gramsci's writings on language have been recognised as an important contribution to developing a sociology of language or a science of language.[3] Interest has also grown in this aspect of his work, first, because of debates about ideology and, second, because of the growth in interest in how human subjects are constituted through language.[4]

THE CHALLENGE OF READING GRAMSCI

Whatever the topic, reading Gramsci presents a particular kind of challenge. From linguistics to politics a difficulty for any reader is that Gramsci undoubtedly has a complex view of the world. This, of course, is true of any great thinker, but in Gramsci's case I would suggest that this is reflected in the very form of his work. Consciously or unconsciously, he made a choice, which has a greater significance than merely reflecting the constraints of prison life, to write in note and not book form. A consequence was to produce an archetypal open text that the reader must recreate each time she or he reads it. This is not to argue that it is correct to attribute to Gramsci whatever the reader wants to transfer onto him. Translating insights from his work into different contexts, and it is a question of translation rather than direct application, must be done carefully. On the other hand, such a text can encourage as well as provide tools for creative political thinking. One reason for the continuing interest in Gramsci, in a moment when marxism is out of fashion, lies in the way in which, writing in an earlier period of crisis of marxism and the working-class movement and of epochal change, he speaks to us because of the questions he asks, and because he seizes on the perplexing, the contradictory, the surprising – those features of society which escape ready classification – as the most fertile and productive points to analyse.

The difficulty readers face is rooted in the way he compacts several concepts into one single note. Rather than an intellectual defect, however, this reflects the multifaceted interconnected nature of reality. It is perhaps not so surprising that he did not write a logical treatise, even though others did in those self-same fascist prisons. However, he makes his writings even harder to follow by the way in which his notes grow out of the seeming minutiae of intellectual and political debate in 1930s fascist Italy. Recognition of the specificity of the roots of his work is important because the usefulness of his writings for us today depends on their first being reconnected to the questions he was asking in order then to draw out theoretical indications for a different context.

Gramsci remains fascinating precisely for these aspects which make him so difficult to read. Our creative reading of him always holds the danger that we stamp our schema, for example, populist, idealist, functionalist, or post-marxist, on him.[5] But his intuitive, sensitive use of the confusion of the new, of the fractured inter-relatedness of reality, of the historically and nationally specific to try to push forward a theoretical understanding of the trends and patterns and possibilities of the present as the basis for helping to create the future escapes many of the obfuscations of contemporary debates. Gramsci is also difficult because of the language he uses. Not because the words are difficult, which they are not, and not because the concepts they refer to are complex, which they often are. But precisely because he uses ordinary or traditional words to signify something new and, further, he often uses the word both in a traditional way and in a novel and sometimes an almost absurd manner.

What is present here is *his* own continuing struggle with language, which undoubtedly had roots in his own background,[6] in terms of the significations carried by individual words, as he attempts to find a way to depict not just new but old phenomena, such as the state or intellectuals, which now appear different because of a leap in understanding the nature of contemporary society. Above all, he cannot *see*, or *comprehend*, these phenomena if they are reduced to one aspect, for example, if the state is only portrayed as having a monopoly of force without reference to its dependence on consent. Yet he also says, explicitly, that methodological distinctions between, for instance, different kinds of intellectual activities are necessary.[7]

He alternates between these distinctions and the unity connecting them, insisting that form cannot be divided from content;[8] that theoretical general-isation is only given meaning by the historically specific; that structure or base is joined organically to superstructure,[9] both using and subverting the base–superstructure metaphor, that while international trends are the context, national developments must be the point of departure. When he uses a word in two ways, one is normally its usual, or 'common sense', meaning and the other is new, indicating an extended or advanced concept which bursts beyond the bounds of the old, such as his use of 'intellectual'.

He is highly aware of this problem of language. The language which is available to him does not very easily accommodate that dual perspective which he insists is necessary in politics. His notes are full of explanations indicating when he is using a word in its 'usual' way and when, on the contrary, it is the 'new' definition which he favours. Indeed the notes are filled with words in inverted commas – a distancing and specifying device – a technique which he shares, for example, with Foucault. Why is there this continuing trouble with language? In part it is related to the increasing com-plexity of the phenomena in question and of Gramsci's view of them. And naming complex socio-political and historical phenomena is not like naming a new mechanical discovery which can be labelled, in some languages, by simply going back to a Greek or Latin root. As Gramsci himself notes, language has an historical and social basis and a word which is meant to have a political resonance and understood by the widest possible sections of the population cannot be created abstractly. In that sense we are often stuck with the old words as developments grow beyond the old significations. Just as ideas often lag far behind 'economic facts',[10] so does language.

If politics remains trapped within a view of reality based on outdated understandings, adequate solutions will never be developed for contempor-ary problems. Gramsci's difficulty with language is related to his very dialectic. That is, his view is that complex tendencies are contained within the historical present which represent influences and continuities with the past, the reproduction of the old but in new forms, and at the very same time problems and possibilities so radical, so revolutionary that their resolution – to the extent that we are able to conceive of it at all – lies in the superseding of a whole historical epoch which spans capitalism and socialism, that is, in a society with a new mode of production, in communism. What is being described here is hard to perceive because it is much easier to see what has been lost or what is being reproduced in new forms than the seeds of the revolutionary contained within current developments. Indeed, readers are challenged because of the divergencies between Gramsci's use of language and more common understandings. This dissonance may well be a sign of an inability to go beyond traditional ways of thinking which impede the comprehension of the possibilities on the historical agenda.

SHIFTING MEANINGS BECAUSE OF
NEW UNDERSTANDINGS

Gramsci is probably best known for his development of concept of *hegemony*. His use of the term is unorthodox. Indeed, he both uses and subverts its meaning as he does with a whole series of concepts, pushing out their boundaries to make them appropriate to changed circumstances.[11] In international relations hegemony has traditionally indicated dominance or power over.[12] In traditional marxist language it indicated the leadership of a class over allies.[13] Thanks to Gramsci it is today used not only in these ways but also to indicate consent and moral and intellectual leadership.[14] It has cultural, political and economic aspects and implies compromises between social groups in which sectional interests are transformed and a notion of the general interest is promoted.

It is important to situate hegemony as belonging to a cluster of words (state, civil society, political society, political, intellectual, democratic, discipline, party, democratic centralism, crisis, historical) whose reference points keep shifting and/or mean more than one thing. These shifts in terminology occur partly because of historical changes which have already taken place and partly because processes are underway which make possible the subversion and transformation of politics or the resolution of what Gramsci calls the fundamental question of political science: the division between leaders and led.[15]

The shifts, for example, in Gramsci's definition of the state, as combining force and consent, as meaning government as well as a much broader range of processes and institutions, manifest the need, first, to connect to an historically and politically defined discourse which restricts its meaning to government, coercion, force; second, to push its meaning to encompass the transformation of political power in the modern period, which was de facto undermining the liberal 'night watchman' state; third, to take account of those questions posed by the Russian Revolution which put the construction of a workers' state and potentially a full expansion of democracy on the historical agenda, and fourth, by fascism's challenge, both practical and theoretical, to the liberal concept of state and practice of politics. The state can no longer be thought of in a restricted sense because of these historical changes.[16]

Thus, while Gramsci insists on the need to differentiate between civil and political society, he argues at the same time that these are methodological or analytical distinctions whose meaning in the real world lies in the forms of the links between the different dimensions of political power – forms which are not *natural* or a *necessity* of a mode of production but *historical*.[17] Historical is in fact yet another example of a word used in two ways by Gramsci: to indicate what is made by human beings in specific circumstances whose parameters are above all national and determined by political intervention, and long-term trends of an epochal and international character which are the wider context of such intervention. Gramsci not only reconstructs Marx's Preface to *A Contribution to a Critique of Political Economy*,[18] but he also reinterprets Marx's famous statement in *The Eighteenth of Brumaire* that human beings make history but not in conditions of their choosing.

It is also well known how Gramsci uses the word *intellectual* to refer to an extended list of categories, to claim that everyone is an intellectual, and generally to confuse us as he breaks with both orthodox liberal and marxist ideas. He asks, 'What are the "maximum" limits of acceptance of the term "intellectual"?', and answers that there 'is no human activity from which every form of intellectual participation can be excluded'.[19] If we examine some of the associated words – connective, organisational, skills, specialist and specialisation, function, division of labour, technical – the effect is both demystifying and confounding. Why does he hold on to a word which he has extended and subverted in this way? Why, when he is convinced of the importance of ideas and ideology, does the concrete illustration he uses of our all being intellectuals come from daily, practical life? Indeed, the example he uses has to do with the skills which come from specialisation and the division of labour: that while we may all fry an egg or sew on a button from time to time, this does not mean that we are all cooks or tailors.[20] Is our being confounded a warning? That is, to the extent we fill the word with an outmoded concept – be it seeing intellectuals as the supposed inhabitants of an academic ivory tower, or the science carriers of a class (as did Kautsky and Lenin), or as members of the chattering classes, or as mere ideologues – we will not understand reality. We will not be aware that any significant debate has moved on.

Gramsci insists that everyone is an intellectual, while making necessary distinctions between different levels of specialisation in intellectual skills and activities, for isolated intellectuals cannot hope to understand reality by force of technique alone. He continues to use the word intellectual, rather than, say, petit-bourgeois or declassé, because a sociological or economic class term is not appropriate while specialist is too limited. Intellectual, in its restricted plus its extended meaning, can indicate the full range of historical and ultimately political possibilities and necessities.

This leads us to why Gramsci turns another expression on its head, *democratic centralism*. As so often in the *Notebooks* Gramsci engages in a double edged polemic, aimed both at Italian fascism and at the working class movement, as he redefines democratic centralism as

> a 'centralism' in movement – i.e. a continual adaptation of the organisation to the real movement, a matching of thrusts from below with orders from above, a continuous insertion of elements thrown up from the depths of the rank and file into the solid framework of the leadership apparatus which ensures continuity and the regular accumulation of experience. Democratic centralism is 'organic' because on the one hand it takes account of movement ... and ... that which is relatively permanent and stable. ... The prevalence of bureaucratic centralism in the State indicates that the leading group is ... turning into a narrow clique which tends to perpetuate its selfish privileges. ... .[21]

How distant this is from the usual connotation of democratic centralism as agreement and discipline enforced from an authoritarian centre. In Gramsci's notes, democratic centralism implies understanding change, movement, diversity, in order ultimately to understand the wider situation. Adapting to change and flows of information and experience into an organisation are necessary if it wants to be an organic part of society and avoid being cut off from social processes. This can never result from the bureaucratic imposition of a party line. Indeed, Gramsci's discussion of democratic centralism as a necessary exchange between different elements echoes his definition of *democracy*.[22] Words such as flexibility, elasticity, practical and experimental are contrasted with mechanical, rigidity, rationalistic, abstract, bureaucratic. And following from this, consider what he does with vanguard, or leadership, or discipline, spontaneity or democratic. They, too, are defined in terms of a function, a problem, and an historical task.[23]

Gramsci defines *vanguard* in its connection to a class and to society at large as 'tied by millions of threads to a given social group and through it to the whole of humanity' rather than viewing itself as 'something definitive and rigid'.[24] At the risk of reinforcing a reductive, Hegelian reading of Gramsci, the word vanguard is defined by him in its *becoming*, or more precisely, for him its meaning cannot be separated from the transformation of the working class and society in the period in which not only the transition to socialism but communism is on the historical agenda. From the more immediate perspective of contemporary problems of politics, when Gramsci considers the classical question of the relationship between 'spontaneity' and 'conscious leadership' or 'discipline',[25] once again, he often puts the terms between inverted commas, signifying his difficulty with the available language. While the terms are analytically distinct, the problem he identifies is the complex nature of the link between them. Their unity becomes conceivable only if posed in terms of creating the conditions for

47

mass politics. Neither their meaning nor this unity can derive from the revolutionary claims of an isolated sect.

These themes were considered by Lenin, and in different ways, too, by Bordiga, the first leader of the Italian Communist Party, whom Gramsci succeeded, and by the syndicalists. This is the political history which informs the traditional reading of these words. Gramsci's wish to break with this history is one reason why he distances himself from them as givens. But if he corrupts or subverts them or pushes them to their limits or argues that as usually understood they are meaningless (as with the case of spontaneity since, he says, 'pure' spontaneity never exists[26]), it is not simply for the sake of polemic. It is because he is convinced that in the contemporary world their traditional, historically constructed meanings are being superseded.

Yet the old or reduced meanings often still have a resonance and are still necessary in specific conditions. Thus, for example, Gramsci defines *discipline*[27] in such a way as to render it almost unrecognisable.

> How should discipline be understood if what is meant by this word is a continual and permanent relationship between rulers and ruled which realizes a collective will? Certainly not as a passive and servile acceptance of orders, as a mechanical execution of a command . . . but as a conscious and lucid assimilation of the directive to be fulfilled.[28]

He defines it in terms of an historical possibility and therefore a political task of overcoming the traditional split between leaders and led. He counterposes it to its traditional meaning, a meaning whose roots lie in institutions like the Church and the military and which has been extended to people's common-sense understanding as the mere execution of orders. This traditional meaning, however, is still appropriate on certain occasions, and thus the word itself has multiple definitions. When Gramsci discusses the significance of the source of discipline, we find still another, apparently absurd, redefinition.

If the discipline originates in an organisation or institution which is democratic, based on a legitimate division of labour, it becomes 'a necessary element of democratic order, of freedom'.[29] 'Democratic' in Gramsci's notes is related to specialisation, division of labour, and a process of creating the conditions whereby there is an organic exchange between leaders and led. That is, it is defined in terms of what Gramsci calls that central problem of political science, the relationship between rulers and ruled.[30] It goes beyond questions of political obligation, and of legitimation or consensus, but does not exclude them. Rather it is posed in such a way that it can create the conditions which will realise what Gramsci considers the full possibilities of the current historical epoch – the political protagonism of ever widening sectors of the population.

Once again words have varied meanings, not only because of the complexity of the past and of the present which construct their meanings today, whether in the heads of specialised intellectuals or in those of mass woman or man, but because this present is part and parcel of a transition to an uncharted historical future. But just as the possibilities inscribed in the present – such as the redefinition of politics which for Gramsci has been put on the historical agenda not only by the Russian Revolution but by the latest developments of capitalism – present unprecedented problems, the awareness of the dialectic, of the present and the future, undermines our traditional way of attempting to capture, and ultimately, control reality in fixed schema.

If reading Gramsci presents problems, it is also intensely difficult to write about him in the logical, rational order which those of us who are academics have all been trained to do as part of our professional, intellectual apprenticeships. His writing, his approach, his language keep escaping and leading us astray. Although Gramsci was aware, and wary of, the unfinished nature of his work in prison, he allowed himself to work on several notebooks at the same time, to consider a wide range of topics, to change and develop his categories and to write in the most fragmentary of forms.[31] What Gramsci does do, of course, is to validate the questions arising from daily life as providing the raw material for advanced, specialist, intellectual labour, and here he coincides with one of the lessons of feminism.[32] And yet he by no means abandons the attempt to generalise, to theorise, to develop the language of today to try to capture process, diversity, particularity. But the meaning, the content, the effective terrain of our knowledge and expertise is always ultimately in reference to the concrete and the historical.

THE THEORETICAL AND THE HISTORICAL

This can be illustrated by considering two other concepts: passive revolution and the historical bloc. Each are terms which have double but interrelated meanings. Gramsci uses them to refer to two levels of analysis: theoretical and historical. Gramsci himself is explicitly concerned about possible difficulties ensuing from this with regard to the concept of passive revolution which, he argues, is useful as a theoretical tool, for example describing the very dialectic of the reproduction of capitalism in the period of its organic crisis.[33] Long-term general, international tendencies are expressed in a series of seemingly diverse, nationally specific, historically concrete political and economic developments. Explaining the capacity of capitalism to survive in the course of change – and thus the possibility both of developing a system of passive consent and the basis for a Crocean, historicist justification of past and present[34] – passive revolution, he warns, can lead to a fatalistic, passive acceptance of trends with no recognition of the new possibilities, even revolutionary implications of historical change. Or, and this is Gramsci's own position, for example in his notes on Americanism and Fordism, analysing such trends need not mean endorsing them but should rather be considered the precondition for constructing alternatives.

Gramsci discusses the historical bloc in only a few notes.[35] He uses it first, to refer to the relationship between base and superstructure. Here he would have been advised to put 'base' and 'superstructure' within inverted commas, because the effect of the term historical bloc is to subvert the traditional marxist imagery. As it describes the complex way in which actual, historically and politically formed classes and groups articulate their relations and form the *basis* or, better, weave of a society Gramsci's approach goes well beyond the base/superstructure metaphor.

The use of the same terms to refer to theoretical and actual historical phenomena has various implications and consequences. First, it is a manifestation of Gramsci's insistence that theory acquires meaning from its usefulness in analysing the concrete. Here he gives great weight to national specificities within the generality of the international, and local differences within the parameters of the national. Thus there is a message about abstraction, generalisation and rational discourse which Gramsci insists must not be confounded with or reduced to schema or mathematical logic. But second, there is a message about politics which also has an echo for theory. For this double usage of passive revolution and historical bloc tells us the following: if long-term tendencies of the reproduction of capitalism and of problems – such as the division between leaders and led and expressions of it such as bureaucracy, which overarch capitalism and socialism – provide the basis of a theoretical concept abstracted from its specific forms, which enables us to comprehend the general and the long-term, its meaning is articulated in concrete forms which are not *natural* but are historically limited and are thus amenable to change, although none the less tenacious and enormously problematic.

The terrain of intervention, our very subjectivity, our identity is the particular. And one type of knowledge is limited to the fragmented, the immediate, the specific. But there are many different kinds of knowledge, and our capacity to intervene effectively and our autonomy, a word much favoured by Gramsci, is augmented by an understanding of the long term and the general, not least because it contains within it the seeds of the corruption of the traditional, of the supersession of the past contained in the present.

Part 2

POLITICAL
INTERVENTIONS

5

EQUALITY AND DIFFERENCE

The emergence of a new concept of citizenship

REAL LIFE AND NEW THINKING

An inescapable dimension of the challenge to socialist politics has been brought home with a vengeance by changes in Central and Eastern Europe: the necessity of reconsidering our relationship to a tradition of political thinking. The word *necessity* is used advisedly, for the rethinking to be undertaken is rendered necessary by the changes of the present period. It is not an optional extra. It is not just a response to the politics of the right but to socio-economic change. What follows is an attempt to think through some of the theoretical implications of changes in women's socio-economic roles in a variety of countries. Focusing on these changes provides a window on a fundamental restructuring of the relationship between different spheres of society in the second half of the century. The fact that most women for most of their lives – including any periods when they have full adult caring responsibilities – are in the formal labour force challenges the adequacy of the concepts at our disposal for analysing the reality before us. It becomes clear how the conceptual division between public and private becomes all the more ephemeral in the light of the complexity of the interdependence between the household, the world of work, and state policy.[1]

What is also being called into question is the *relationship* between contemporary and traditional political thought and how, more generally, to relate to the past. As the socialist regimes have crumbled and democratic socialist parties have sought to reconstitute a basis of support in different countries, a critique of marxism has widely resulted in throwing away one tradition only to be accompanied by a renewed interest in liberal political thought. After years of intense theoretical debates informed by marxism, or a version of it, in which other traditions were either ignored or dismissed, there is the sensation that the answers were there all along if we had only looked beyond the provincial influence of our leftist ghetto.

What is at issue is how to avoid being fettered by old concepts – which prevent us from knowing reality. Instead we must pose those questions which are appropriate today. Here I would argue that, if we do re-read the liberal tradition in order to arrive at a better understanding of our present predicament, we need to recognise the historical, concrete, and political nature of the concepts we are dealing with. This is a contentious issue given the left's history of superficially dismissing 'bourgeois ideas'.[2] However, far from reducing a tradition to its historical period or to the 'needs of capitalism', we can both better understand our task and learn from that tradition if we are more sensitive to the historical dimensions of the ideas we inherit.

When Hobbes, Locke, or others wrote, they tried to produce concepts which were useful in intervening in the reality confronting them. They addressed a moment when the existing political traditions no longer seemed to provide a framework for posing the classical political questions because of concrete social, economic and political change. We cannot fully appreciate their ideas if we do not introduce this historical and political dimension. It is much more than an academic question for, if we are to learn from them, we must be equally sensitive to the need to arrive at concepts which are adequate for our period. In asking questions about the elements of continuity with the past and in trying to ascertain those which indicate fundamental change, we must be able to live with the uncertainty of not being able to rely on *any* pre-existing schema while at the same time seeking to learn the lessons from thinkers from the past.

And here we can *also* learn from the way that thinkers like Marx and Gramsci approached their intellectual work. We could do well to pose some of the same questions which they posed – however critical we may be of the answers they arrived at. For example, we too could ask: what messages do the major socio-economic changes of the day carry for rethinking politics? Further, how can we separate the *forms* of these changes, which have been specific – say, to Britain under Conservative governments, as compared to changes in another country with a different history, culture and balance of political forces – from long-term, deep-rooted trends which can tell us about the possibilities and constraints of a whole period of historical change?

The first lesson which we can try to learn in reconsidering our relationship with the various traditions of political thought is the 'not to be taken for granted' nature of the questions before us, however obvious they may seem. The second is the productiveness of allowing the uncertainty, ambiguity, and discomfiture inherent in a period of transition and crisis to serve as the humus of the creative development of new thinking, informed but not trapped by the past. The resulting knowledge is likely to be of a higher quality if we give ourselves permission to be tentative and acknowledge that knowing reality is an art as well a science. The pieces that do not slide easily into our old categories might well contain the seeds of new understanding.

CIVIL SOCIETY AND CITIZENSHIP

In recent years the concepts of civil society and citizenship have gained a prominent place in debates on the left. In addition, after a period in the shadows, the concept of equality is once more under discussion. These ideas not only have a history as ideas but cannot be dissociated from a whole historical epoch: the development of modern, post-feudal society and the modern state. Acknowledging their history helps us to comprehend their novelty in their own time, to analyse their utility today and to understand the historical and political reasons why we are still obliged to make reference to them. If concepts like civil society and citizenship cannot be 'put in the loft'[3] as outmoded ideas, it is for very real reasons. Yet, for other equally real reasons, we cannot simply adopt them as an alternative to the impoverished thinking which has so long dominated left political discourse. Contemporary conditions require us *both* to use these concepts as they acquire new meaning *and* to go beyond them.[4] If, for example, we historicise the concept of citizenship, we would have to examine the terrain on which it is exercised today. That terrain includes the welfare state. What comes into play is a highly complex and differentiated relationship to the state mediated through a wide range of institutions,in which the differences between people, according to resources, needs, family situation, point in the life cycle, and work history are as significant as equality before the law or equal political rights.[5]

The abstract nature of recent discussions about the concepts of civil society and citizenship, although responding to a very real political context, has occluded the possibility of these concepts being enriched to make them more useful for us today by rooting them in their concrete terrain. This by no means diminishes the importance of the need for legal guarantees and protection of civil liberties. Yet the abstract and general nature of much of the literature has meant that questions of race and nationality have not had the weight they deserve given the differential effects of government policy on sections of the population. Nor has the extensive and rich feminist literature, which offers a critique of an ungendered concept of citizenship, found a response in the dominant debate. Only recently is citizenship being redefined to include social rights, largely due to feminist work on the welfare state, despite T.H. Marshall's inportant essay in the immediate post-war period outlining the evolution of civil, political, and social rights.[6]

Interest in the concept of civil society in Britain was in part a response to the re-organisation of the state–society relationship under Conservative governments. However, the debate was given particular impetus by developments in Eastern Europe, where the concept of civil society has served such an important political purpose deriving from both its analytical function and its normative claims.[7] To a lesser extent, renewed interest in the possibilities of a regenerated and empowered civil society in the West is informed by an awareness that the fight for a progressive politics cannot take the form of a defence *tout court* of the welfare state and traditional social democracy.

Yet there is a danger in the way much of the discussion has been posed. Again, it has been abstract, not rooted in what is happening in society. Ironically in focusing on the political form of changes, that is, on the way this period has been moulded by a particular kind of politics, the political implications of underlying socio-economic trends – for example, the increased participation of women in the labour force, or the increasing complexity of individual and social needs – have often been obscured. That is, the *necessity* of rethinking the role of the state as a result of these underlying changes – which are not be controlled or caused by any political force – has tended to be hidden. Thus while there has been some acknowledgement of the need to rethink the role of the state, it has, in the main, been in response to a political and ideological offensive, and consequently, has assumed a defensive character: 'we, too, are critical of the state.' It has not been derived from an analysis of socio-economic conditions. It has not reflected an awareness that we are in fact *constrained* to rethink the state as society changes. To this extent it has, in fact, failed to replicate an important dimension of the tradition of political thought which we inherit.

Traditionally, going back to the classics of liberalism, but also to Hegel and the early Marx, the definition of civil society was always connected to the emergence of the modern state. A more recent example is Gramsci's argument that the potential for the expansion of civil society and the reduction of state power is rooted in the concomitant complexities and contradictions of the state and of civil society. In fact, Gramsci continues a long tradition of political thought when he asks: what do socio-economic changes tell us about the classic question of political science – the division between leaders and led? And yet, he goes beyond this tradition when he argues that because of the development of society, a new, unprecedented question is on the historical agenda: the possibility of overcoming that division. This question was also posed by Marx, but it was considered with new urgency by Gramsci as he reflected on the first concrete attempt to build socialism and the latest developments of capitalism. A further expansion and development of civil society which was the precondition for an unprecedented development of democracy became conceivable while also posing difficult new problems.[8]

What is missing from many contemporary debates is a parallel analysis of the potential and the problems inherent in the most recent developments of society, which cannot be reduced to the fact that one party or another is in power. The focus on civil society has tended to ignore, or at least to take for granted, the other side of the coin – the state – even though the condition of one implies the condition of the other. If, for example, there is a move away from an overly centralised, hierarchical, and bureaucratic organisation of services throughout Europe and a recourse to delivering social provision in new forms which override the bounds of private and public[9] – if the state is assuming an enabling rather than a providing role – this is because the complexity and diversity of social needs *require* a new relationship between civil society and state. Any renewal of civil society, of necessity, implies the reconstruction of the state – not just less of it but something different with a different web of relationships with society.

But what? It is, of course, easier to criticise 'the old' than to analyse 'the new'. Perhaps given the widespread disillusion with grand designs and technocratic utopias – what the post-modernists call metanarratives – intellectual modesty is hardly misplaced. Yet perhaps the task itself is misunderstood. If intellectuals are increasingly aware that they cannot spin utopias out of their heads, perhaps their vocation should be to concentrate on trying to ask the right questions of what is already happening before our eyes in order to understand the possibilities of what *might be*.

They might ask what possibilities, dilemmas and contradictions are contained in a major socio-economic change such as the dramatic increase of women in the formal labour market or the complexities of meeting social needs in a modern welfare state. Or what the dynamic of social reality reveals about concepts like civil society, state, citizenship, equality, difference, public, and private. This leads to the question whether the categories commonly used are adequate to capture the full potential of the dynamic of this pulsating, fragmented, contradictory society. For example, an analysis of the material fact of millions of women combining the public and private spheres, family needs and participation in formal paid work, in new forms in different countries, leads to new ways of thinking about concepts like the individual, equality, and difference.

THE INDIVIDUAL, EQUALITY, AND DIFFERENCE

A key feature of the debate about civil society is a reassertion of the civic role of individuals. The concept of civil society as it emerges from contract theory and liberal political thought cannot be separated from the notion of an autonomous, separate individual: a universal figure whose essence is defined in terms of his (sic) relation to the rule of law, and whose equality stems from eliminating from this relationship all indications of social status, socio-economic position, race, gender, etc. Hence the symbolism of Justice blindfolded. Just as the emergence of civil society, the rule of law, and the modern state were great advances, so the insistence on the universal aspects of the citizen, detached from specificity and difference, was an advance on the bonds of feudal society. Status no longer determined the formal legal relationship between citizen and state.

These progressive features are not negated by recognition of its gendered character, or by the fact that a new set of circumstances leads to further advances and new contradictions.[10] As legal and constitutional guarantees of civil rights were slowly established and the franchise extended, the fight for an expansion of democratic political rights in turn opened up the possibility that the struggle for social reforms and social citizenship rights could be placed on the political agenda. What were previously defined as private needs could be articulated as demands addressed to the state because of a concomitant development: the granting of political rights to individuals went hand in hand with the increasing weight in politics of organised groups. The civil right of association provides the possibility for individuals to enjoy a corporate presence in politics, as members of groups. Citizenship comes to signify both the legal, constitutional representation of the individual, first men and then women, and *de facto* representation of organised groups.

As the meaning of citizenship is expanded, the conditions are created for a major change. Civil and political rights allow for social needs to be articulated as demands on the state by political parties and pressure groups, and leads to the expansion of social policy and state intervention in society. This results in a complex and contradictory situation in which the relationship between individual and state, and hence the nature of citizenship, is transformed both politically and socially through the establishment and expansion of the welfare state.[11]

What, then, are some of the ways in which the abstract concept of the individual, despite its limitations, still functions and why is it – or at least a version of it – still of use? First, while it is posed as universal and abstract, the notion of the individual implicitly recognises difference. Human beings are defined as separate and individual and as motivated by particular rather than universal needs and desires. The liberal notion of equality before the law, that is, equal protection and opportunities, the assertion that irrelevant differences should play no part in preventing individuals, *however different they are,* from competing with each other under the same set of rules, continues to be a powerful claim. Within this framework, differences are not ignored but relegated to the social sphere and subtracted from the application of the rules of the game. The legitimacy of the law and the rules governing institutions such as in employment or education depends on the impartial application of what are presumed universal norms.[12] What is constituted is a hierarchy in which the universal, the general, and the abstract as dominant while the particular and the concrete are subordinant. The particular is understood as threatening to the social order if not kept within the bounds of the rule of law because individual needs are primarily viewed as separate and contradictory.

Yet if these questions are considered from a more recent point of view, there is another dimension. From the perspective of the needs of the individual in the context of the welfare state and with the increasing participation rate of women in formal paid work, the picture is one of complexity and social interdependence. In terms of the responsibility we each have as adults to care for ourselves and others – children, partners, parents – and to cover the myriad needs of households, the needs of one person are very different from another.

In modern conditions of the welfare state and advanced industrial society, when both men and women are in formal, paid work, these differences have entered the public arena. They can no longer be conceptualised as private. In addition to being structured by gender and by contemporary forms of the sexual division of labour – in which women have the main caring responsibilities but in which they are also likely to be in the formal labour force – the fulfilment of needs and the definition of differences depend on a much more complex set of conditions and institutions than previously. These depend on the services which are available but also on the organisation of work and of time. Any concept of the individual adequate to contemporary conditions must include these complexities and these differences. Moreover, the relationship between individual and state is mediated by a web of institutions which overlap the bounds between civil society and state. This calls into question much of the conceptual framework of liberal political thought which was posited on a direct relationship between individual and state *at the very same time* as other of its precepts such as the rule of law, founded on just such a direct relationship, are as significant and important as ever.

The concept of the individual can be viewed from still other more recent perspectives, not available to the founders of liberal thought, for example psychoanalysis. It is clear that concrete individuals, you and me, each have different life histories and both complex and evolving inner dynamics and identities. These can only be understood as processes in which individuals are both the responsible subjects and the objects of inner and outer in-fluences. We are each unique, however much we may have things in common, and however much the outsider, the professional or the intellectual might be able to discern patterns over time or across society. We have different points of view. However constrained by influences inside and outside ourselves, by institutions and practices, our subjectivity and identity are highly individual and complex.

On different levels and from different perspectives we need the concept of the individual. But this does not mean that its content can remain what it is in liberal political thought, or that the criticisms of this notion of the abstract individual and of the particular concept of equality which accompanies it can be ignored. The most familiar criticism is that social conditions make it impossible for all individuals in fact to enjoy the full benefits of the protection of the rule of law and of civil rights because of the different cultural, economic and social resources. In addition, a marxist approach would criticise the universality of the notion as ahistorical and as obscuring the inevitable structural imbalance of power between individuals who are, in fact, situated in classes, an imbalance which is imposed by the relations of production.

More recent anti-racist and feminist critiques open up new dimensions. These go beyond a claim for equal opportunities since they are informed by the recognition of the differentiated effects of an equal application of the rules to people who are different. On the one hand, this is because the rules themselves contain assumptions which are far from neutral or universal. On the other, the very notion of the universal, by silencing differences, derives its very meaning from subordinating or marginalising the other, the specific, the particular, the different.[13] On a practical level, equal achievement premised on the integration of everyone into the dominant model is impossible. Consequently, these critiques assert the value and validity of different identities which derive from ethnicity, nationality, religion, and gender.[14]

Criticism of the abstract, universal dimensions of the concept results in a complex redefinition of the individual, as member of a group, a category, a gender, yes, affected by the rules in a particular way because of sharing certain characteristics with others, but whose identity is meaningful in so far as it is redefined in its concrete peculiarity and individuality: in its separateness, in its multidimensionality, in its moment – that is, its stage in the life cycle – its differentiated, specific, mediated relationship to the state. In a sense, what we have in common is our separateness, our uniqueness, the fact that we are different, our sense of being alone. Deconstructing the abstract concept of the individual, helps us to recognise something else: viewed from different facets of our identity, we each belong to a partial group, we are each an 'other', whatever our ethnicity, gender, nationality, however privileged or not we may be by the structures of power relations, opportunities, and inequalities within which we find ourselves.

INTERDEPENDENCE, COMPLEXITY, AND A NEW CONCEPT OF CITIZENSHIP

What has been inserted into the political process is a contradiction which is a result of the expansion of democracy and the extension of civil rights. Combined with the need for greater state intervention as modern industrial society developed, as people fought for and gained the vote, and as they organised in parties, trade unions, and pressure groups, the old utilitarian aim of making the state responsive to people's demands took on a new meaning. The expansion of the welfare state was, in part, the result of the insertion into the political agenda of a range of social needs. The relationship of the individual to the state began to be defined in terms both of equality and difference, equal treatment by the law and differentiation according to needs. I am a citizen of a state and therefore possess certain rights. Those rights, civil, political, or social are the same for all citizens, but the needs of individuals vary enormously. From the point of view of the individual, since our needs, not just our resources, vary over the life cycle, so does our relationship to the state.[15]

The contradiction has also been inserted into the world of production.[16] The principle of economic organisation in the modern period, which applies both to socialism and to capitalism, is that the worker is paid for the job done, all differences being left behind. There is a parallel with the principle of formal, legal equality, and there are also parallel criticisms of the gendered and racialised character of both the application of this principle in practice and the universality implied in it. Equal access to jobs and equal treatment at work is the ideal and the goal, the object of the fight for equality. If people have different cultures or needs outside of the world of work, they are supposed to be left behind, to be addressed through the market, the servicing work done by women, or the state. The organisation of work is blindfolded, just like Justice, as it is confronted by the concrete social figures who in fact bring with them a huge range of needs which are highly differentiated at any one moment.

This has always been the case in modern industrial society, but once these social figures are increasingly women, less and less can needs be said to belong to another sphere. The classic reserve army of carers, women, as they straddle work and private life bring into the open a contradiction which was hitherto hidden by the sexual division of labour. Paid work impinges on their ability to satisfy social needs; and their responsibility for social needs both impinges on their lives in the productive sphere and, consequently, their financial wellbeing whether from wages or benefits such as pensions related to work history, and manifestly cannot, and never has been, consigned to the state or to the market.

What is immanent in the situation is the necessity of a transformation of the very logic of production in which Marx's definition of communism, 'from each according to his [sic] ability, to each according to his needs', has to be gendered. It can no longer be reduced to an economic calculation, and but must be forced to take account of social organisation. The centrality of paid work, and the overdetermination of our lives by rigid, inflexible jobs, is being challenged no less by individual needs than by economic transform-ations. This is the context of a further redefinition of citizenship, of social rights, to include the rights of daily life and the right, for men as well as women, of 'time to care'.[17] If we look at even the most advanced welfare states, the Nordic countries, we cannot conceive of all caring needs being taken over by the state, the market, or even voluntary organisations in civil society. We, women and men, need to be guaranteed time to care – for our-selves and others – and flexibility throughout our working lives in the organisation of work and social institutions to reflect a politics of time. What is being asked of the state here is something traditional: legal regulation. But its object is novel and indicative of a new relationship between state and society, between the state and the individual: to enable, to facilitate our individual and social creativity. Changes of this nature are subversive of a whole order. They are revolutionary, but they are not utopian because they reflect the real social needs of millions of people.[18]

From this perspective, the private, the social, the economic, the political, civil society, and the state form such a web of interdependencies that it is difficult if not impossible to 'think' them separately. Yet, if these categories, like the concept of citizenship, are still used and have a significance, and consequently are still necessary, changes in society, in daily life, mean that in fact they are being reformulated and enriched. Their increasing complexity reflects the complexity of society itself. To the extent they remain simple, general, historical, abstract, they cease to represent this reality, rather like the intellectuals who use them.

UNIVERSALITY CHALLENGED

The introduction of gender into our way of thinking undermines the universality of traditional conceptual schema. The rich feminist literature which has placed gender on the intellectual agenda is underpinned by the daily experience of millions of women. Most adult women negotiate the various spheres of society as adults with full caring responsibilities who nonetheless engage in formal paid work, with all the constraints this implies. They live their lives in social institutions built on assumptions, values, and symbols, which alienate and incapacitate them. What they, we, experience is the impossibility for women to feel at ease in a world made according to a male model.

What intellectual reflection has retrieved from obscurity is that this model is male, in part because the public world has been shaped empirically by those social figures who have in the main constructed it, men. Perhaps more significantly in terms of any project of transforming the conditions of domination and subordination, realisation that our very conceptual framework and our symbolic order provides a structure and a justification for these conditions. The political system, the world of work and theoretical discourse are all premised on a concept of the universal which maintains the pretence of being abstract and general. The way institutions are organised, the rules which govern their practices, our language and concepts (e.g. the rights of Man), our notion of reason itself, present themselves as blind to gender, as they pretend to be universal.[19]

We can deconstruct the pretence of the universal, and uncover this blindness by working from two perspectives, one historical and one ahistorical. As it has developed in modern, post-feudal and then industrial society, and acquired conceptual form in the Enlightenment, the pretence of blind, neutral universality has contributed to the concrete, historical subordination and marginalisation of women and legitimised the historical domination of men. The relegation by modern thought of the specific, the concrete, the other to a lesser status was part of an attempt to comprehend, order, and control reality through the establishment of general, universal categories. This project goes back to the Greeks but acquires a particular power with regards to the mass of the population as it informs a web of institutions and forms of social provision which affect their lives intimately, as the universal, the general moves beyond the province of philosopher kings to structure the thinking of civil servants, policy makers, and social scientists, professionals, and practitioners in state services.[20]

The inadequacy of modern, universalising thought is further revealed by focusing on another, highly contentious, aspect which can be argued is ahistorical: the fact of there being more than one gender. What it is to be female or male, their internal complexities, the interdependency between the definition of one and the other are historically, socially, culturally determined. The argument is not derived from biological essentialism. Biology is in any case but one aspect of a much more complex phenomenon, and its significance is transformed by social and technological change. The internal complexities of masculinity and femininity signify that we can never think one as the opposite of the other. Further, as we are each a different mixture of femininity and masculinity but our identities are overdetermined by one or the other, it is impossible to conceptualise androgyny. Whatever this means for a particular, concrete individual, however our gender identities are constrained, regulated, influenced by rules, norms, symbols, ideas, practices, and cultures related to our biological, bodily being or our social roles, it follows that gender differences will be redefined but not eliminated.

The need to think about gender, then, is not only an historical or political phenomenon although there are concrete, historical and political reasons why it has been put on the table now. Feminism and the women's and gay liberation movements have had an important impact. But the need to conceptualize gender difference does not derive from a movement which manifests in the public arena a preconstituted set of differences. It is not a constitution of an interest like other interests which may or may not be incorporated into the political system like economic and class interests have been. Instead, it is derived, as argued above, from something much more fundamental. Our identities are structured by gendered relations which permeate institutions and practices. No project based on a universal which seeks to eliminate gender differences altogether can be successful.

What is, however, on the historical agenda is another project: the construction of a terrain – and the ideas and institutions and practices appropriate to it – in which differences and conflicts exist and are recognised and in which a dynamic, organic differentiated concept of unity replaces the false premises of traditional social and political institutions and practices. We have to think about how to create a woman-friendly world, in which women as well as men can be at their ease, a world made for women *and* men. Constructing such a world would contribute toward overcoming not only the alienation of women, but also that of men. Further, we might also be enabled to *recognise* ethnic differences but as aspects of a multifaceted diversity in which we begin to comprehend how we are each part of some minority – albeit some more privileged than others. What is being inserted into the very foundation of politics is complexity and conflict as the irreconcilable difference implanted in the gendered structure of our identities confronts the universalistic pretence of social and political institutions and theory. One inference is that it is impossible for women (or men for that matter) to leave their gendered identities behind when they are actors in the public sphere. Our identities as gendered beings need to be recognised so that women no longer have to act in the public sphere as surrogate men.

WHEN DIFFERENCE BECOMES DIVERSITY

It is not surprising that there is great hesitancy to embark on this road. Difference *has* been and is being spoken – in private, in the form of sexual and other stereotypes, as part of a public and private structure of domination and subordination. Disadvantage and discrimination not to speak of persecution have been and can be the result. There is still the need to fight old, outmoded concepts of difference. But we must be under no illusions. The institutions and practices which bear the marks of the old are the product of the historical domination of one gender. The concept of the universal or the practices of these institutions which are incapable of speaking gender or difference construct the subordination of women.

Blinding ourselves to difference does not mean that it ceases to exist. Overcoming women's subordination in a world made for one gender, whatever the social organisation, and the possibility for an enriched, complex concept and practice of equality to be created are both related to understanding that the expansion of freedom of the individual depend on removing the constraints of the universal while maintaining what has been achieved by the painful stuggle for equality. We arrive at the notion that, if the concept of universal equality before the law, in which irrelevant differences play no role is manifestly still necessary both in terms of civil rights and equal opportunities, it rests alongside the necessity of thinking difference and specificity: a necessity imposed upon us by socio-economic change, the consequent transformation of social needs, articulated or not, cultural developments, the new ways in which we articulate our subjectivity and perceive our identity, and advances in intellectual perception which render the notion of the individual both complex and problematic.

What can be observed are a variety of challenges to traditional political science and politics. These represent a challenge to the role of the intellectuals as experts and to social policy making. By introducing difference, complexity and conflict into the foundation stones of political and social theory and practice, the task of politics and of social policy changes even though many old values remain as useful as ever. Tolerance and respect reinforced by civic, cultural and, where necessary, legal guarantees and practices are the precondition for diversity to become a social asset rather than for difference to constitute a threat.

What is made necessary is a process in which differences and highly differentiated needs are addressed in their specificity and peculiarity. This is one in which it is recognised that the universal can be as misleading as the particular and in which the need for rethinking the democratic process and democratic institutions derives from the very development of the modern period. We are experiencing the re-articulation of the meaning of the individual and the emergence of a new concept of citizenship. We are living in a period in which the old lines of public and private, of state and civil society, are being transformed whether we like it or not. Further, what is being scrutinised in new terms are the conditions in which women particip-ate in public life, be it in the state, the productive or the social spheres. The forms of transformation taking place between and within spheres differ from country to country according to both historical and political traditions and the balance of political forces. Comprehending, let alone intervening, in this reality is a daunting task. Questioning the universal does not inexorably lead to abandoning any attempt at general comprehension and remaining confined to partial, occasional, haphazard knowledge, as much of the debate on post-modernism would have it. Rather, we forced to begin to construct a new way of thinking and of understanding reality in all its increasing complexity and diversity.

6

BACK TO THE FUTURE

The resurrection of civil society

Rather than used analytically, the concept of civil society has been mobilised ideologically in countries as diverse as Sweden and the United States to argue that the state should retreat from welfare provision. In the years immediately before the collapse of communism it served a similarly political function in the very different circumstances of Central and Eastern Europe. In focusing on Gramsci's ideas, I suggest some approaches which might help us to understand how we can learn from thinkers from earlier periods. Building on Gramsci's method, but going beyond his conceptual schema and most of the current debate, I then argue that no concept of civil society which is adequate today can ignore relationships within and between family, voluntary organisations and state or the gendered configurations of real civil societies. This in turn helps us to reformulate our concept of the political. Above all, Gramsci helps us to understand that we must not idealise civil society.

I would tend to agree with those who argue that civil society should not be extended to all phenomena outside the state,[1] but I would cast the net widely. I would extend debate to those conditions of its existence which are to be found in earlier thinkers but currently need to be resurrected: the family and gender, plus an important contemporary phenomenon, voluntary organisations whose functions can often be civic or mobilising.

'CENTRE' AND 'PERIPHERY': THEORETICALLY GENERAL OR HISTORICALLY AND SPATIALLY SPECIFIC

Writing on civil society in English[2] is marked by some special features. First, this literature has tended to reproduce a split between the conceptual and normative terrain of political and social theory, on the one hand, and recent historical and contemporary empirical and political analysis, on the other.

The exceptions are rare.[3] Second, theoretical discussion is generally allocated *de facto* to those writers positioned in 'the centre', broadly the Anglo-American world. That is, the task of developing philosophical abstraction and conceptual universality is implicitly assigned to those who, it is assumed, no longer need to investigate the concrete and particular features of their own societies. Much of the recent literature from these perspectives takes for granted their already supposedly completed modernisation in the by now 'post-modern' world (although within this debate the term is rare) in which the history of civil society belongs to the past, having reached an acme, perhaps degenerated, and perhaps now in need of regeneration.[4] Concrete analysis is therefore relegated to the perceived need to explain the deviation from the norm of the 'periphery', countries whose histories and social realities are at variance with the paths of development of Britain and the United States.[5]

Third, in only a few cases is it implied that the conceptual schema of the social and political theorists and the very mode of analysis need to be rethought in the light of knowledge derived from different kinds of concrete studies of other experiences.[6] Fourth, it is these latter studies,[7] plus work done by feminist scholars[8] which insist on the need to think about the nature of different kinds of *state* at the same time as focusing on civil society and to extend the discussion to take account of the consequences of the development of civil society on the construction of gender and the social and political role of the family and kinship networks.[9]

Fifth, the use of civil society as a strategic concept, that is, as part of an analysis of what *is* in order to understand how to achieve what *might be* tends to come from writers who are concerned with immediate political questions of transition.[10] Finally it is only by considering some of the empirical dimensions of the transition which former communist countries are undergoing that an attempt is made to consider the 'pros' and 'cons' of really existing civil society, not only in Central and Eastern Europe, but in the United States, both today and in De Tocqueville's day.[11] It is noteworthy that in most if not all cases, those who reflect on theoretical dimensions in the light of empirical and historical considerations, and not the other way round, are authors who are 'outsiders' in relation to the Anglo-American debate, in terms of empirical focus, personal histories, theoretical perspectives, or a combination of these.[12] There is a marked paucity of analysis of the contours, or dynamic, or weave of actually existing civil societies in, say, Britain or the United States, or Italy, or they go by another name.[13]

HISTORICAL AND METHODOLOGICAL CONTEXTS

On the whole the Anglo-American debate about civil society remains highly abstract with little relation to concrete reality.[14] In considering the relevance for social and political analysis, not only of Gramsci's concept of civil society and the ideas of *any* earlier thinker, it is vital to know about the societies which they were reflecting upon and about the debates within which their ideas were inserted in order to help us to decide what is historically limited about their concepts, and what can still provide insights for us today.

We would argue, on the contrary, that any consideration of the relevance today of Gramsci's concept of civil society must begin by explaining the context into which he was intervening, before going on to try to clarify some common misapprehensions about his ideas. His writing, it can be argued, is both much simpler and more challenging than many commentators have recognised.[15] It will then be possible to suggest some limitations in his ideas, many of which, it must be said, are not restricted to him but apply to other thinkers, not least most contemporary commentators on civil society. These include the lack of attention to the significance of the evolving voluntary, non-profit, or 'third' sector, or to the family and gender.[16] The important question is not so much whether he provides a theoretical model sufficient in itself for our theoretical needs, but rather whether his ideas help us to do the rethinking which *we* need to do in changing circumstances even if his ideas inevitably only partially fulfill our own analytical requirements.

WORLD WAR, EXPANDED STATES, NEW KINDS OF MEN AND WOMEN: THE RECOMPOSITION OF PUBLIC AND PRIVATE

When Gramsci was writing, the expanded role of the state was a central political issue from the Soviet Union, Nazi Germany and fascist Italy to New Deal and Latin America. The related question of planning was widely debated throughout Europe. Furthermore, the experience of the First World War, but a few years behind, was decisive. The First World War showed the capacity of the state in exceptional circumstances to organise society as never before, and to depend on both economic structures and political consent in an historically unprecedented way in order to wage war. Although its aftermath in many countries shook the very foundations of their political systems, they were remarkably resiliant. In the 1930s Gramsci's reference to trenches as fortifications of the state was far from abstract. The extension of state activity and the mobilisation not only of military forces through conscription but also of society more widely meant that any differentiation between civil and political, or indeed civil and military, corresponded to only part of reality. Such a distinction, in short, simply did not capture the new weave of threads connecting different parts or aspects of society, or the nature of state power in the twentieth century.

Public and private and the relationship between the two were also being recomposed in a myriad of ways: from the creation of parks and garden cities; the building of dams and highways; the reclaiming of land and electrification; and the construction of monumental buildings with public money; to widespread attempts at social engineering. The development of mass cultural forms, including film and radio, the expansion of modern retailing, or, in some countries, the regulation of alcohol were only some examples of changes in the public sphere which had an important impact on the private sphere.[17] Traditional social relations, including gender relations, were being challenged by the projects of building socialism in the Soviet Union, remaking and 'purifying' German and Italian society, and producing the kind of workers suited to a Taylorised assembly line. The family was the site of interventions – from Detroit to Rome to Berlin to Helsinki to Moscow – as traditional socialisation no longer seemed to guarantee desired outcomes and certainly not the noble women and men needed to construct new societies.[18]

Changing values, controlling behaviour and motivating consent, both in economic production and in maintaining allegiance to (or at least passive acceptance of) the state, were not abstract debates but entailed practical policies, public or private, such as Henry Ford's attempt to interfere with the private lives of his workers. Gramsci's notes on what he calls Americanism and Fordism capture much of this. Hegemony had roots in the workplace, the home, the school and the cinema.

THEORETICAL AND POLITICAL IMPLICATIONS

These practices *also* had consequences for theory. The state and political power, the role of intellectuals, experts, and politicians, political organisation, the configuration of society, the significance of strategies to maintain hegemony could only in part be understood using traditional concepts. The words might remain the same, but their meaning was changing, not because of intellectual debate but because of the effect *on theory* of profound economic, social and political change which was beyond the control but *also* produced in part by the activities of political parties (and Gramsci defines these widely), social movements, and economic actors.[19] Gramsci investigated these changed meanings as he attempted to take account of the consequences for both theory and political intervention of what we would now term the cutting edges of historical development, and the latest thrusts of modernisation. Only a few commentators have attempted to analyse Gramsci in these terms.[20]

This is the context in which Gramsci resurrected and redefined a traditional concept, civil society, little if at all used in contemporary debates. But why this concept? Because he needed it to help him to comprehend several contemporary developments: the resilience of capitalist regimes despite profound economic and political upheavals; the success of fascism in Italy, a movement which arose in civil society, outside 'normal' politics; and the differences between Russia and the West.[21] A certain kind of revolution might have been possible in 1917 in tsarist Russia where an atrophied state, emptied of effective power, could be toppled in the absence of civil society, but not in the West. Yet, by the 1920s and 1930s, this very lack of a developed civil society presented an enormous problem for developing a fully fledged socialist democracy.

Gramsci argued in the famous letter to the Central Committee of the Communist Party of the Soviet Union in 1926, just before he was arrested, as Stalin was consolidating his power, that the Soviet Union could represent a model for the working-class movement in the rest of the world only in so far as it expanded consent, or hegemony, as socialism was constructed.[22] This required the development of a modern civil society, the real bulwark of the new system. Gramsci develops the concepts of civil society, and the notion of hegemony which is integral to it, to help him to understand what most of his contemporaries in the working-class movement did not – the complex nature of state power in the twentieth century not only in capitalist society but in the process of building a new, democratic, socialist society.

Yet Gramsci employs the term in a self-conscious, reflective and analytic way. Civil society had to be revalued as a *terrain* which had an impact on *politics*, and was a measure of historical advance. But civil society itself had to be scrutinised. The way it was organised, the ideas, practices and social relations which were manifest, the struggles and conflicts between different groups and institutions with varying degrees of autonomy from the state *conditioned* politics and were in turn conditioned by laws and by public policy more generally. Consequently for Gramsci civil society is an *analytical* concept *not* a normative one. Although marking historical advance, the outcome of a 'civilising process', it could be far from civilised. Contemporary examples of 'uncivil' civil society in Western and Eastern Europe, North America and elsewhere are not hard to find. Civil society could throw up a fascist movement which would suppress much of civil society itself, or, Gramsci would argue, it could provide the basis of an increasing democratisation of politics.

Gramsci writes that he *often* employs the concept of civil society (implicitly but *not only*) in the way Hegel used it[23] referring above all to the ethical role of the state, to the lines of connection between state and society, and to the structures, practices and ideas through which consent to the social order is achieved and to the roles of the intellectuals.[24] In that sense, effective political power in the modern world was not a one-way process of political management. Nor could it be understood without an adequate comprehension of the nature of civil society in the concrete because civil society in its nationally and historically differentiated institutional forms and contents *conditioned* state power and the activity of political parties, and was inevitably conditioned in turn.

Gramsci was *both* analysing contemporary reality *and* considering how state intervention might be changed from transformation from above for ends determined by the few into facilitating the liberation of human capacities.[25] When he argues that the achievement of democracy and implicitly socialism implies the expansion of civil society and the shrinking of the state as 'normally' understood, as a lawmaking and enforcing body, as coercion,[26] Gramsci is engaging with several precise intellectual and political traditions: Catholicism, economic liberalism, Italian philosophical idealism, fascism, and Soviet socialism.

IDEAS IN AND BEYOND THEIR CONTEXTS

After the Risorgimento, the Catholic Church claimed to represent civil society in contrast to the political society of the state, and did everything it could to undermine the legitimacy of the political order,[27] which enjoyed such a narrow basis of consent that 'Italia reale' was commonly contrasted to 'Italia legale'. Gramsci disagreed with the Church's claim to represent the whole of Italian civil society as he analysed the unified state's limited hegemony, itself in part a manifestation of the opposition of the Church.[28] Civil society could not be represented by *any* one institution, be it church, party, or state.

Gramsci's multifaceted polemic with the philosophers Benedetto Croce, Giovanni Gentile and Ugo Spirito is relevant. Croce formed part of a Southern Italian Hegelian tradition which advocated a leading role for the state and for the stratum of intellectuals to which he belonged in modernising and industrialising Italy. Croce was little help, however, in understanding the contemporary political and social roles of different kinds of intellectuals,[29] that is, the complex weave of civil society which constituted the terrain of battle over what would be the predominant influences in that process of change. Italian fascism understood much better than Croce the nature of modern mass society and the implications for state power. Criticisms of Gramsci's concept of civil society as dangerous utopianism and precursor to totalitarianism are misconceived.[30] Gramsci is unambiguous when he argues quite clearly *against* the ideas of Gentile, Spirito and other fascist thinkers more generally on the role of the state, maintaining that political society and civil society could *not* be conflated.[31]

Further, he is explicitly, and courageously, given his prison conditions, critical of Mussolini's idea of creating a totalitarian state.[32] It cannot be stressed too strongly that Gramsci argues, both analytically and strategically, *against* claims that political society should or even *could* absorb civil society. Fascist ambitions to unify society through a single party and through the totalitarian state which could represent all social forces by eliminating the need for a plurality of organisations in civil society[33] were no more valid than the claims of the Catholic Church to represent all of civil society[34] or, significantly, *any* other political party.[35]

The implications of this argument for *any* regime, including the Soviet Union, are clear. A link which might at first appear unlikely is provided by Gramsci's critique of the assumptions of economic liberalism, another site of his discussion of civil society.[36] The state, Gramsci argued, was not the be all and end all, as his criticism of Jacobinism makes clear.[37] But could the state, defined as coercion, in fact wither away?[38] Gramsci considered the terms in which this traditional marxist question could be posed as a concrete political project which was not doomed to demagogic utopianism while confronting the irrefutable statism of the 1930s. In his view any notion of the state simply withdrawing and leaving a vacuum was unrealistic in modern society. This is why he disagreed that the liberal ideal of a nightwatchman state, adopted by parts of the social democratic movement, could serve as the model for the withering away of the state.[39] A civil society which becomes more complex, as organisations within it take on new tasks, and articulate new needs, is part and parcel of the transformation of the state so that its ethical content expands,[40] the state increasingly reflects social needs, and its coercive role diminishes. This perspective is different from claiming that the existing state could simply do less and less, providing minimal protection for society, with no more responsibility for its welfare than that of a nightwatchman, in the absence of the full development of civil society and extended democratic control.[41]

CIVIL SOCIETY AND THE DEMOCRATISATION OF POLITICS

This leads us to Gramsci's preoccupation with the limits of the Soviet experience in providing any kind of model for socialism. No less than with his argument with Mussolini, Gentile, and Spirito, or his critique of Croce, his notes on civil society in this context are both analytical and strategic. The 'war of movement' of the Russian Revolution does *not* provide a model precisely because the 'East' did not have the modern civil society which existed in the 'West'.[42] The only strategy appropriate for a whole historical period in which a complex civil society is a sign of historical advance[43] was a war of position. If a modern civil society does not exist before a transfer of state power, it must be created.[44] In the absence of the development of civil society, the state remains in Gramsci's terms backward, i.e. predominately coercive, enjoying at best a highly restricted hegemony over society. Because it can only depend on limited consent, it must consequently rely on force, and the conditions for a fully developed socialism, defined by Gramsci as the extension of democracy, are aborted. In the 'East' a fully fledged civil society had to be constructed as an integral aspect of the democratisation of a modernised Soviet society. Indeed, the real conditions of transitions to democracy in Central and Eastern Europe, South Africa and elsewhere in the late twentieth century demonstrate that such a concern for the development of civil society is just as relevant today.

Gramsci was not only reflecting on the Soviet Union but considering what differentiated socialism from other statist regimes, not least Italian fascism, when he links a period of what he calls statolatry or state worship to an economic-corporative transformation in which infrastructural elements needed to be built, a limited first step in changing society. His worries are apparent when he argues that this must be considered temporary and exceptional in the early stages of building socialism.[45] He also considers the case in which organisational plurality is eliminated,[46] and explores the possibility of a progressive as well as reactionary Caesarism.[47] In the context of a widespread belief in the benefits of state intervention in the 1930s which extended across the political spectrum, his concern to analyse what were world-wide trends rather than condemn them is understandable even if with hindsight today this could appear damning. This is meant as more than a gloss to 'save' Gramsci now that we see much more clearly than he the tragic defects of the Soviet system. After all, he was clearly concerned that what he hoped would be temporary features, shared with fascism in many respects, were contingent on specific conditions and would be eliminated. He was wrong.

The concrete problems of a transformation of state power and the development of civil society necessitated, he argued, a moral and intellectual transformation of the order of the French Revolution or the Protestant Reformation.[48] The development of civil society extends democracy to achieve a 'societá regolata' in which an ethical state regulates in the sense of guiding society rather than coercing it.[49] This mode of governing (the Italian *regolare* is translated into English as 'to guide or govern or regulate') is no longer conceptualised as the Hegelian product of the knowing few, but in relationship with an increasing capacity for self-government, posed not as a utopian ideal but concretely and in all its extreme difficulty. The state is defined as civil plus political society and the suggestion that civil society will supersede political society entails an increase in the democratic and ethical content of politics and the decrease of coercion.[50]

The battle for a progressive politics had no choice but to engage on the terrain of civil society. It was no accident that authoritarian regimes feared and tried to control civil society whose development was not spontaneous but could be facilitated or hampered. It both influenced state policy and was affected by it. The qualities of this terrain would determine the qualities of a country's democracy as much as the constitution or the political system. A fully developed civil society was a political project to be achieved. It would not be the automatic outcome of economic transformation[51] and even less brought about by an identity between party and state.[52]

73

THE LIMITS OF SPATIAL METAPHORS

Gramsci argues that while civil and political society can be understood *methodologically* as different levels of society, *empirically* (in the context of his notes on the roles of intellectuals in organising hegemony),[53] there is no definitive division between the two: he is trying to portray differentiation, connection and simultaneity using terms which are spatial metaphors. But depicting civil society and political society as occupying different spaces brings with it problems. The inadequacy of the metaphors with which Gramsci struggles is confirmed by the different 'positions' he assigns to civil society, as composed of fortifications or trenches sometimes portrayed in front of, sometimes behind, and sometimes 'beneath' or encompassed by the state.[54] Further, the concept of historical bloc effectively supersedes both the structure/superstructure metaphor and wraps around the civil society/state distinction.

TODAY'S SOCIETIES TELL NEW STORIES

No discussion of civil society today which remains at a purely abstract level and relegates history and analysis of actual societies to 'the other' can be complete or provide the preconditions for incorporating ethnicity, sexual, and wider social diversity organically into our analytical frameworks. Second, going beyond Gramsci's work, a greater and greater role is being played *in civil society* by what is called the voluntary, the third, or the not-for-profit sector, by non-governmental organisations which constitute a new weave of the threads between state and individual.[55] The state is not just doing less, but in its new role as facilitator, as regulator, and usually also as financier of the activities of these organisations its function is changing. Certainly the voluntary sector should not simply be celebrated. National specificities have to be borne in mind as well as the political instrumentalisation which can take place in referring to idealised, ideological portrayals of civil society and of voluntary organisations, as if they were alternatives *tout court* to current provision, not least in political debate from the United States to the Nordic countries. At the same time, these developments, in their different forms in different countries, *might* constitute some of the conditions for an increase in democratic control, a development of civil society, and a transformation of the state.

But is this civil society? Not all organised activity or social institutions that exist outside the state can be defined as civil society, for example, in the black economy, or the criminal world, or the family. But the campaigning activities of voluntary organisations qualify them, and the very servicing activities of women, and men, can no longer be called simply private and particular. In conjunction with, say, schools, or other institutions, these

activities often provide the basis for civic and ultimately political participation.[56] Indeed, private tragedy can provide not only the motivation but the
organisational basis for civic and political activity.[57] Prompted by Gramsci's
example, our concept of politics and of civil society must therefore change
and expand if we are not to lose important aspects of contemporary society.
Certainly, if we are to make use of *any thinkers* from the past, we have to
historicise them, decide what is still relevant and what we need to develop for
ourselves.

OLD CATEGORIES REFORMULATED OR
BACK TO THE FUTURE

Gramsci retrieved the concept of civil society to reformulate it to help him to
understand modern conditions in which society outside of but related to the
political sphere was increasingly organised and counted politically. An
element which we must reinsert in our conceptual schema, and which is
missing both in Gramsci and in most contemporary discussions of civil
society, is the family, both as a 'corporate body' and in terms of the effects
on individuals. Today no understanding of civil society, of the political
order, or indeed of the economic sphere, can do without a conceptualisation
of gender and other identities, or fail to consider the consequences for
thinking about civil society of the state of relations in the family. The very
constitution of the terrain of civil society has effects on gender identities as
women and men find the social and political spaces they inhabit expanded or
constricted.[58]

Yet if family, civil society and state, however defined, do not occupy the
same space, and have different rhythms and logics and cannot be reduced
one to the other, nor can they be conceptualised in terms of separate,
discrete *places* or *times*. Hegel's model of family, civil society, and state, in
ascending order, for all its historical and conceptual limits, at least provides
us with the sense that all three elements must be conceptualised simultaneously and are interrelated in their differences. However, if writers like
Hegel and later Arendt include the family in their discussions, it is relegated
to a lower order, its particularity and mode of cohesion contrasted to the
potential of civil society for the assertion of individual capacities within a
competitive framework for Hegel or of the public sphere to offer the space
for rational discourse for Arendt. Family roles are important but of lesser
value. It is easy, then, to slip to devaluing what is in fact a precondition of
the social order and to place in the shadows one, if not the only, source of
the gendering of economic and political institutions and the weave of
relations between them.

The project of developing what might be termed a user-friendly society,
discussed from the Nordic countries to Italy, is related *both* to the question,

in Gramsci's terms, of an ethical state and 'una societá regolata' which is more responsive to human needs, *and* to a reconceptualisation of the democratic activity of women and men,[59] that is, of politics. These are but some of the dimensions of a discussion of civil society which both takes account of recent significant developments and is newly aware of the significance of traditional concerns, recast in a modern light. It is in this sense that we can learn from Gramsci's own thinking as he asked old and new questions about the potential of the latest historical developments.

BEYOND DICHOTOMIES

The transitions we are living through reveal the inadequacy of traditional categories and force us to go beyond simple divisions between public and private, however defined. The old boxes of market, public sector, civil society, state are not self-contained entities. Rather we could say that the different spheres or levels of society invade each other. Writing which refers rhetorically rather than concretely to civil society or to community, or to the family, and ignores women's and men's concrete roles within it and in society at large, or the informal networks between friends, or the messy, highly differentiated, difficult to define voluntary sector, is simply inadequate however theoretically or journalistically polished.[60] It cannot be stressed too strongly that engagement with the concrete will contribute to better theory and improved theory will help us to understand and to shape change. The journey from theory to reality and back is a road well travelled but too often forgotten. Gramsci is one who can help us to find our way.

7

BEYOND PESSIMISM
OF THE INTELLECT
Agendas for social justice and change

> Cynics inside the Labour Party and in abundance beyond in the
> media like to prove their independence and powers of professional
> scepticism by scoffing . . .; to display enthusiasm, interest or under-
> standing is to depart from the unwritten code. All politicians are
> knaves and propagandists; all their ideas are confused, inadequate
> or boil down to the same old left/right divide in the end.[1]

In the absence of understanding clearly the complex analysis which lies at
the bottom of the new directions of so much New Labour policy, most
critics do not have much more than soundbites. This reflects the enormous
gap which exists between policy announcements and a more profound
understanding of the analysis which underpins them. Consequently, the
desire for change easily turns into diffidence and suspicion that what is
being advocated is just electoral calculation. Yet it is also obvious that much
of the country has been impressed by Blair's leadership of the party and
transformation of Labour's policy agenda. The negativity of so many
academics, journalists, pressure group campaigners and others on the left is
therefore all the more striking. This negativity dominated the period before
a Labour government was elected on 1 May 1997 and after a brief honey-
moon, and despite continuing popular support, old habits have reasserted
themselves.

   Prior to putting the notion of a stakeholder society on the agenda in early
1996, Blair reflected on the widespread suspicion and dismissal of his ideas
as a move to the right. An interview with him in *The Observer* just before the
1995 Labour Party conference, noted that

> one of the remaining problems is to persuade the liberal-left
> intelligentsia . . . to abandon their pessimism of the intellect and
> adopt some optimism of the will. 'There [is] a very great defeatism

77

that [grips] the left intelligentsia. If I can put it politely, there is a distinction between the Guardian-Observer left and what I would call the broader Labour supporters in the country. . . . What I would like to see more of on the left is genuine intellectual debate.'[2]

This was referring to the oft-quoted phrase which Antonio Gramsci used on the masthead of *L'ordine nuovo*, the radical newspaper he edited in Turin after the First World War.[3] The original phrase, 'pessimism of the intellect, optimism of the will', meant that clear, hard-headed analysis, undistorted by any illusions, had to inform the determination to make the world a better place. But it also meant that realism on its own without political will can lead to resignation to the status quo.

SHAPING CHANGE

The roots of this dialectic between human knowledge and the capacity to intervene in nature can, of course, be traced back all the way back to the Greeks. It is certainly found in Machiavelli's depiction of the interplay between princely virtù, or what we might today call leadership skills, on the one hand, and fortuna or chance, on the other. In *The Prince* Machiavelli joins incisive analysis of the attributes needed by a political leader to overcome the chaos existing in the Italian peninsula to a passionate plea for a united Italy. It is no accident that later, writing in a fascist prison in the 1930s, Gramsci builds on this Italian tradition and uses the term 'Modern Prince' to challenge Mussolini's claim to follow in the footsteps of Machiavelli's Prince, and to be the heir of the Risorgimento, as the *duce*, or the leader who can complete Italy's imperfect unification and modernise Italian society.

In *The Prison Notebooks* Gramsci writes that modern society and twentieth-century politics is so complex that no one individual could provide the leadership needed to transform society. Such leadership – or Modern Prince – could only be provided by a political party able to forge a collective will to transform society in a progressive direction.[4] Gramsci describes a particular kind of party and politics capable of analysing social and historical development as it reaches out to learn from the experiences of the widest possible cross-section of society and from what we would now call the cutting edge of socio-economic change. On the basis of what is *possible* and what is *necessary*, the aim is to develop a strategy to achieve what is *desirable*, and in so doing provide a focus for gaining widespread and continuous popular consent.[5] Whereas Lenin was most concerned to establish doctrinal correctness and party discipline,[6] Gramsci was much more worried about political isolation when a party loses touch with reality and when unity becomes purely mechanical.[7]

The first key to retaining consent to a party's policies was to make sure that they reflected the real needs of the vast majority as they actually lived and not as some political ideology or political force wished that they did.[8] This was why the party had to be deeply rooted in the society. Second, these policies could only succeed if they were based on the understanding that historical development was not a mechanical, inevitable, mystical process. Rather, it was the product of human activity. But neither was it within the control of any single political force. Referring again to Machiavelli, Gramsci examines the complex relationship between analysis of the situation confronting a political organisation, a reality in which, he argues, the aims of that organisation are themselves an element, and the attempt to transform that reality in line with new political priorities to influence the direction of change.[9]

Historical change could not be stopped, but it did provide opportunities for progressive politics as it brought both advances and losses. That was the lesson Gramsci drew from the impossibility of simply opposing one of the major challenges of his period, what he called Fordism, that is, assembly line production as developed by Henry Ford, and the 'scientific management' of Frederick Taylor. Some American trade unions and, indeed, some conserv-ative elements in Europe, had tried to oppose these trends but had been defeated. Nor, for a progressive politics, was it possible simply to endorse the productive potential of these developments as representing 'progress' and 'rationality' as did a wide range of people from the fascist right to the Bolshevik left.[10] Any progressive potential could only be fulfilled by a fundamental rethink about the enhancement of the skills and knowledge of the majority of the population. This was the precondition for a creative contribution to a democratic discussion about the uses to which expertise and technological advancement could be put in relation to a progressive political agenda.[11]

Just as Gramsci himself was clear that Lenin and the Russian Revolution provided no model for the West European left,[12] much of Gramsci's writing is not relevant for us today. What still *is* absolutely relevant, however, is Gramsci's special insistence on the need to base politics on a clear understanding of the nature of change and the experiences of the widest possible sections of the population in order to unite people and to earn their support for a progressive transformation of society. This is what Gramsci meant by hegemonic politics.

Fortunately, our situation today is quite different from the traumatic post-First World War period. However, we are living through major political, social and economic transformations that are leading to a level of political confusion unprecedented in recent times. As the century ends, it is becoming more and more difficult to determine what is progressive and what is not. How often today the word 'left' seems to connote 'leftover' or indeed at times reactionary. This is meant in the historical, post-French Revolution sense of *reacting to* a major change by looking backward to an *ancien régime*. On the other hand, claims by the 'right' to be radical, for all the changes which have been initiated, are hardly borne out, at least if we understand the word as a fundamental reorientation of society.[13] As Ross McKibbin has commented in the *London Review of Books*, Conservative government policies in fact preserved significant aspects of British society, for example, the Beveridge welfare state, but 'in an utterly degraded form'.[14] There is no shame, then, in feeling anxious because the old goal posts not only keep moving, but the boundaries of the political football pitch seem so blurred.

After the election, the Labour government continues to surprise and to exasperate many in almost equal measure. Aiming to change politics itself and to tackle social exclusion in a holistic manner, it has set itself a large task. Before being able to see what is constructed on the ground, anxiety and ambivalence can only be contained within pre-existing categories of judgment. Scepticism is understandable until results are concrete. But while a major transformation in British society and politics requires skilful political management, it also needs to harness wider energies and enthusiasms. It is appropriate therefore to reflect on some of the roots of government policy and reactions to suggestions for change.

SOCIAL JUSTICE IN A CHANGED WORLD

Indeed, anxiety and confusion marked the reception given to the most ambitious attempt since Beveridge to redefine and to reorganise provision for the social and economic wellbeing of the British people, Labour's Commission on Social Justice Report.[15] Much if by no means all of what is being attempted by the Labour government reflects the analysis which it outlined. 'The size of the problem,' the report states in the introduction, is so great that there is 'no "quick fix", for the UK's difficulties.'

> if politicians or others suggest that there is, no one should believe them. . . . (O)ur world is so different from that which William Beveridge addressed fifty years ago, and it is now changing so fast, that there is no way in which the prescriptions that suited an earlier time can merely be renewed, however much goodwill, money or technical sophistication one might hope to call up in their support.[16]

Echoed subsequently in Blair's idea of a stakeholder society, the report maintains that in addition to social justice being an ideal in its own right,

> economic success requires a greater measure of social justice . . . Squalor and crime carry enormous economic as well as social costs;

unemployment uses resources simply to sustain people who might sustain themselves and contribute to the economy. . . . Social justice stands against fanatics of the market economy, who forget that a market is a social reality which itself requires trust, order, goodwill and other forms of support. . . . Social justice does indeed attend to the needy . . . but in doing so it can be an enabling force for everybody . . . something that society requires because everyone's quality of life is dependent in part on a high degree of social well-being. This conclusion, that social justice is not simply a moral ideal but an economic necessity, is at the heart of this report.[17]

The dimensions of the change which the report's perspective depicts and the dramatic nature of the UK's predicament which it describes require a leap of imagination to reformulate the very terms of the debate. This has confounded people and led to no little anxiety. The UK's problems, it argues,

are not simply the product of Conservative mistakes. The causes reach back well before the onset of the Conservative administration in 1979, and they will not be tackled by trying to recreate the country that existed before that. . . . The reality was that the foundations of the post-war settlement had been destroyed by national and international change.[18]

If the 'tragedy of the 1969s and 1970s was that the Left, which had created the successful post-war settlement, failed to come to terms' with change, 'the Right, which grasped the need for change, failed to understand what was really needed.'[19]

Agreeing with the statement made to the Commission by Bill Morris, General Secretary of the Transport and General Workers' Union, that 'many of the principles on which the post-war welfare state was based still hold good today,' the report argues that,

If the values of the welfare state – opportunities, security, responsibility – are to have real meaning in the future, then they will require new institutions and policies to give them practical effect. We have no option but to engage with the three great revolutions – economic, social, and political – which are changing our lives, and those of people in every other industrialised country.[20]

The argument that socialist values remain the same but that the way to achieve them in a changed world is different would become a central theme in New Labour.

The report described how the UK has been left behind by the global economic revolution of 'finance, competition, skill and technology', while neither government nor employers have caught up with the social revolution which has taken place 'of women's life chances, of family structures and of demography' even though 'social change has been faster and gone further in the UK than in most other European countries'. Nor do political institutions escape the challenge, particularly 'the UK's old assumptions of parliamentary sovereignty and . . . its growing centralisation of government power'. The political revolution 'involves a fundamental reorientation of the relationship between those who govern and those who are governed'.[21]

DOUBTS, CONFUSION, AND NEGATIVITY

Reflecting on the general response by academics and others on the left to the publication of the Commission on Social Justice report in October 1994, what is striking is the negativity of most of it. As Christopher Pierson has written:

> The Commission's Report has faced that mixture of weary cynicism, vested interests and quack cures which seem to greet any attempt at deep-seated welfare reform. It finds itself condemned in just about equal measure for having been both too bold and too timid.[22]

It would be worthwhile considering some of the reasons for this negativity. It is one thing to feel pessimistic confronting the scenario of economic mismanagement and institutional arteriosclerosis depicted by Will Hutton in *The State We're in*.[23] It is another to give up all hope of influencing change for the better and to mistake the attempt to depict the nature of current trends, in order to ground policy in a clear assessment of the dynamic of contemporary reality and the way millions of people live their lives, with an outright endorsement of those trends.[24] Weary cynicism, or pessimism of the intellect without optimism of the will, leads to defeatism. After all, as Gramsci also argued, the way to undermine the old is to construct the new.[25] But if this optimism of the will is to result in real change, it cannot be based on what we would wish but what we endeavour to construct in the difficult conditions we face, conditions which, as Marx pointed out, are not of our choosing. Wishful thinking by another name is ineffectual utopianism.[26]

The problem is determining what is indeed new, and progressive, and how to achieve it. If this cynicism and negativity are understandable, they are ultimately a self-fulfilling prophecy. Valid reasons for being doubting Thomases (and Thomasinas) are certainly not hard to find. There is, of course, the collapse of old certainties in this post-modern, post-fordist, and post-communist yet still socially unjust and violent world. Scepticism is rational, and holding on to the old tenaciously is understandable, until new arrangements are shown, concretely, to be better than the old. There is also the habit, strongest in academia perhaps, but which, as Will Hutton notes, marks a whole style of polemical debate, of a type of critique which tells us what is wrong but often does little to draw out what is positive or useful in the contributions of others or in policy proposals which do not conform to favoured prescriptions in which individuals have an intellectual, political or professional investment.[27] Here, too, are vested interests of a sort which need to be taken into account, especially as the depth of psychological investment must not be underestimated.

However, if this psychological investment is at the root of much of the confusion, perhaps most importantly, some of the political messages coming from New Labour are no less confusing, to say the least. Before the election, mixed with soundbites, by-election leaflets and comments which seemed recycled from the Conservatives' dustbin of black propaganda were radical policy proposals like abolishing the assisted places scheme and GP fundholding, transforming the House of Lords, establishing a Bill of Rights and a Freedom of Information Act, holding a referendum on proportional representation, providing for Scottish and Welsh devolution, applying a windfall tax on excessive monopoly profits, signing up for the Social Chapter, legislating for a minimum wage – and the list thankfully goes on. Yet even as many of these are being enacted, governing leaves room for confusion and mistakes. It is not surprising, therefore, that there is so much wavering between pleasant surprise and well-worn paths of cynicism.

One possible response to what is being proposed is to play the 'up the ante' political game, where it is considered left-wing to oppose any suggestion for change by raising the stakes. Even those of us who have no interest in participating in this particular game[28] are nonetheless still left with the doubt whether the mixed messages from Labour are intentional. What appear, at least from the soundbites which the media pick up, opportunistic moves not to offend combine with heartfelt and inspiring ethical commitments together with convincing explanations why an up-to-date and realistic analysis of the world requires a different radical strategy today.[29] The desired effect may be to unbalance the opposition, but the result is very often disenchantment, and the closing down of spaces for constructive criticism.

FEARS AND DESIRES

Beyond this confusion, there are genuine psychological reasons why it is easier to make a negative critique than join in constructing a progressive alternative at the very moment that change seems most possible. On the one hand, there is the fear of loss, and, on the other, the anxiety of having to assume responsibility without being able to blame someone else. The familiar is held onto for dear life, however uncomfortable, be it the memories of long, hard fought battles, and defeats, or cherished beliefs. We hold onto *everything* for fear of losing *something*. It may appear highly contradictory, and both politics and individual psychology *are* contradictory, but going beyond blaming others for defeat, accepting one's own responsibilities, leaving isolated opposition and joining a majority, and after so many years plunging into the unknown, can feel very dangerous. Worries about losing what we know, however imperfect, for what we do not are quite real. Vested interests are not just material but are the result of psychological and ideological investments as well. Until alternatives are up and running, hope cannot be attached to anything concrete.

Furthermore, a strategy to dampen down expectations given harsh realities, however politically intelligent in the long run, can easily feed widespread cynicism about any possibility of change today. And yet, reaction to the Social Justice report also reveals an enormous desire to believe that Britain *can* be changed for the better. As one participant in a discussion on the Social Justice report commented, 'At first, I was worried about what would be lost, but then I thought, I would be delighted to live in a country with the kind of provision it argues for.'[30] That person was thinking about, for example, universal nursery provision, the possibility to combine part-time work with part-time benefits, a minimum wage, a Jobs, Education and Training programme to ease the transition into work and between jobs, the right to a minimum second pension with pension contributions guaranteed even when unemployed or not employed from choice, for example, while caring for a child – in short the kind of programmes aimed at eliminating the kind of social exclusion that large sectors of British society suffer at the moment. Early Labour government policy reflects many of these proposals. But what is certain is that unless widespread consent is developed around the kind of fundamental reforms that the report calls for, given the very real difficulties of getting a complex society to shift in new directions, much of its promise will be stillborn, even with the most optimistic and determined political will in the world.

BEYOND BEVERIDGE

But developing such active consent to a major shift in perspective will not be easy. The Social Justice report came out of a very different context than the 1942 Beveridge Report. An official government document, the product of a civil service interdepartmental committee with Beveridge the only non-civil servant, Ross McKibbin points out that it had 'an "official" character which raised expectations that it would be implemented'. Discussed widely in the armed forces, '(i)n many ways, and quite deliberately so, it summed up what the Allies were fighting for'.[31] The Beveridge Report was a cornerstone of wartime national unity and encapsulated hopes for the reconstruction of peacetime Britain. As McKibbin so well describes:

The long queues outside HMSOs; the hurried reprintings; the intensity of public discussion and, to judge by wartime diaries, private discussion as well; the enormous publicity given to Beveridge by the *Mirror*: all contrived to give the Report a social centrality inconceivable today.[32]

Fifty years later the situation was dramatically different when the Commission on Social Justice was set up by the late John Smith, then leader of the opposition in the wake of Labour's 1992 general election defeat. Created as an independent, broadly based group, chaired by Sir Gordon Borrie, it was at arms length from the Labour Party and far from effective political power. The difference could hardly be greater than the excitement which greeted Beveridge and the way in which its message was spread and its proposals discussed, although the need was hardly less. The Commission was set up in a moment when the argument for dropping the policy of a minimum wage and for targeting benefits such as child benefit was gaining ground. The question was bound to arise then, and is still relevant – in a period when even the Nordic welfare states, often looked to as providing a model of advance, are facing serious challenges – whether any of the 'principles on which the post-war welfare state was based', referred to by Bill Morris,[33] when Britain itself seemed to many to provide an international model, could be adhered to by any party seeking to form a government. The conclusion it came to has to be reiterated: society, and especially its economic performance, cannot do without adequate social provision.

By the time the report was published in the autumn of 1994, after almost two decades of neo-liberal Conservative governments, international economic restructuring and UK decline, and a dramatic increase in social polarisation,[34] the need to go beyond restoration to reconstruction was becoming more and more obvious on the centre left.[35] The Commission on Social Justice report was the most ambitious amongst several important publications from the centre and left of the political spectrum addressed to reconstructing the British welfare state and the economy. Although they vary in perspective and policy prescriptions, their very proliferation was a manifestation of a widespread conviction that it is impossible to go back to the *status quo* from before 1979, nor would it be particularly desirable. There are real differences in perspective, but there are also real points of contact and overlap both in analysis and prescription. Indeed, James McCormick and Carey Oppenheim argue that far from Labour filling in a blank sheet, there is a broad left-of-centre consensus on which to build.[36] However much this is true, there still remains the fact that as long as debate focuses on details without a wider understanding of the underlying analysis, there is a danger that the opportunity for a radical, progressive reconstruction will be opposed by those who feel the loss of what they know and fear the unknown more than anything else.[37]

A REPORT LITTLE READ AND LESS UNDERSTOOD

The Social Justice report sparked widespread press coverage, but the changes in the Labour Party's Clause IV soon came to dominate debate, and discussion about the report soon died out. Yet, without the process being very clear to anyone not involved, and without it being the *only* source, the report's impact, if not its detailed proposals, is gradually becoming evident in Labour government policy. But because of its length, wealth of detail, and breadth of scope, going well beyond Beveridge, few have read it. Those who have are faced by a document which steadfastly refuses to be organised into the kind of categories, policy proposals, frames of analysis or concepts which most people are familiar with, and which describes an expansion of choice which is lacking at the moment and which many people find hard to imagine.[38] The report goes well beyond Labour's traditional, and simple, commitment to a redistribution of financial resources, while still highlighting the costs to individuals and to society of increasing poverty. To grasp what is radical in the report, and in much Labour government policy, requires an investment of time, good faith, hope, and optimism – quantities which far too few people will have.

Interrupted temporarily by Labour's landslide victory, it has been easy for the negative reaction of sincere doubt, weary cynicism and vested interests noted by Pierson, plus backward-looking leftism, to colour reactions to change. The very desire to get rid of the Tories and the euphoria after the election tended to silence most outright opposition from the centre and left for a while, but the doubt remains whether most people really understand the radical nature of the changes suggested.

POLITICAL CONVICTION ROOTED IN ANALYSIS

So on what grounds can it be argued that this report is radical, progressive, and deserving of support? First, it puts women at the very centre of its analysis and their life chances at the core of its proposals. We are well beyond tokenism here.[39] Second, it puts overcoming poverty and providing the conditions to achieve greater social justice at the very top of the agenda. And third, it is convincing because of its mode of arguing from the grain of change that it is possible to influence it for the better. It all adds up to a fundamental and welcome shift in perspective. Its ambition is no less than to refound the welfare state in Britain considered in a world perspective, posing questions for the next two decades. It is a radical document not just because of its concerns, but because of its mode of analysis: it joins pessimism of the intellect with optimism of the will. It goes well beyond Labourism where the old left/right divide so often ran between grand rhetoric and resigned pragmatism covered with a gloss of moralism. With few exceptions Labour programmes, whether influenced by the Labour left or the right, have never been derived from an analysis of contemporary trends in order to shape the future. What is emerging here is an attempt to ground conviction in analysis. The Social Justice report has contributed to that process.

A NEW DEAL FOR WOMEN

The debate has certainly come a long way since the 1980s when *Women and the State*[40] was published. At that time very few analysts focused on the dramatic social changes taking place as more and more women were entering formal, paid work at the same time as having major family responsibilities, or discussed the implications of these changes for the organisation of the welfare state, in the broad sense, the world of work, and the household all of which still assumed the primacy of a male-bread-winner.[41] Today all these spheres still continue largely to operate according to a logic which ignores the fact that very few women are full-time house-wives for more than a short period in their lives, and that most households depend fundamentally on their income from paid jobs to keep above the poverty line.[42] That is, major social institutions operate in a way which is in contradiction with the way millions of people in fact live. One of the main reasons the Social Justice report is so progressive is that it defines the social revolution which has been taking place, above all, with regard to 'women's life chances, family structures and demography'.[43] Indeed, the preconditions for eliminating poverty and transforming the economy are organically linked in the report to establishing what has been called in the Nordic countries and elsewhere a new gender contract[44] in which the relationship between work and family needs changes, and in which women, and men, are given the possibility to live more flexible and productive lives with greater freedom of choice and fewer constraints.

More concretely, to give just one example, counting part-time work for pensions and other benefits without penalising the partners of the un-employed, backed by a minimum wage and guarantees of employees' rights, would especially help women and their families.[45] Analysing trends does not mean endorsing them, but understanding change is the precondition for developing policies to influence outcomes for the better. The report does not *advocate* part-time work. Rather, it recognises that part-time work is convenient for many people at different times in their lives.[46] As it argues,

> Full employment in a modern economy must recognize that, for both men and women, the world of work has changed funda-mentally. In the 1950s, full employment involved full-time, life-time employment for men; in the 1990s and beyond, it will involve for both men and women frequent changes of occupation, part-time as

well as full-time work, self-employment as well as employment, time spent caring for children or elderly relatives (as well as or instead of employment) and periods spent in further education and training. Forty years ago the typical worker was a man working full-time in industry; today the typical worker is increasingly likely to be a women working part-time in a service job. Already, there are more people in Britain employed as childcare-workers than as car-workers.[47]

Far from endorsing those labour market trends and management strategies which make part-time work a synonym for insecurity, and flexibility the equivalent of marginalisation, or those social policies which encourage some households to be 'work rich' with two, exhausted, partners in employment, and others kept 'work poor' because benefits are withdrawn if either works even part-time, the report describes a series of interrelated policies which will facilitate women, and men, to combine family, education and training, and paid work in ways which suit new living patterns. For example, an immediate priority is placed on free, universal nursery education, which is considered the 'first goal' of investment,[48] and on a learning bank to be drawn upon over the life cycle.[49] Justice across genders, a greater contribution by men to household responsibilities, minimising the current loss to the economy and society more generally of women's skills, and better educational opportunities for all social groups at different ages are some of the aims of the report. These are connected to its radical perspective in arguing for a redistribution of time and not just money between the genders and over the life cycle and the clear influence of feminist debates on social policy, economic organisation and citizenship.[50] One yardstick by which to measure the outcomes of Labour government policies can be found here. Another is the extent to which social exclusion is eliminated.

TOWARDS A SOCIAL STRATEGY OF INCLUSION

The report's damning critique of poverty and of the increasing inequalities in British society has contributed to putting social exclusion back at the centre of the political agenda and also, if not explicitly, to the setting up of the Social Exclusion Unit in the Prime Minister's Office. Describing the state of Britain, it explains,

In January 1994, a 28-year-old Birmingham engineer sent us his payslip. He earns £2.50 an hour – £101 a week. 'I am scared to put the heating on as I would not be able to afford the electricity bill,' he told us. 'Please do not tell my employer I wrote to you as I would be straight on the dole'. . . . For those at the top, these are the best of times. For those at the bottom, horizons are even narrower than they were a decade ago and the gap between rich and poor is greater than at any time since the 1930s. For most people – those in the middle – insecurity and anxiety are rife. Comparison with the past is important. . . . But the real comparison – the comparison to shock anyone concerned with the future of this country – is the one between what we are and what we have it in ourselves to become, the gap between potential and performance. Most people in this country are doing less well than they want to and less well than they could, if only they were able to learn more, work more productively (or work at all), live more safely, more securely and more healthily. Too often, opportunities are distributed not on the basis of ability, but on the basis of ability to pay; not on who you are but who your parents were; not on the basis of merit, but on grounds of race or gender.[51]

The fact that it speaks in the language of inclusion, considering the needs of the vast majority of the population, without losing sight of the situation of those who are excluded is one of the main features which recommends its approach. Another is the conviction that expectations can and must be raised. 'Doing better than we used to is not good enough when [other countries] set their sights far higher.'[52] The report talks about a flexible, intelligent welfare state to help people into work and to enable individuals to change jobs 'upwards' rather than be trapped in low skill, low pay jobs or no jobs. The object is not to eliminate uncertainty, which is inevitable, but insecurity, deskilling and long-term unemployment.[53]

In an argument now familiar on both sides of the Atlantic, education and training, understood widely over the life cycle are presented as the necessary precondition, if not guarantee, of economic regeneration.[54] This flies in the face of Tory arguments that the way forward consisted in keeping wages down and in preserving the kind of labour market flexibility which encourages low investment in skills and to suit the needs of poor employers rather than those who work. Indeed, the report turns the usual argument on its head: it maintains that social justice is a prerequisite for economic success.[55]

Throughout the Social Justice report there is a strong argument for universalism with redistributive consequences. It is important to avoid confusion here by differentiating between targeting and means-testing. Taxing allowances or benefits for those earning at the higher rate signifies targeting the *affluent*, *within* universal provision, *without* a means test for the poor as usually understood. The same is true of the *right* to a second, 'topping up' pension for those people whose pension provision falls below a certain level, most likely because they do not have an occupational pension, or in periods of unemployment, because of caring responsibilities, or part-time work. In fact, with regards to redistribution, the report is much more ambitious than the usual definition which relies so heavily on higher income tax. Much can be achieved, it argues, from changes in existing tax allowances, while a minimum wage and facilitating women's contribution to household incomes would help to cut down on the *de facto* welfare subsidies given to poor employers who pay low wages.

The report follows best Nordic practice in linking labour market strategies with family policy.[56] It expands our horizons and demands a new way of thinking as it takes into account life cycle perspectives for women and men to facilitate a better fit between individual and family needs for employment, for care work, and education and training when the likelihood of lifelong, full-time, family wage male employment has almost disappeared. In short, the report argues that a radical rethink is necessary, that tinkering is inadvisable, and that a return to the past neither possible nor desirable since it would be inadequate for today's needs.

There are, of course, problems. The special needs of the disabled within work and not and the necessity of providing for those who are not able to undertake paid work, for example, those with severe disability, are not adequately considered.[57] Those *not* in waged work must be part of the included. The report is not perfect. Racism is named as one of the major evils to be eliminated without being given due prominence. Some issues are fudged. There are contradictions, even major ones, between helping people *now* and building for the future. As Ruth Lister writes,

> A new Labour Government, committed to social justice and the extension of citizenship, will need to combine the kind of long-term structural strategy proposed by the Commission with some immediate help for those who have been the main victims of over a decade of redistribution from the poor to the rich.[58]

In its early days, the Labour government has adopted a strategy of combating exclusion without raising benefits.

Indeed the difficulty of achieving a shift in direction cannot be underestimated. What is outlined by the Commission on Social Justice is a complex package, not a political manifesto, and leads to the question of where to start and in what order. Although some things are clear priorities, if Labour chooses to pick some parts but not others, the outcomes may well not be the progressive ones hoped for. What is required is a long time span, at least fifteen years, and the question arises how to organise and maintain consent around such a programme of reform, and how to keep a government in power devoted to this kind of change. This, of course, necessitates consent across a larger section of the population than the Labour Party has traditionally achieved, at least without the horrific experience of a world war to galvanise support, and, even more crucially, maintaining consent over a long period. The implication that the electoral system should be changed to some form of proportional representation to allow a more pluralistic form of government is not spelt out. And finally the economic perspective in the report leaves open questions of how an expanding economy in Europe can be achieved, and which policies should be pursued to ensure that enough jobs are created. What to do if jobs are not created quickly enough is unspecified, although the door is left open to some type of guaranteed income outside the labour market.[59]

There have been several critiques by political philosophers of the definition of social justice in the report, and the argument in it that *those* inequalities which are unjust (implying that only some are) should *where possible* be eliminated, suggesting that the elimination of inequality is to some extent contingent on what can be achieved. Certainly there is an ongoing discussion to be had about the conditions which are necessary to bring about greater social justice.[60] But it is desperately short-sighted to miss the contribution the report has made to opening up a wider discussion about social justice because it does not *in the abstract* provide a perfect definition. These questions are complex in the extreme.[61] One thing is certain, the radical perspectives in the report will never come to fruition unless current cynicism and pessimism are undermined by different narratives of what is possible and needed, and the argument won that the inadequacies of old patterns of welfare can only be addressed by the kind of fundamental rethink which the report exemplifies. Only so much can be done until new provision is in place, but there should be no mistake. We are not only talking about technical changes in rules, regulations, and benefit levels. What is required is a major cultural shift in which the habits and assumptions of lifetimes are at stake and a collective will for a major reform has to be painstakingly constructed. Fear of loss can only be overcome to a limited extent until alternatives are in place.

This, then, is an invitation to engage in a much more adventurous and imaginative debate than has taken place so far. This is even more urgent after the election of a Labour government which aims to tackle social exclusion. The Commission on Social Justice report is aimed at improving the lives of all those who are ill served in one way or other as things are and who deserve something better, not only the socially excluded but society more generally, an attempt at hegemonic politics if there ever was one. What is at stake are not just documents or detailed policy proposals, but fundamental questions about how the future can be influenced and how we determine what is worth fighting for, what is feasible, and how to achieve it. In short, how we can construct a version of change which is progressive, for change there will be, as sure as death and taxes. Analysis of society as it *is*, in an international context, for any decent social science or political strategy, can help us to think about what it *might* be, no less today than for Marx or Gramsci. That is precisely what the report sets out to do.

Certainly many people, inside the Labour Party and in the country, including many on the Labour backbenches, and likely some also on the frontbench, remain to be convinced about the validity of an analysis which differs in fundamental ways from what is so deeply ingrained, and the policy conclusions to be drawn from it. Even more important is the work still to be done to make the analysis intelligible, the policy conclusions acceptable, and the conviction convincing to the country at large. We must not underestimate how difficult it is to convey policy let alone complex analysis, or how necessary for that analysis to exist in dialogue with the widest possible range of ideas and experiences and for experts and politicians to listen, to learn, and to reflect. The Labour Party does not have a tradition of debating the rationale of policy, as opposed to resolutions. It cannot do it on its own inside or outside Parliament. But a Labour government cannot do without such a debate either. Tony Blair may talk in terms of common purpose rather than collective will but what is required is a widespread understanding of the nature of the dilemmas facing Britain in order to construct a better place in which to live. The hope, desperation, and excitement ensuing from a change of government might make it possible to forge a new hegemony, a widespread consent which will inevitably be full of contradictions and diversity, but rooted in unity around a project to renew Britain. The Labour government and the Labour Party need to be tolerant and to accept constructive criticism, to keep people on board, to maintain and renew consent, to construct a hegemonic politics.

As the Commission on Social Justice report argues,

> Ours is a long term strategy, designed not to amend a few policies but to set a new direction. That is what people want, and that is what the country needs. But the fact that change will take a long time does not mean that there is time to spare; it means that we have to get on with it. Ours is a call for urgent action. . . . When the challenge is so urgent, our timescale of ten to fifteen years may seem too long. Imagine, however, that fifteen years ago, government had determined to invest the revenues from North Sea Oil in the long-term development of the UK economy; that ten years ago, it had embarked upon a programme to expand nursery education; that a Jobs, Education and Training programme to prevent long-term unemployment had been initiated five years ago, and a welfare-to-work reform was already under way. We would not be living in utopia, but this would already be a very different country. What we need from government now is willingness to help develop a political and economic culture in which long-term strategies can flourish.[62]

It remains to be seen if the Labour government elected on 1 May 1997, or any other government, can meet this challenge.

8

FROM REALISM TO CREATIVITY

Gramsci, Blair and us

(T)o understand what is Modern as opposed to new is, for politicians, a way of seeing how the shape of the man-made world can make a stronger, fairer, healthier and wealthier society. Or it could be.

(Jonathan Glancey, *Guardian*, 17 November, 1997)

Not everything that is new is modern. And not everything that is old is old-fashioned. Jonathan Glancey was criticising the assumption that Canary Wharf Tower, Tony Blair's choice for a meeting with Jacques Chirac and Lionel Jospin, was the best example of a forward-looking, modern, New Britain. He argues that,

> Throughout Britain, and up until the eighties, local councils, education authorities, universities and other public or publicly minded bodies fused Modern architecture to Modern ideologies . . . not simply to create the shiny and new, but to modernise class-divided, low-wage Britain. . . . New Labour has inherited [the] Thatcherite penchant for fancy dress and has yet to separate in its mind the New from the Modern. The former is all about fashion; the latter about the health of the body wearing the latest clothes.[1]

Glancey's argument about modern architecture extends beyond the built environment to the architecture of society more generally. It reflects both the widespread scepticism about New Labour amongst sectors of the population and the broadly felt need to modernise. It is striking, however, how Glancey defines objectives, 'a stronger, fairer, healthier and wealthier society', which Blair and his government would claim to share.

93

> Without social justice, without modernisation, without mutuality and solidarity there will be no prosperity. . . . A high level of social cohesion is not just urgent in itself; it is essential for an efficient and prosperous economy, which is why we have to bring together a drive for economic efficiency with that for social justice.[2]

Holding Blair to account for his modernising vocation implies sharing many of his objectives while reserving the right to criticise the means chosen to achieve them. This enlightened if sharply critical engagement with New Labour links to wider issues. A deep-seated and highly conservative cynicism about the possibility of change for the better is reinforced by the fear that what is put forward as new and exciting merely represents the repetition of old, oppressive power relations in new guises. At the same time, the desire to modernise and to escape from the fateful consequences of an increasingly polarised society reflects the conviction that there is no returning to pre-1979, that restoration is not an option.

Whatever our reservations, the thrust of New Labour represents a necessary political shift to the future. As the Commission on Social Justice report argued in 1994:

> Our world is so different from that which William Beveridge addressed fifty years ago, and it is now changing so fast, that there is no way in which the prescriptions that suited an earlier time can merely be renewed, however much good will, money or technical sophistication one might hope to call up in their support.[3]

But will change be for the better? If we cannot go back to the past, can we look forward to a fairer, more inclusive, less polarised society?

FACING THE FUTURE: REALISM OR FATALISM?

For all that the future rather than the past is on the agenda, most of our present concerns share points in common with urgent questions which were being posed many years ago. Many of the dilemmas facing political leaders at the end of the twentieth century were described by the Italian Marxist writer Antonio Gramsci in a fascist prison in the 1930s as he thought about the problems facing the left in his time. Claims by a wide range of public figures from Mussolini and Hitler, through Roosevelt, to Stalin to represent the 'future' were a challenge to anyone committed to forward-looking, progressive politics.[4] Throughout Europe, North America, and elsewhere political, economic, and social projects were launched during the 1920s and 1930s to modernise productive systems and infrastructures, to respond to popular pressures for a better life, and to create a 'new' generation of men and women better suited to the demands of a modern society. Grand reclamation projects, public building and art schemes employing modernist architects and artists, and education and social welfare policies were presented as forward-looking.[5] Then, as now, political legitimacy and political commitment were reinforced by arguments that what was being created was 'rational' and 'needed'. Debates raged about which policies were the best response to the need to modernise. At the same time opposition came from both left and right to pressures for change.

As Gramsci rethought left politics, he reflected on an urgent issue: how to avoid passive resignation to seemingly overwhelming historical trends without resorting to schema which were utopian because they had very little basis in reality and therefore little chance of success? The question, he wrote,

> is one . . . of seeing whether 'what ought to be' is arbitrary or necessary; whether it is concrete will on the one hand or idle fancy, yearning, daydream on the other. The active politician is a creator, an initiator; but he neither creates from nothing nor does he move in the turbid void of his own desires and dreams. He bases himself on effective reality, but what is this effective reality? Is it something static and immobile, or is it not rather a relation of forces in continuous motion and shift of equilibrium?[6]

In posing this question Gramsci was building on a long tradition of political thinking from Machiavelli to Marx. In *The Prince* Machiavelli described the capacities, or 'virtù', which a leader needed to develop in order to grapple with 'fortuna', or fate, and to be able to achieve a united Italy. Marx argued that human beings make history, but not in conditions of their choosing.[7] Just as no one can choose their biological parents, we cannot choose our historical context, but neither do we simply have to face the future fatalistically.

POLITICAL LEADERSHIP AND POLITICAL RENEWAL

Gramsci was struggling with issues which are still central to today's politics. Any project which aims at creating a better society must take account realistically of things as they are in order to help to create what might be. Change is inevitable but the forms which it can take vary and are amenable, within certain bounds, to political intervention. The question therefore is not *whether* to reform but *which* reform. Politics and policy choices matter but so does effective reality. The challenge is to analyse this reality as a dynamic with constantly shifting relationships between different social, economic, and political forces. Moreover, it is clear that deep-seated social and economic trends in all their complexity can never simply be reduced to the aims of politicians or policy makers. Outcomes are often unintended. Social creativity exists *despite* what governments do. The only thing to be taken for granted is that no historical transition can be understood as all good or all bad. If we are to avoid falling either into cynicism, resignation and pessimism or utopian wishful thinking, it is important both to seek out the spaces for inventive political practice and to take the measure of the constraints which impinge on progressive outcomes.

Of course, much of Gramsci has been superseded, and certainly care must be taken before we recast Blair into a contemporary Gramscian Modern Prince, which in any case, Gramsci argued, in modern circumstances had to be much more than a charismatic leader and implied a transformation of parties and politics more generally.[8] While we, and Blair himself, might speak of a modernising 'project', a term which *The Economist* has attributed to a Gramscian influence,[9] it would be wrong to see this as a preconstituted, finite objective. A 'project', as those impatient to see the 'big picture' may perceive, can imply something unfinished, in the making, to which many different actresses and actors not only may, but, must contribute, rather than what Gramsci criticised as 'a cold utopia' or merely 'learned theorising'.[10]

Today's use of 'project' rather than the more dirigiste and ideological 'programme' is therefore significant. 'Programme' comes from the political language of the past and can imply that final destinations may be determined from on high with little regard to the process of arriving at them or to whether they reflect widespread social needs. In contrast, given the increasing complexity of society, any serious reform can only be realised through harnessing the diverse energies, skills, and different kinds of knowledge in the wider population.

Although the word 'project' goes beyond Gramsci's own terminology, it nonetheless captures something significant in his approach to politics.[11] He argued that politics in the modern period entails constructing widespread consent around alternatives which are in part 'created from scratch' but which also reflect 'historical necessity'.[12] Political leadership, according to Gramsci, required a sense of direction, goals, a conviction that society can be different, and a strategy to unite disparate groups into a 'collective will'.[13] This requires an intellectual, moral, and cultural reform which in turn must be rooted in economic change.[14] Widespread and active consent around social and economic reforms is the precondition for creating an alternative society. Gramsci described this process as the establishment of an alternative hegemony.[15]

Such an alternative hegemony, or widespread support for a different project for society, is not, however, easily constructed. Building and maintaining popular support for fundamental change will only be possible, given the inertia of society, if reforms correspond to real needs and are justified by changes in the way millions of people live rather than reflect 'idle fancy' or 'daydreams'.[16] Adequate knowledge of societal change, however, requires more than 'learned theorising'. Information from the widest sectors of society is necessary to ground any hegemonic reform. Hegemonic leadership, therefore, cannot be based on a party which is cut off from the wider society.[17] Effective leadership, and Gramsci argued this was true even in the constrained conditions of clandestinity, requires both expert knowledge and a web of connections to the wider society which could teach party members and therefore the leadership what they needed to know to keep up with rapid change.[18] This is connected with his description of the party as 'a school of state life', which develops leadership skills but is also an exemplar, for better or worse, of politics more generally.[19]

Long-term, modern, progressive outcomes are only possible by attempting to shape historical change that is already underway, deep rooted, and that cannot be reversed. Politics which goes with the grain of change does not mean endorsing the forms which it has taken hitherto. If it succeeds in connecting with and influencing the way that institutions, cultures and people develop and interact with trends and tendencies that we cannot control, it operates on the 'terrain of effective reality' to create and initiate rather than simply to reinforce a status quo.[20]

EARLIER PARALLELS TO TODAY'S CHALLENGES

The possibility of creative political intervention which was realistic yet progressive was sharply posed by the debates about modernisation and rationalisation in Europe in the 1920s and 1930s,[21] as it was after the Second World War. Cataclysmic destruction, the Russian Revolution, waves of popular militancy, and the emergence of the United States as a world power and cultural model contributed to the desire to reconstruct not as things were in the past but in new, modern, better ways which reflected the needs of the mass of the population rather than those of tired, and often displaced élites. This applied as much to the social and economic structures of society as to the physical fabric.[22] Today the need for reconstruction and popular support for reforms may not appear as urgent as in the aftermath of the devastation and dislocation of the two world wars. But few would doubt that ecological dangers and globalisation pose enormous challenges. Naturally as the century draws to a close we have to update our thinking to take account of new developments which no thinkers from earlier periods could have analysed, least of all Gramsci, but we can still *also* learn from the past, from the insights of thinkers contemplating previous challenges even when we recognise their limitations.[23]

Certainly Gramsci's notes on Americanism and Fordism[24] have particular resonance for debates today about what it means to promote a progressive form of modernisation. And if we think laterally, these notes can provide useful perspectives on the contemporary phenomenon of globalisation. In particular, they help us to consider whether varied outcomes could result from different political responses to the pressures and possibilities coming from such a major historical transition.[25] Gramsci was fascinated with the multiple dimensions of this major push towards modernisation and rationalisation of production and of society more generally in the 1920s and 1930s. Americanism and Fordism took its name from the United States and Henry Ford's mass produced Model T Ford and marked a new era internationally, which no political force and no regime could ignore, and indeed many embraced. So-called scientific management and assembly line production for a mass market involved both brutal discipline and high wages for sectors of workers. Gramsci noted that

> it was relatively easy to rationalise production and labour by a skilful combination of force (destruction of working-class trade unionism on a territorial basis) and persuasion (high wages, various social benefits, extremely subtle ideological and political propaganda).[26]

These developments also signalled the advance of mass retailing and important changes in popular cultural production, consumption and in gender roles as policies to create different kinds of workers resulted in interference in even the most intimate details of private life.[27]

Large-scale mass production also provided a model for social provision as political compromises were struck between the representatives of business, labour and other social forces, in the context of serious economic and political crisis. In the face of the fear of a repetition of the Russian Revolution and the spread of fascism, progressive social and economic policies emerged in a number of countries, for example, guarantees of paid holidays, legal recognition of trade unions, and other social provision. At the same time, an expanded role for the state could serve a variety of ends depending on the political project and the forces in the field. Nazi Germany, fascist Italy, and the Soviet Union were only some examples of increased state activity. There were also widespread calls for more active state intervention to rescue society from the effects of the depression, for example, in Popular Front France, New Deal America, Social Democratic Sweden, and in Britain, by Lloyd George, the young Macmillan, and, of course, Keynes. The responses to economic and political challenges shared many features, but the specific outcomes derived from specific factors, above all, from the political aims and capacities of different groups and individuals.

Gramsci was as interested in the varied reactions to these developments as in analysing the complexity of what was a major historical transition.

> The reaction of Europe to Americanism merits . . . careful examination. From its analysis can be derived more than one element

necessary for the understanding of the present situation of a number of states in the old world and the political events of the post-war period.[28]

In another note he wrote that the problem,

is rather this; whether America, through the implacable weight of its economic production (and therefore indirectly), will compel or is already compelling Europe to overturn its excessively antiquated economic and social basis.[29]

The dilemma facing the left concerned what attitude to take towards Americanism and Fordism. At one and the same time as capitalism faced its most dramatic economic crisis ever, new wealth was created amongst sectors of the working class as well as the population more generally. Yet such developments also devalued old skills and led to working conditions which in many ways could be much worse than those they replaced. The very trends which undermined so many of the dearly held assumptions of the traditional, skilled working class of the day and defeated the opposition of trade unions until new organising strategies were pursued, for example industrial unionism, also undermined old economic and social élites.[30] Moreover they were portrayed as the height of modernisation and the irresistible way of the future not only by those whose economic interests were immediately involved or by sectors of Italian fascism[31] but by the Bolsheviks who greatly admired the increased productivity and dynamism of this American model.

CREATIVE RESPONSES IN TIMES OF TRANSITION

What Gramsci managed to contribute in his dense and difficult notes was to argue that such trends, while they could not be reversed, could be shaped by those who understood what was potentially progressive within them. He pointed out that skilled workers in Italy were not against innovation per se.[32] Technical, scientific, and managerial change *could also* become the basis for social and political renewal – but with a proviso. The model could not simply be adopted as it was but had to be transformed within a different political project 'to turn into "freedom" what is today "necessity" '.[33] A precondition for this to be possible, however, was a fundamental transformation in the relationship between the management of such a transition and changes in the knowledge and skills of the population which implied much more than management from on high whether promoted by Mussolini, Stalin, or Roosevelt.[34]

Gramsci's vision rejected the assumption, held across most of the political spectrum in a wide range of countries, that the expansion of state activity was by definition progressive. This was no mean achievement on the left in the 1930s but perhaps not surprising given the activities of the fascist state. The danger was, and is, that management of change from on high may supplant active contribution to renewal from below so that progressive outcomes are undermined at the same time as many popular demands may be addressed in a more or less authoritarian, populist, or corporatist manner. Gramsci called this passive revolution, or, another term he used, revolution-restauration, ultimately a conservative strategy of managing change which both transforms society in important ways and conserves many traditional hierarchies as it responds to certain popular demands while pre-empting popular participation.[35] Gramsci acknowledged that recognising that 'every epoch characterised by historical upheavals' might result in a passive revolution could lead to defeatism and fatalism.[36] That was why it was all the more important to develop an alternative strategy capable of gaining active consent rather than rely on largely passive acquiescence. A precondition for building such an alternative hegemony was to base it on 'necessary conditions' and 'actual reality'.[37]

Creative yet effective political intervention required negotiating the line between resigned pessimism and unrealistic optimism. Reading contemporary reality as preventing progressive political intervention leads to resignation. Such hyper-realism denies there being anything potentially positive in contemporary challenges and consequently is unable to develop a strategy of politically creative intervention to achieve different, more progressive outcomes. Gramsci writes that,

> 'Too much' (therefore superficial and mechanical) political realism often leads to the assertion that a statesman should only work within the limits of 'effective reality'; that he should not interest himself in what 'ought to be' but only in what 'is'. This would mean that he should not look farther than the end of his own nose.[38]

The alternative, however, is not unrealistic optimism.

> If one applies one's will to the creation of a new equilibrium among the forces which really exist and are operative . . . one still moves on the terrain of effective reality, but does so in order to dominate and transcend it (or to contribute to this). What 'ought to be' is therefore concrete. . . .[39]

Rather than remain trapped in generic opposition, the real challenge was to understand the contradictory dynamics of a complex process which was neither a given nor could be ignored but was itself the product of policies and interventions by many different actors and organisations. Gramsci was perhaps thinking of his own role in prison when he wrote of Machiavelli that his aim was to show 'concretely how the historical forces ought to have acted in order to be effective'.[40]

100

A HEGEMONIC POLITICS FOR OUR TIMES?

Gramsci's courage in challenging many of the political orthodoxies of his own day was remarkable. Tony Blair's attempt to remake Britain poses similar questions to those put forward by Gramsci about the role of political leadership and the new kind of politics and political party appropriate for the twenty-first century. Certainly Gramsci has been appropriated by such a wide range of interpreters that mere citation is no proof of his relevance today let alone comparisons to Blair. *The Economist*'s link between the bold heterodoxy of Blair's thinking and Gramsci's, via the influence of the think-tank Demos, one of whose founding members was Martin Jacques, formerly editor of *Marxism Today* is, however, not completely fanciful.[41] Whatever its derivation, a strategy which attempts to expand the basis of consent to a project of renewal has the potential of becoming, and remaining, hegemonic over a wide field of allies.

Of course, if Gramsci's ideas are to be meaningful today, they have to be developed to take account of contemporary realities. Appeals to identify with a new, modern project for Britain are one aspect of the attempt at hegemonic politics. The goal of tackling social exclusion while improving the quality of universal provision of services like health and education is a fundamental part of broadening who 'we' are, certainly beyond a self-defining 'left', in order to link those who are now excluded, marginalised, and poor to the vast majority of the population who all depend on public services. This is in fact, if not in words, a politics of expanding the basis of hegemony, to create and strengthen consent, in order to found what Gramsci would have called a new collective will.[42] The desire for broadly-based support should not surprise us. Gramsci argued that the need to maintain and broaden consent to reconstruct society went hand in hand with undercutting the potential appeal of the opposition. At the same time, Gramsci was quite clear that the success of a progressive strategy required both a moral and intellectual revolution and the development of concrete policies which, if they corresponded to real needs, would bind the population to the national project.[43]

There are even points of contact between Gramsci and New Labour on much more specific aspects of policy, for example, education. The objective of raising the education level of the widest possible majority of the population was one that he would have strongly supported. Indeed, we might even be reminded of Gramsci's criticism of those who pretend that learning is easy because they fail to validate the experience of those children from less privileged backgrounds who find it anything but.

> Many even think that the difficulties of learning are artificial, since they are accustomed to think only of manual work as sweat and toil. . . . This is why many people think that the difficulty of study

conceals some 'trick' which handicaps them – that is, when they do not simply believe that they are stupid by nature. They see the 'gentlemen' – and for many, especially in the country, 'gentlemen' means intellectual – complete, speedily and with apparent ease, work which costs their (children) tears and blood, and they think there is a 'trick'. In the future, these questions may become extremely acute and it will be necessary to resist the tendency to render easy that which cannot become easy without being distorted. If our aim is to produce a new stratum of intellectuals, including those capable of the highest degree of specialisation, from a social group which has not traditionally developed the appropriate attitudes, then we have unprecedented difficulties to overcome.[44]

Gramsci was thinking about a very different society, but his engagement with the concrete problems of his own day including the harnessing of the intellectual potential of wide sectors of the society could not be more relevant today.

THE ART OF POLITICS

It may not be easy to recognise a compact, articulated preconstituted hegemonic project in New Labour in day to day coverage in the media of government activity and political debate scattered though indications are of an overall vision in speeches, documents and policies.[45] There is nevertheless preliminary evidence of an awareness that for democratic politics to regain the confidence of the population new channels of communication and of opinion research are needed. Testing the ground through focus groups or by other means, careful reflection on what works and does not, enhancing the roles of people who have a great deal of knowledge and skills to offer as well as needs and desires, for example through citizens' juries, acknowledging the functions of organisations in local communities and civil society more broadly could all amount to the beginning of a different kind of politics which implies that no single political party or group of policy makers has all the answers. Behind it all, according to Michael Kenny,[46] may indeed be the attempt by Blair to construct a new social coalition, or what Gramsci would have called an historic bloc,[47] around a wide set of social issues to underpin the Labour Party in a much longer-term sense than people often imagine. After all it was Gramsci who thought of blocs as porous and multi-faceted and who drew out the implication that, in the modern period of mass politics, the consent of diverse groups had to be earned and maintained through compromises and concrete reforms.

The new political language and the refusal to consign to the right many issues of concern to a wide sector of the population could be a sign of aiming to create the basis for a radical restructuring of British democracy rather than a passive revolution. Indeed, Gramsci developed his concept of hegemony as a recognition of the changing nature of political power in the twentieth century and the *political* significance of civil society. Analysed rather than idealised, the attributes of civil society were an indicator of the democratic nature of a society. If its democratic, pluralistic potential develops, coercive aspects of the state could diminish.[48] New Labour policy seems, in fact, to struggle to find the balance between enhancing the democratic potential of civil society by facilitating local, community responses to major social challenges and assuming a prescriptive leadership role with regard to institutional and private activity. What is undoubtedly true, and Gramsci helps us to be sensitive to this, is that the nature of politics is in large part defined by the changing and tangled relationship between state and civil society in different countries in different periods.

No one thinker, however brilliant, can absolve us of doing the thinking we need to do for ourselves. And Gramsci was someone who, for all his theoretical insights, underestimated the threat of Nazism and fascism to world peace, did not specify how fundamental human rights are for progressive politics, and did not use gender as a category. His view of the party as a protagonist of change is in large part superseded. Yet, as Stuart Hall has demonstrated, applied sensitively to new questions, with political and analytical intelligence, Gramsci remains a precious intellectual resource.[49]

Gramsci is a remarkable source of inspiration for anyone trying to embrace change, but also trying to think and act politically to shape it for progressive ends. Much of Gramsci's originality came from a courageous recognition of the part which the failure of the left had played in the victory of reactionary forces and in the inadequacy of traditional understanding to grasp the theoretical and political requirements of a progressive politics in the twentieth century. His insistence on the significance of ideas, his interest in how they are constructed, and contain within them diverse and often contradictory elements; his conviction that people do not simply absorb, but reject or work with, ideas thrown at them; and his understanding of the democratic potential of civil society are all reasons for thinking that his ideas are still relevant today. Not least, he helps us to be aware of the danger that the potentially progressive features of the contemporary historical transition may rapidly dissolve into a passive revolution is real. Indeed, with New Labour now in power, it is easy for politics once more to be defined in narrow Westminster terms.

Yet while scepticism about the likelihood of progressive outcomes of New Labour's political project is perfectly understandable, above all in the period before many concrete results are there to be analysed, we should be careful not to be close-minded. New possibilities open up with reforms which break through old logics. Slowly, the way people view themselves and the world is unsettled, and new spaces are created for new exchanges between ideas, cultures and structures. Should reforms as significant at the end of the century as the National Health Service was in the late 1940s, for example, good quality childcare which begins to be taken for granted, or lifelong learning become a reality rather than a slogan, this could help raise the aspirations of the British to what might appear the heavens today. British common sense could shift in profound, and deep-seated ways. Bolstered by constitutional change, a new social consensus – or in Gramsci's terms, hegemony – would become more difficult to undermine even with a different government. At the same time, elements of proportional representation in the Scottish, Welsh, and Northern Irish assemblies, and in elections for the European Parliament, all mean that more than ever consent will have to be earned. An intellectual and moral reform is both a precondition and a result of such change. It will never be the mere reflection of the wisdom of experts. For example, as it becomes integrated both into the national psyche and accepted as integral to children's experience, socially provided childcare could be a factor in still further change in women's and men's views of their roles with regard to both professional and parental responsibilities, and also help to place children's needs on the political agenda. Beginning to provide some of the conditions which are necessary to enhance the abilities of people with diverse special needs could initiate a process of rethinking paid work and social provision on the road to creating a more people-friendly society.

Yet at the very moment when change is possible and the talents and skills of creative and innovative people are so needed, many feel betrayed, offended, and bypassed because the terms of debate are so altered and new allies are courted. We have to grieve if we have a sense of loss and then move on, to go beyond expecting parental figures to be perfect, to recognise the positive and the negative, to assume our own adult responsibilities, to analyse what is missing and needed, and to consider how it can be supplied. The implication is, of course, that we are also treated as adults by Blair and company. The danger, as Peter Hennessy has written, is that scepticism, 'the necessary intellectual condition for improvement', gives way to cynicism.[50] Those who are unable to contribute to radical renewal with good will but with critical faculties intact will be left behind. At the same time the forces for change must be open to hearing those voices who offer constructive criticism. Most dominant left traditions find it remarkably difficult to acknowledge that such openness is not an option but a necessity for social renewal. Gramsci helps us to understand that building an alternative hegemony requires leadership which resembles conducting an orchestra rather than commanding an army.[51] All are stronger for having to meet the challenge of co-operation between diverse talents. All are weaker without it.

Part 3

REFLECTIONS AND
EXPLORATIONS

9

RETHINKING SOCIALISM
New processes, new insights

The more challenging the period, the more urgent it is to find the space to reflect, and to allow ourselves to be tentative. We who earn our living as intellectuals must cast arrogance aside. Any polished end product may be the result of individual intellectual effort, but it inevitably reflects a collective process. However 'expert' someone is, however much someone has read, ideas with any claim to validity must be tested and based on *listening* and most importantly on *hearing* as they take account of the responses they elicit. Academic seminars and specialist conferences provide one kind of terrain for this, party commissions and independent think tanks still others. Nor should we forget private conversations. Small discussion groups are perhaps one of the most 'thinker-friendly' because of the opportunity they provide to share some thoughts and get feedback. Along with private conversations, they can provide rich 'food for thought' and help to overcome some of the isolation which intellectual work forces on those who engage in it.

Having a practical object or a political commitment or even belonging to a group or working with others is useful but not sufficient if debates continue to reproduce old ideas as answers to out of date questions. That new thinking which somehow manages to leap out of the traps of old dichotomies, while taking from the past insights which are still useful, and which aims to innovate in ways corresponding to the needs of a new epoch, must be grounded in the messy, often confusing tangle of developments while allowing for uncertainty and ambiguity.

UNSETTLED AND UPENDED

We are without any doubt living through extraordinary times and any attempt to rethink socialism is little short of daunting. The Central and Eastern European socialist regimes have collapsed. We read in the newspapers, hear on the radio, and see on television reports about what is being destroyed, and what is left behind. Without personal contact it is more difficult to get a sense of what is being created in the spaces opening up. In the West old certainties are undermined by financial crises, as people lose jobs and homes, as we walk past people sleeping on the streets, as even once steadfast regimes like the Swedish welfare state cease being a beacon of light. Yet while socialism has collapsed, capitalism certainly does not seem to work all that well. In Britain it cannot house a significant section of the population adequately. In the United States it has not been able to provide good health care for all. Those starving in sub-Saharan Africa or who are struggling on a pitifully small pension in Russia have little to thank capitalism for. But what, we ask, is the alternative?

As we think about an answer, we can, and must, each examine our own feelings about this situation. For it is a period which inevitably requires reflection, the deeper the better, as much as reading, or listening or talking. The process of self-reflection must not be short-circuited precisely *because* of the *necessity* of trying to go beyond our individual limitations, the narrow confines of the groups and places we each inhabit, in order to try to connect with society more widely. We must be in touch with our own feelings, and relate our thinking to them, if we are to have any chance of being with touch with others. That is, a rethinking which shares concerns with others must come from the inside as well as the outside. We need to listen to our hearts as well as our heads and to reflect on *our* daily experiences to begin to check whether our ideas and our policies are valid. How else can we have empathy with others, however much we recognise the distance between different experiences? And if we do not listen to ourselves let alone others, how can our activities, our ideas, our policies have a ring of authenticity on the one hand and of necessity on the other? How can they attract, and reflect, more than a handful of intellectuals unless they *feel* right? In other words, how can we construct a politics which connects with wider sectors of society in forms which are appropriate to the present moment?

Putting *feelings* on the agenda is hardly the usual mode of proceeding for rethinking politics, or indeed, for engaging in intellectual activities. The usual mode in its most dogmatic form is to lay down the line, to give the definitive version. At best this implies using ideas to capture reality. We are supposed to subjugate our feelings and to conquer our uncertainty and ambivalence as we search for the certainty of generalities outside of ourselves. The dichotomy which has been set up historically between thinking and feeling has been much criticised, not least in important work by feminist writers. But can we overcome the seeming contradiction between a naive belief in the obviousness of reading our feelings and a sophisticated, detached intellectual analysis? Can we understand how subjectivity can itself be a *resource* in expanding our comprehension of the social order?[1]

Although you would never know it from the bad press political parties receive, this question also has to do with the need for a new kind of party.[2]

108

As political parties try to redefine themselves and find it difficult to regenerate, many people search for alternatives and talk about social movements or civic groups or whatever else seems to provide an unsullied organisational form.[3] Yet if history has irrevocably undermined the parties of old, our problem is how to move from a party which sees itself as the be all and end all (a vice of social democratic parties no less than communist ones) to one, or better, ones which see themselves as *part* of an overall process in relation to and alongside other organisations which organise people and ideas, which represent interests and serve political functions. Parties are needed to formulate political programmes based on a vision of society as it moves into the future which reflect and influence pressures for change. They are needed for an effective democratic process answerable to the electorate and responsible for the actions of governments and policy makers. They are needed as an important mediator, if by no means the only one, of knowledge about society as it connects with some sense of a collective project to which millions of people are willing to lend (and I mean lend, not grant once and for all) their allegiance.

It should be obvious that this is not just any old party. Nor is it an organisation which already exists although some of its *attributes* have existed. Much of what I am talking about concerns how the political can be reflected in a new way in an organisation which is deeply rooted in society, which functions as the conduit for ideas and feelings, which listens and tries to understand, and which connects those understandings to knowledge at a higher, societal and indeed international level, that is, to policies and political programmes. This is what mass social democratic and communist parties used to set as their task. Admittedly it was in a manner which is today increasingly inadequate since the complexity of society and consequently of governing requires manifold channels of knowledge and sources of creative policy making. Moreover, the imperatives arising from this situation have enormous implications not only for rethinking the party but also the state.

ON THE GROUND AND DOWN TO EARTH

Yet if the current situation requires parties plus a myriad of other organis-ations, institutions, and processes, we *still* have to have our ears on the ground, to learn from people's daily lives, their aspirations and needs how-ever they are being defined. This is not because of some populist vocation, but because the name of the political game is the need for popular support, not only and crucially for elections, but because any policy worth its salt has inevitably to be translated on the ground by millions of people as they simply get on with life within the confines of the possible and with the dreams of the desirable. Of course the forms and content of these needs are contested and constantly evolving, and are the product of a myriad of

109

influences, structures, and agencies. But *whatever* we encounter, and *however* far from any particular political vision we may have, popular aspirations are the context and the mediator of any politics and policy.[4] Given that the experience of any of us or of our families, friends, workmates, acquaintances is inevitably circumscribed, we can only come into contact with a minute part of this society directly.

We therefore depend on what others know and communicate, and overall we require some kind of evolving, never fully defined, always contestable synthesis as the basis for constructing what Gramsci called a collective will. But the processes and outcomes, the collective will which is negotiated, I would suggest, if they are to succeed in renewing society must reflect the complex texture of contemporary society, the *depth* of individual experience, and qualities of openness and tolerance which can ensure its ongoing renewal. We need to hold together the subjective and the analytical. However finely honed the intellectual argument, however convincingly argued a political position, however complex a policy analysis, if it is to be translated *on the ground*, it must be firmly rooted in this reality, and it will be constantly tested as society changes.

The question of knowledge and understanding is not an abstract, theoretical matter. It is very down to earth and concrete. As Marx wrote, 'The educators must be educated.' To change his language somewhat, we who have come some way down the road to articulating political ideas, who organise or manage or educate in the work we do, who aim to intervene to change society for the better, need the confidence that our politics are valid, confidence in ourselves, but eventually and much more importantly confidence from wider sectors of the society. And we cannot achieve that confidence simply by being in an organisation with a particular name, or because our hearts are in the right place. Our politics can only be validated if it is rooted in the profound needs of our society.

The greatest danger in such a rapidly evolving situation is to assume that we already know all the *questions*, let alone the *answers*.[5] Yet that does not mean that none of the old questions are useful, or that we have to throw away all the old categories. Quite the opposite. What it seems to me is happening is that some very traditional questions are reappearing in new, and sometimes rather old forms. At the level of intellectual debates, for example, there are attempts to reformulate very traditional questions about the nature of citizenship, the problems involved in arriving at the common good in conditions of pluralism and diversity, the tensions and contradictions within liberal democracy which can serve as the motor of a process aimed at improving democracatic practices. What is too often missing, however, is an understanding that social and historical change require the development of new and adequate conceptual apparatus.

The inadequacies of left thinking and the disastrous aspects of socialist regimes do not mean that traditional ways of thinking, such as liberalism, however much it is still relevant, however dressed up in inspiring, radical language, are sufficient to analyse the dramatic changes we are living through. At the same time, being 'post' something else, identifying with a 'post-ism', be it post-marxism or post-modernism, runs the risk of simply repeating the insights of Locke, or Rousseau, or Nietzsche, or Freud in language much more convoluted than they ever employed. Many debates in philosophy and social theory, sometimes carrying the name of post-modernism, have been essential in liberating us from the dead weight of those ideas which prevent us from seeing and seeking to understand the multifarious and complex nature of social reality. But, to put it crudely, the baby has all too often been thrown out with the bathwater.

BACK TO REALITY

Debate is often posed at such an abstract level that there appears little if any recognition that we need continually to move between theoretical abstractions and reality and back again. Theory, it seems, has little if anything to learn from the material nature of the structure of society, or from people's daily lives. It is easy therefore to lose sight of some inescapable if very old-fashioned features of society. Let's jump to the specific and the concrete: school league tables, flawed as they may be, highlight how *class* differences can still determine educational achievement. The same could be said of health statistics or other indices. Yet we should all be aware how class is but one of a configuration of factors and how any automatic, knee jerk response to facts which assumes an obvious protagonism of some mythical working class (mythical in the sense that it tends to be conjured up in its superficial generality) is completely inadequate politically.

At the same time it is truly difficult to maintain the kind of multiple perspectives which we need. Again this is not a question of theory but of something very concrete. As I sat recently in a sparkling new international class shopping mall in the outer London suburb, Kingston upon Thames, where I teach, I thought to myself how very distant metaphorically the society it represented was from what in spatial terms was just up the road, inner city Brixton, where I live. *Both* realities must be taken account of and the similarities as well as the differences enter into our frame. After all, unemployment and house repossessions are a reality in Kingston just as material gratification is alive and well in Brixton. Yet, we must not under-estimate the challenge such a mixed reality presents to us both analytically and politically.

To consider another question, when we speak about developing civil society, we need to realise two things. First, that we must study what is *already going on* in civil society, in both organised and unorganised ways. Second, civil society cannot be conceptualised in limbo. It is always in some relation with the state. We cannot avoid the traditional concern with the state, yet this concern has taken on a new meaning in a context where the state/society relationship is being reorganised so dramatically in such a wide range of countries. With regard both to civil society and to the state, if we fail to begin with studying what is already going on, and instead assert a politics which we weave out of our heads, we risk at best being irrelevant and at worst failing to connect with precisely those elements which could constitute the basis for progressive advance. The development of policy which is worth fighting for because it is appropriate for what is *really* going on and is not just proceeding in well-worn channels or reflecting the untested ideas of a few experts must derive from a reflection on the actual processes of society, the ones we like but also the ones we do not.[6]

REINVENTING GOVERNMENT: THEORY LEARNING FROM PRACTICE

Any attempt at 'reinventing government',[7] must learn from an examination of those practices which are developing in public institutions as the people who work in them try to 'push back the walls' of the constraints they face and take advantage of the new spaces which are opening up. I am thinking here of everything from local authority service contracts to new teaching practices to equal opportunities policies and attempts to get what is good out of community care legislation. That is, we have to study those inter-mediate levels and to listen to those people, the practitioners, who are trying to do good jobs, to develop more democratic practices, and at the same time to maintain some kind of job satisfaction within the most difficult constraints. To learn about the concrete dimensions of citizenship in a country like Britain today, we could do well to study, for example, the local service contracts which a number of local councils have introduced between specific services and their users. These required detailed and concrete thinking, service by service, about how to give people some effective control to make the contract meaningful.[8] Other examples are the attempts at more democratic and empowering practices in social work,[9] good community care practices provided by voluntary sector services run by users, practitioners and managers together,[10] and the development of effective multi-cultural and anti-racist policies.[11]

If our politics and our rethinking does not build on the good practice which is already being developed by focusing on those achievements which, incidentally, cannot be claimed by *any* single political party, by creating the conditions to fulfill their potential, and not least to fund them properly, then our very vision of what is possible and desirable will not be grounded in concrete practices. Theoretical debate, however stimulating and inspiring, would then remain floating in the air, unrelated to ongoing processes, real

112

problems, and concrete structures. We will be reproducing the worst aspects of traditional intellectual practice without effectively feeding into a process of political regeneration. We will remain out of touch and out of date. As we aim at a strategic dimension, not only nationally but internationally, we will be trying to reinvent the wheel without the benefit of the knowledge and experience of those who constitute the concrete link between citizen and state.

What is actually being suggested is something which can be found in Marx and in Gramsci. Marx provided what remains an incisive critique of attempts to develop philosophical and social thinking as if it could be generated without reference to the historical, socio-economic context. He and Engels based their prognosis of socialism on what they understood was the potential of capitalism generated from an engagement with the cutting edge of contemporary developments. Going well beyond them but developing many of their ideas in the 1920s and 1930s, in a period of enormous political and theoretical crisis, Gramsci was sharply critical of political parties or intellectuals who acted as if they had nothing to learn from the ongoing, complex historical process. He analysed the latest historical developments while criticising the limitations of existing theory to give us some of the most creative and original insights into twentieth-century society, insights which managed to escape the sterile dichotomies of contemporary debates. The point is not to have any illusions about the possibility of basing the analysis which *we* need *today* on thinkers whose own works are full of limitations. Moreover, there are many different sources of wisdom. But at the same time, we should be open to learning from the way they worked, and from the criticisms they made of abstract, detached intellectualistic pretence.[12]

THE RESOURCES FOR A NEW UNDERSTANDING

Learning and thinking about social change must be tackled by *all* reforming political organisations, wherever in the political spectrum, but no political party in today's conditions can hope to accomplish this task on its own. There is a *functional* need for non-sectarian openness and democratic change. We must go beyond even the most open communist tradition informed by Gramsci, and we need more political and intellectual resources than even a reforming Labour Party or think tanks can provide, essential as they are. Society is simply too complex, and the amount of knowledge required too great. One consequence of the complexity of social needs is the inevitability of diversity and flexibility if social provision is to be adequate. And if we begin to reformulate our idea of how this is to be accomplished to include fundamentally the state but as a facilitator (and funder) as much as direct provider, with much policy being invented in a creative way 'on the ground' and probably 'on the move' as well, then we also have to rethink the party which can no longer be conceived of as an all-knowing, all-providing organisation. Further, given that a different kind of party is a necessary but not a sufficient condition, what is required is a regeneration of a whole range of organisations: from trade unions, women's groups, voluntary, civic, ethnic and other minority organisations, to professional associations and, crucially, educational institutions.

This means embarking on that intellectual and moral reform described by Gramsci when he discussed the 'political' question of the intellectuals. By this he meant not just the academic élite but all those in society whose jobs and training mean that they organise institutions or ideas, who connect people in civil society, in the state, or link the two: the experts, the managers, the professionals, the technicians, the practitioners, in short anyone with some kind of advanced education or training. Gramsci chose the word 'reform' with care. It indicated the kind of sea change in the way people view themselves and their socio-economic roles, from top to toe of the social ladder, associated with the Protestant Reformation or the creation of a modern secular society. Elements of a transformation of this order are already under way within the difficult conditions of the present. And since these processes *are* already under way, we can be comforted that we are not simply idealistic utopians, cut off from the needs of our neighbours or indeed out of touch with our own.

Out of the anger with the failure of what is no more and the vast distance between, on the one hand, what is needed and, on the other, what seems to be within our grasp, between the necessary and the possible, it is so easy either to reject all of what went before or to hold on for dear life to the familiar. Or someone comes up with a formula which seems to be original but which is created in a very old-fashioned, outdated way, that is, by intellectuals who are detached from ongoing processes.

Rethinking socialism inevitably implies rethinking how we go about things, individually and collectively. The ends will never be achieved if the means are not the right ones. And if the means are faulty we will not, in any case, know what those ends are or could be. This rethinking, then, is a task on the agenda for everyone who is trying to make some kind of sense of the present situation. It may be easier to come up with a slogan or mobilising call or neat theoretical formulation than to contemplate the brutal reality that what is needed has to be painstakingly created. It is not created in conditions of our choosing, to paraphrase Marx, but what we *are* able to create, for politics is a creative process, will depend on how far it harnesses the potential, expressed or not, of people and sectors of society who would never turn out on a dark winter's night to a meeting.

A good starting point is to add to our usual sources to include conversations, films, novels, television programmes, plays, whatever – and our own deepest feelings. Let me give you a few examples of how I have been given a much greater understanding of some major issues and profound questions by batting them around in my own mind and gaining insights from unexpected sources. I would emphasise insights rather than solutions. They all concern women. I think that both changes in women's lives, the contradictions they and the households in which they live encounter, and the theoretical and political advances made by feminism give us an important basis for a real advance in understanding.

The first story has to do with a woman who was my daughter's child-minder some years ago. She was a single mother with two primary school age children who had applied several times to return to a job part-time which she had held before as a lab technician in a large London teaching hospital, but she never even got an interview. By sheer coincidence her mother used to work in the personnel department of this same hospital, and she explained that they simply would never consider anyone who had small children. Hearing this story made something click. First, what might seem obvious, the justification for the law on equal opportunities, and the fact that we had to make sure that it was enforced. The rules of entry to jobs and the practices of personnel departments should resemble justice blindfolded, i.e. disregarding irrelevant differences, keeping childcare responsibilities out of court. This single, concrete example drove home to me that the traditional liberal democratic guarantee of equality before the rule of law still needs to be fought for and applied equitably.

Yet there was also something else. This specific, concrete woman *did* have responsibility for the care of two small children. While entry to a job should not be blocked because of this, once she was in a job (and she finally did get one), she could not in fact leave this responsibility on the side, and no one anywhere in the world, however good the childcare provision, has come up with any possibility of doing that.[13] What we (and this includes me) need is a transformation of the logic of work itself to be able to develop adequate flexibility to address the different caring responsibilities of both men and women in different points of their life cycles. This is difficult to imagine, but while it would be revolutionary, it is not utopian because it reflects the concrete needs of millions of people, even if it goes beyond the logic of much if not all contemporary working life. Of course, this concrete example was deciphered by me through lenses which I had because of some reading and knowledge of theoretical debates, but I understood the theory so much better from thinking about the concrete dimensions of this woman's life, and my own life and the lives of other women I knew. This kind of engagement helped me to understand how it is necessary both to fight to make liberal ideas of equality opportunities real and to construct a new terrain in which different needs can be addressed. Taking this one step further and relating it to discussions about women and different welfare states, I arrived at a much better understanding of the highly differentiated relationship we each have with the state, not only through the system of laws but mediated by the institutions of the welfare state and how our citizenship is much more complex than it once was.[14]

The second example has to do with something I have been puzzling over for a long time. Why is it that in Britain, unlike say Italy, or Finland, or a number of other countries including non-European ones, women experience such guilt and anxiety over combining paid work and childcare responsibilities? Yes, there was the influence in the post-war period of oversimplified psychoanalytic theory as mediated by social policy and inadequate social provision.[15] But why did it seem to stick to women's guts in Britain, at least amongst the ethnic majority, in such an uncomfortable way? Why do so many women in Britain see childcare as an *individual* responsibility? (And I stress the word responsibility – the place of joy and desire has all too small a place in discussions.) What gave me some possible clues to greater insight into this, or at least further questions, came from an account of a friend's emotional experience having been evacuated as a 6-year-old child to the United States at the beginning of the Second World War with her sisters, changing from one set of relatives to another, before finally being reunited with her parents at war's end. Could it be that the trauma of a *policy* of evacuation, where parents had to take the responsibility of *choosing* but in conditions of fear and loss, as opposed to unforeseen and unchosen separations which involved so many millions in Europe in the last war,[16] scarred the national psyche so deeply that discussions of childcare are overdetermined by it? And didn't the fresh memories of millions of women of the difficult conditions of combining work and childcare in wartime, which were only partially mitigated by the existence of nurseries and the benefits of an independent wage, influence the desire for 'normality' at war's end, sex stereotyped that it might be? And could a further contributing factor be the emotional experiences of early separation of a small, but influential minority of people, whose parents have sent them to boarding school, who have formed part of the nation's élite?

When it comes to developing a policy of good quality, socially provided childcare, could these in part explain some of the resistances? When they are reinforced by the lack of experience of good quality provision, which, for example, as a Danish friend told me, makes it as automatic in Denmark for a parent to decide to place a young child in a nursery as it would for British parents to send their children to school, we are talking about long-term historical and cultural factors which shape the context for policy making. Of course anecdote does not provide systematic knowledge, but combined with reading and research, it can provide leads and ground more abstract discussion.[17]

And finally, a very different example. A few years ago at the London Film Festival I had the good fortune to see the latest Istvan Szabò film, 'Sweet Emma, Dear Böbe', about the experiences of two young women teachers in contemporary Budapest, and to hear his comments afterward. 'Sweet

Emma, Dear Böbe' is about coping and survival. It is a moving, at times funny, and also incredibly sad story about how tough it is to survive a change of regime, low income, the need to take a second job, the loss of ties with family and rural culture, the experience of living in a hostel with no privacy, the upheaval of an institution where colleagues constantly accuse each other, pupils could not care less about learning, and where one's previous training, to teach Russian, is worth nothing. Added to these were the torments of loving a man who cannot respond to your needs, the institutionalised sexism of the police, and some, little, humanity and joy.

What was striking was the sympathy and understanding with which the characters were portrayed. When Szabò responded to questions about the bleakness of it all, the role of religion, the conditions of making films in post-communist Hungary, and so on, he told some stories from his own life, explaining that since he was born in 1938 there have been eight changes of regime in Hungary. He described how he learned about the situation of these teachers from the inside through long discussions, showing them the film before it was released. And he said some things that I will never forget: 'It is really hard to live through these changes. Some people make it and some don't. People need to believe in something. Our future lies with the education of our children. I had already made several films about opportunistic men. Now I wanted to show the story of a strong woman.'

It is an equivalent authenticity, sensitivity, and dedication of our talents and skills to a politics which is rooted in the depths of our society and in a reflection on our role as intellectuals, in the wide Gramscian sense, which must be the basis of our rethinking socialism. There are no any easy prescriptions for accomplishing this, but at the centre of our agenda there must be an expansion of our ways of seeing, hearing and understanding, and a critique of the inadequacies of all those prognoses and programmes which seem to have little if anything to do with daily life, whether they come from the academic world, the civil service or left intellectuals. We have to stay in touch with the positive things which are being created as well as provide a critique of the negative features of society. We need to wed policy making, the reconstruction of organisations, and theorising to the lived experience of millions of people. Only then can we hope to regenerate ourselves and our politics.

10

DEAR PARENT . . .

INTRODUCTION

The emphasis on education in strategies for economic and social renewal in the UK, the US and elsewhere not only call teachers and schools more generally to account for teaching methods and for outcomes much more than in earlier periods, but place explicit responsibility on the shoulders of parents. The context in which this is taking place place has been formed, at least in the UK, by attacks on 'progressive education' from the right and by eighteen years of Conservative governments. Reflections on personal experience as a parent a few years after Margaret Thatcher was elected provided the occasion to test some insights from my professional life, from work on Gramsci's ideas on the intellectuals.[1] It seemed to me that the right captured aspects of parental experience which should not be ignored by the left. Although much has changed in school organisation since my daughter was in school, the basic features of the parent–teacher relationship have evolved very little.

No right-wing campaign about education would have a chance of success if it did not relate in important ways to elements of popular experience. Although children and young people are the subjects and objects of education, the experience which is invoked by the right is that of the parent. The appeal is particularly effective because schools are outposts of the welfare state, involving a very large part of the population in daily contact. Not only does concern for their children's education strike an emotional chord in the parents, but schools are supposed both to account for themselves and to create a working relationship with parents. Schools are more open than other state institutions, and are markedly different from most other parts of the world of work. This has not always been so, and it is the product of many battles not yet concluded which have produced new demands and new expectations amongst parents which the right has responded to in its fashion.

IDENTITY PARENT

'Parent' is a blanket term leaving class, sex, and race unspecified. Millions of us think of ourselves as parents alongside our other identities, and certainly we are addressed as such by schools. When the right claims to represent the interest of parents, it may obscure differences between them while emphasising individualism – but that does not mean that the subject 'parents' does not exist. A parent has a particular kind of responsibility for and relationship to a child. To be a parent is to relate to the needs of a particular child or children and to do what is 'best' for them. 'Best' is determined purely by the fact of parenthood. At the same time a person is addressed as one amongst many parents by an institution and by people in that institution. The school relates to 'parents', rather than to manual or white-collar workers, to black or white people. With regard to sex, on the other hand, because it is overwhelmingly women who normally are in contact with the school, the image invoked is often the mother, at times the mother and father, but rarely the father as such.

A person's identity as a 'parent' is reinforced in several ways. In the first place parents relate in the main to teachers, and others such as educational psychologists, all of whom are defined as specialised experts by training and work. That they, too, might be parents and/or black, white or from a working-class family is usually suppressed as irrelevant to their work role. The most significant dimension of that relationship is constituted by the difference between the parent and the professionals who are linked by a child: one has a parental relationship to the child, the other has specialised skills. The relationship will be affected by sex, race, and class differences but is not defined by them. Second, the right can address a universal 'parent' because we are defined as such by the state. Since the state took over education in the last century, all parents have the right and the obligation to send children to school. Third, parents are organised as a group vis-à-vis the school and are the constituency which elect parent governors. There are therefore real ways in which parents are constructed as a group by the school, whatever the dominant political discourses, even though divisions and differences within that group can be just as important as elements of unity.

IN LOCO PARENTIS

There is no typical experience of a parent in relationship to the school. However, one's own experience can be taken as symptomatic though not representative of experiences shared by many parents, and valuable in understanding how the right has succeeded in mobilising parental opinion. The comments here reflect my having a 6-year-old daughter in primary

119

school. If I face certain problems despite a job which gives me a degree of self-confidence and training in higher education, I can assume that some of these problems are experienced by others with a different background. For me the school meets two needs: childminding and specialised education – in that order. *In loco parentis* means to me first of all that my daughter is the school's responsibility during school hours and mine and her father's at other times. Statistics and personal experience indicate that childminding is a crucial function of the school for the overwhelming majority of women. It is school which makes it easier for mothers to seek a job, although most will have no choice but to organise their working lives around school hours.[2]

For many of us the way the school day and the school year are organised is a major problem, but then so are working mothers a 'problem' for the school. The increase in mothers with young children in the workforce means that far fewer parents are 'on tap'. A school closed for half term, for use as a polling station, or for a strike, or for a training day, disrupts parents' lives in a way that it simply did not some years ago. This childminding function goes against the grain of the professional training of teachers whose job it is to teach. Moreover, my needs as a working parent often contradict their personal needs as workers. To fulfil their own domestic responsibilities they depend on a particular organisation of the working day and year.

HIGH STANDARDS FOR ALL

Education is important in itself, of course. Parents feel passionately about the education of their children. Meetings on language and numbers skills at my daughter's inner-city, mainly working-class school are always well attended – by parents from different class and ethnic backgrounds. If claims about a decline in basic skills are influential, they relate to a real concern. They connect with the high expectations of a good education and life chances for all children by a mass of parents brought up under the welfare state. The standard of judgment is not the past: we have lost all collective memory of how bad things used to be before, for example, the Second World War. More is being demanded of schools than previously.

The right's answer is to reorganise these higher expectations around a model which is presented as meritocratic based on individual achievement. Parents can see the inadequacies and failure of the British education system. If an élite in fact benefits unfairly from the present system in ways which remain obscure and mysterious, why not support a plan which is put forward by the right as benefiting all those with ability, whatever that means?[3] The widespread concern about children's need to acquire basic skills relates to an awareness that those without these skills are trapped at the bottom of the heap.

PARENTS AND PROFESSIONALS

In fact, schooling is a mystery to parents. However open a school, what goes on during the school day remains a blank. According to my daughter, undoubtedly protecting jealously the achievement of a separate experience, they 'never do anything'. If I were to drop in – and like most if not all parents I can't because I have a job – I would only be a distraction. It would require considerable extra time and effort, in resource terms, plus a new attitude, for a teacher to explain the philosophy behind the methods used. I am favourably impressed with the individual treatment children receive in my daughter's school: each child has individual reading and maths schemes. But this undoubtedly advanced attitude presents real problems for all parents interested in their child's schooling. In the absence of a written report, a tangible piece of paper giving the parent an assessment, however inadequate, we depend on the odd comment.[4] But with or without reports, how do I know what to expect, let alone whether things are on the right track? And when is it appropriate to expect more? If my child is being considered as an individual, what view of her capacity does the teacher have? Is it the same view as mine? Which is more accurate? Is there an acceptance of a stereotype or something less than 'full' potential – for whatever reason? Will I appear pushy? Or will I be fobbed off with compliments?

Parents feel vulnerable when they talk to a teacher, because they see themselves as dependent on the latter for their child's welfare. Dependence and vulnerability hinder a positive relationship as does relating to a person simply as a professional. The teacher must disguise that he or she is a worker seeking job satisfaction, who may need support, and who is often drained by various demands; the teacher may also be a parent. The teacher appears as someone with specialised teaching skills. But all parents 'teach' whether they realise it or not. Of course we aren't professional teachers: we aren't specifically trained and our involvement is concentrated on one or a few children over a limited period. We don't specialise in teaching. It occurs alongside everything else we do in the home and at work, but we know something about teaching. If parents complain that education can't always be fun, could it be that, through their practical experience, they feel there is a grain of truth in the saying, 'If at first you don't succeed, try, try again'?

Professionals who specialise in teaching have thus developed some of the skills we all have, however embryonically.[5] To the extent that this expertise appears as a monopoly of knowledge, the property of the teacher, un-explained to the parent, it constitutes a barrier between parent and teacher. Just as a skilled mechanic has a better chance of fixing a car than someone who can simply use a spanner, teachers know more about teaching than parents. Defensiveness about maintaining a monopoly over skills, whether it takes an archaic professional or corporate trade union form, however, divides teachers from parents. There are real difficulties in overcoming this division which must be recognised if they are to be broken down. It is very difficult, for example, to explain the principles of the new maths to most of us who have learnt, some of us badly, the old. And yet from the point of view of what parent and teacher have in common – an interest in the education and development of the child – an increase in parental knowledge so that parents can reinforce the educational process at home is precisely what is needed.

At the same time as asking a great deal of schools, parents are also well aware of how much children learn from other sources, in particular from television, but also from friends, babyminders, parents. Certainly most of the facts and much of the vocabulary they learn comes from television. The level of knowledge held by children today is vastly higher than when we were young. How do schools relate to that?

COMMON AIMS DESPITE DIFFERENCES?

Neither Parent Teacher Associations nor school governors' meetings provide a suitable forum to talk about most of these things. The structure of consultation between parents and teachers does not permit parents to raise questions about what they feel deeply but find difficult to articulate. What may appear to teachers as a threat to their professional status needs to be confronted in the course of discussion. There is a need for debate and one of the preconditions for the success of such a debate is clarity rather than inhibitions about the differences between teachers and parents, between parents of different races, classes, sexes, between generations. At the moment it is usually just too embarrassing to talk about these things. If it is ever to be possible, impediments to such discussions must be put forward as a problem to be overcome. This is the precondition of our talking about the need for compromise and considering the political question: compromise about what, for what, within which parameters? Only then can we consider how a democratic progressive politics can be created out of our differences. If, on the other hand, some parents do not always go out of their way to participate in the life of the school, it probably reflects a very rational calculation about an investment of time and effort and the probable outcome. Middle-class concern is but one expression of this calculation. Elements of unity can be built around an awareness that for the vast majority of parents the state system is the only choice. If the right has been able to harness a widespread sense of dissatisfaction, the onslaught on state education of recent years can only be combatted by a recognition of the reality behind this dissatisfaction in parental experience, an experience which also contains goodwill, and the hope for a better future.[6]

AFTERWORD

There have been major changes in the education sector in Britain, some of which address a number of the issues discussed above. Since the Education Reform Act of 1986, the first of several under Conservative governments, the way schools in England and Wales are governed has changed substantially, with local management of schools holding out a promise of parental involvement. Local education authorities no longer have the kind of power they once did. Accountability for professional competence is more transparent as the performance of schools is measured through inspections and the publication of test scores and exam results. Reporting on individual children is within a standard format. But while parents can get involved more in discussions about the curriculum and teaching methods and although more educational demands have been placed on them through 'contracts' and homework, the promise of parental power has in the main been unfulfilled, and the ability to intervene in issues to do with an individual child's education is still circumscribed. Despite all the changes in formal structures, the fact that parents, from a wide variety of backgrounds, know something about teaching, although they are not specialists, still rarely figures in the relationship between parents and teachers.

11

SUBJECTIVE AUTHENTICITY, CULTURAL SPECIFICITY, INDIVIDUAL AND COLLECTIVE PROJECTS

Although much has been written about the social and political roles of intellectuals in modern society, the sociology of knowledge, and the philosophy and methodology of social science, social scientists tend to be pre-occupied with analysing others, not themselves.[1] The structural constraints on the ways intellectuals work, the history of academic disciplines, or the international variations in academic cultures and practices may all be investigated within various subject specialisms, but they also form the largely unspoken context of our professional daily lives. Demystifying our practices may undermine the basis of authority, but it is also a precondition for a more open and honest relationship with our roles. This tentative exploration of some themes which derive from a reflection on years of academic work is far from being definitive, and it comes not only from the head but from the heart. The aim is to open a conversation – not to close it.

One of the best sources for a reflective discussion about the relationship between the concrete person who is writing, the product which is created, the 'voice' in which it is written, and the world at large is literature. The German writer Christa Wolf explains that writing is not a question of 'mastering' reality, nor is it 'some kind of ecstasy or taking refuge in the inaccessible recesses of the so-called artistic labour process',[2] but rather it is 'a process which continuously runs alongside life, helping to shape and interpret it: writing can be seen as a way of being more intensely involved in the world'.[3] Her comments in an interview are rooted in a particular context, the debates in the GDR in the late 1960s and early 1970s, and are a response to a question about her refusal to make a distinction between 'story-teller' and 'prose-writer'. They draw on an essay, 'The Reader and the Writer'.[4] But her approach is suggestive for a sensitive consideration of our own modes of working and our relationship to the tasks we undertake in a different context and in different fields.[5]

In the social sciences there is an increasing awareness that academics and other intellectuals as well as practitioners such as teachers or social workers mediate and shape 'reality', which itself is never an unproblematic category. There is also a recognition, at least among some, that we never start from a neutral position.[6] But rarely do we reflect on the relationship between the individual intellectual and the intellectual project which is undertaken. It is perhaps not surprising that some of the most insightful work in this direction comes from feminists. That 'lack of ease' which women experience in a world which has historically predominantly been shaped by and for men has led feminists to query what is considered knowledge and how it is produced.[7]

There have been impressive feminist reconstructions of epistemology and of the philosophy of science, and feminist analyses of the inadequacies of fundamental, hegemonic categories of philosophy as the 'master' discipline overseeing all others.[8] Addressed more directly to sociology, the work of Dorothy E. Smith challenges many of the practices present in a broader canon of empirical work. In *The Everyday World as Problematic*[9] she suggests that by starting with the ordinary experiences of women we can arrive at a complex ethnomethodology revealing structures and processes in society and at the same time help the *object* of our study to become a *subject*.[10] And from another perspective, Gayatri Chakravorty Spivak uses her transnational experiences to analyse the provincialisms of academia, and dissects the specificities lurking beneath its pretence of that universalism which marginalises and 'tokenises' those like herself defined as the 'exotic other'.[11] She explains that,

> I find the demand on me to be marginal always amusing. . . . I'm tired of dining out on being an exile. But the question is more complex than that. In a certain sense, I think there is nothing that is central. . . . [I]n terms of the hegemonic historical narrative, certain peoples have always been asked to cathect the margins so others can be defined as central. Negotiating between these two structures, sometimes I have to see myself as marginal in the eyes of others. . . . I'm never defined as marginal in India, I can assure you.[12]

Beyond the question of marginality/centrality, we need, of course, to avoid reducing the attempt to generalise about the world to the biography of its author, and her or his cultural or geographical specificity. At the same time, acknowledging how knowledge may be 'situated' in specific contexts opens difficult questions, but it can also lead us to consider further dimensions of intellectual practice. For all the writing on social research methodology and the sociology of knowledge and of intellectuals, integrating reflection on our practice beyond a nod in the direction of methodology is none too easy. The possibility, and the limitations of, expanding our repertoire of intellectual tools to include subjectivity as a *resource* in expanding our comprehension of the social order is easier to treat as the *object* of study rather than incorporate it into reflective practice.

Christa Wolf, in the context of a fight to justify a particular creative space,[13] describes writing as involvement in the world. Talking about her work she says,

> This mode of writing is not 'subjectivist', but 'interventionist'. It does require subjectivity, and a subject who is prepared to undergo unrelenting exposure . . . to the material at hand, to accept the tensions that inexorably arise, and to be curious about the changes that both the material and the author undergo. The new reality is different from the one you saw before. Suddenly, everything is interconnected and fluid. Things formerly taken as 'given' start to dissolve revealing the reified social relations they contain and no longer that hierarchically arranged social cosmos in which the human particle travels along the paths pre-ordained by sociology or ideology, or deviates from them. It becomes more and more difficult to say 'I', and yet at the same time often imperative to do so. I would like to give the provisional name 'subjective authenticity' to the search for a new method of writing which does justice to this reality. I can only hope that I have made it clear that the method not only does not dispute the existence of objective reality, but is precisely an attempt to engage with 'objective reality' in a productive manner.[14]

It is obvious that engagement is crucial to her definition of her role when she concludes,

> that form of retreat which seeks to keep one's own inner passions apart from the burning issues of the day causes your creativity to wane and you're left with the kind of artistic activity about which nothing bad can be said apart from the fact that nobody – particularly its producer – feels it to be necessary.[15]

Reading laterally, going beyond Christa Wolf's discussion of modes of literary production as she tries to blur the boundaries between essay and fiction,[16] can this tell us something which is of use in considering *our* role as social scientists? After all, she actually differentiates her approach from that of sociology.

> I don't observe these phenomena in a remote detached manner, as a sociologist might; I have to call my own self into question as I write. My approach is subjective, but at the same time social . . .[17]

126

Can we conceptualise *our* work as subjective, social, and productive of useful, new knowledge while we call ourselves into question?

WHY THE WRITER DOES NOT EXIST –
OR DOES SHE?

Social science and other academic literature is usually written in a style which is careful not to betray that both the author and the reader are real human beings.[18] One reason for this hesitancy, and it is an important one, is that we 'hide' because of our fears of exposure and vulnerability.[19] A dispassionate style may also be connected to the all too frequent retreat into terminology which can be understood only by those *already* introduced to a certain discourse. The particular closure and narrowness of these jargons or languages is in fact a relatively recent historical phenomenon and only became hegemonic in the social sciences in the post-war period.

In the Anglo-American world and those influenced by it, there are at least two important sources of a detached social 'scientific' way of writing. First there is the continuing influence of the traditional idea, going back to the last century, and even earlier, which defines true intellectuals as above the fray of politics, the proverbial 'ivory tower'. This idea was taken up in the 1920s and 1930s in opposition to those who insisted on a political role for intellectuals,[20] and relates to the second, more immediate, source: the rejection in the US and in Britain by European refugees and native born intellectuals alike of both ways of working and modes of thought which seemed to have led to the catastrophes of the 1920s and 1930s. What became reified instead was a dispassionate approach to knowledge of society which could technocratically inform policy but whose authorship was portrayed as neutral and uncommitted.[21] This style was exported and was well received, for example, in West Germany or the Nordic countries which had been influenced by German pre-war and pre-Nazi social science, and where the break with this tradition had left a vacuum. It had less influence in France or Italy whose intellectual and political traditions admitted a political role for intellectuals even if the form of this role was contested. In Italy an exception, where the view that intellectuals should be uncommitted held some weight, was amongst those intellectuals who were trying to create a space for themselves between two dominating and contending positions, Christian Democracy and Italian communism, and even they tended to be aligned with a political party.

In contrast, in the US, where academics were particularly isolated by anti-intellectual populism and cold war anti-communism, a resort to 'neutral science' could provide links both to a populace which equated technology with progress and to governing élites who defended a restricted notion of democratic competition influenced by Schumpeter and pluralist theories against the presumed negative outcomes of political activism.[22] There is, then, a *history* to a particular way of working and style of writing which means that it is not the *only* way.

There is also another aspect to be considered. It is connected to the expansion and specialisation of knowledge, the institutionalisation of disciplines, and larger numbers of people with advanced training. This is, in turn, linked to the increasing intervention of the state and to state policy which is informed by the picture of society painted by social but also natural science. Foucault has discussed the constitution of certain discourses while Bourdieu makes other connections between knowledge, institutions, and power. Gramsci on the other hand helps us to read it in terms of the reproduction of a split between those rational if less well trained human beings, the intellectuals of daily life who are the vast majority of the population, and specialist, professional intellectuals.[23]

A final dimension is subjective and psychological. The closure of academic language probably also reflects the need of intellectuals to feel part of a community in order to overcome the alienation, anomie and isolation of academic work.[24] How many of us have whispered to ourselves, 'It's nice to speak the same language, to have the same agenda, to be on the same wave length.' Expertise, a common language, and special forms of rhetoric or ways of speaking can be experienced as protection, armour, comfort. They produce a communality, a community, an identity. But they keep out the 'others' who cannot understand, who look at things differently. They are also an attempt to establish 'discipline', as anyone will acknowledge who has resorted to an inaccessible language to prevent children knowing what is being discussed. These closures apply both between disciplines, discourses, associations, journals, and institutions, and between professional intellectuals, on the one hand, and everyday rational human beings on the other.

Earlier thinkers did not employ particularly specialised or obtuse language – although it may appear so today. For them analysis and rigorous argument could coexist with the passion to make a political intervention. Not just Machiavelli and Marx, but Hobbes, Hume, and J.S. Mill spoke more or less directly to an audience employing the 'normal' language of the educated of their time and revealing their intellectual and political passions as they wrote. This directness did not detract from the profundity of their messages, the rigour of their arguments or the development of new concepts. Nor could it be confused with simplification or popularisation. It did not mean that their ideas were accessible to large numbers of people. But there is a sense in their writing that a voice is speaking which is missing in so much modern academic literature.[25]

The fear of the 'I' and the relegation of subjective, particular experience as a lesser form of knowledge also has a history and was no less shared by an earlier generation of intellectuals than within present day academia. The critique of the impermanence and narrowness of the accidental, the occasional, the subjective and the search for overarching categories, deeper and more universal knowledge and laws has over time developed as one of the normal practices of philosophy and social science. This has been part of a traditional attempt to understand, and therefore in some sense achieve a greater control over reality which in fact goes right back to the ancient Greeks and extends throughout a contemporary social science mediated via social and economic policy.[26] It is also a question of establishing intellectual authority by removing any indication of the specificity, and inevitable limitations, of the writer.[27] By denying the existence of a specific human being who has an individual biography as the source of what is written, we simply delude ourselves. Any argument that true scientific work must be detached from the person doing it or its context simply ignores the fact that *all* knowledge is an intervention of *one* sort or *another*.

THE 'LOCALITY' OF INTELLECTUAL WORK

If we recognise the 'I', we will realise that any piece of writing is always coming from somewhere. Whatever style is employed, work in the social sciences is always de facto tentative, provisional and inserted in one debate or another, never *the* debate. However much intellectual work advances knowledge, it always has a locality, a spatial and time dimension.[28] It is *always* historically delimited, however much it may carry messages which transcend time and place. A piece of work is *always* coming from a specific, 'provincial' starting point because of the individual's particular intellectual history. That history includes training in subject areas which are more or less narrow and certain intellectual and cultural traditions which have national and linguistic boundaries.

We write according to what we have read and the conversations we have had in a particular language or languages. Anyone who has had the opportunity to step outside one tradition of debate will realise that the same words do not always share the same meanings and that shared assumptions have very different outcomes if the national setting is changed. This is, of course, why contact across countries and cultures is so stimulating and enrichening. But travelling across boundaries can also be very unsettling as we once again begin to realise our vulnerability and the fragility of our knowledge and our need for intellectual maps and lexicons.

The written material we have access to is linguistically determined, and depends, even when we can read a particular language, on what others are reading, i.e. on the 'state' of the debate.[29] The particular configuration of the debate also informs how new and original material is received. It is decoded with reference to existing schema and arguments. We make sense of the new in terms of the old. The forms of the debates, who is influential within them, and the way questions are articulated follow certain intellectual itineraries

129

and mirror certain power relations and institutional arrangements rather than necessarily reflecting what is intrinsically valuable. Intellectual authority is crucial. Moreover, *who* says something can often be as important as *what* is said. As Gayatri Spivak points out as she analyses her own experiences in this academic world, relations of forces *do* exist and regulate the conditions of production of our knowledge, its transmission and mediation.[30]

This does not mean that research never travels well, or that lessons are invalid outside their 'natural habitat'. If material from one place is applied with caution and sensitivity to different national realities, the result can be creative new combinations. It is important, however, to acknowledge that we can never comprehensively encompass the different viewpoints. Each of us inevitably makes strategic choices, explicit or not, reflecting the impossibility of universal knowledge. Since we always run the risk of being buried by the literature available, we are more likely to read commentaries and what is derived, rather than the 'master/mistress' him/herself. Unless they are the specific object of specialist study, it is rare to re-read thinkers who have influenced us. Our memory of what they have written tends to become more and more reductive. We so often work with our *idea* of their work and with what others say it is. This reflects a real problem. We need to absorb and synthesise difficult thought and to move beyond studying the 'masters/mistresses', whomever we define as such. Otherwise we fall into mere scolasticism. We need to move on. But it is striking how much academic debate is formed by oversimplification and attacks on straw men and women.

At the same time as we recognise the limits of our work as intellectuals conceived as the product of *individual* enterprise, we would do well to understand that, whether we realise it or not, we are *always*, de facto engaged in a collective, shared project. We depend on others and are formed by others as we learn from them and engage in debate with them. Whereas the actual production may be in an individual form, and the specific content the result of individual insights and creativity, that work is always the product of a particular history and culture, and it always intervenes in a specific preconstituted space or spaces and connects with some aspects and not others.

Our work cannot help but be selective and incomplete however much we seek solace in identifying with a particular debate or intellectual community. There are always other debates, other communities, other literatures which we have not read and which could bring light to bear on the questions we are examining. This is only frightening if we aspire to a 'traditional intellectual' view of our role and do not comprehend that we are each (individual and lonely as we may feel as we struggle to produce something) de facto part of a much larger collective project to which we each contribute in a modest way. We *need* each other for the intellectual resources which we cannot individually possess given the functional necessity of divisions of labour.

This is related to a very real dilemma. How do we maximise the possibility that we are not each continually rediscovering the wheel or missing important insights which we may not even know exist? Is knowledge always developed in parallel but ultimately separate paths as Vico suggested? Or do we unavoidably have a spatially, culturally, historically specific road to follow, in part because of the inevitable limitations of our knowledge, but also – and perhaps more importantly – because of the need ultimately to relate to a specific national context? For example, when we are examining a question like childcare, and investigate 'good practice' in other countries, we have to return 'home' to analyse the specific conditions – political, economic, social, cultural – of translating these lessons into concrete practice in a national terrain. The longstanding custom and practice of human actors and structures and the intellectual and emotional connotations of words such as 'care' in a particular context constitute the real terrain in which knowledge is translated into policy and put into effect at 'home'. That is, in order to learn from *others* we have to know *ourselves* and what it is about our culture which is specific. This is something that others, who come from different cultures, can help make us sensitive to, on one condition, that we do not simply see them as lesser versions of ourselves or as exotic others who have nothing to teach us.

Yet recognition of the national rootedness of knowledge in, say, the UK and the US is rare unless it comes from these exotic others. How many articles in the social sciences specify the national parameters of what is presented unless it is analysis of the 'other'? How many while drawing data from just one national reality begin with the admission, 'In Britain' or 'In the US', (let alone specify a region within)? The specificity of those parameters are ignored, and the information and arguments contained within them are presented as universal. In the social science literature coming from the 'centre', broadly the Anglo-American world, numerous articles are written as if the author has no nationality, no ethnic specificity, indeed often no gender. As a Canadian colleague said to me recently of a piece of research, 'It is interesting, but the trouble is, the author does not realise that she is American.'[31] Specificity is of the 'marginal' and – be they Finnish, Polish, Bengali, or Afro-Caribbean – those defined as such must speak in the language of the marginal, about their own situation in workshops or on panels, are rarely acknowledged to have anything to teach more generally.[32]

This is a substantive problem. There is a real need to learn about the situation of other countries. Yet details must be repeated over and over because, however expert the audience, unless its expertise is narrowly specialist, that knowledge is inevitably circumscribed confronted by a different national reality. By the time the specificities of, say, the condition of old age pensioners in Hungary are described, any more general message is not heard.[33] The 'centre' acts as if it has nothing to learn about *itself* from these 'others'. The lack of training in lateral thinking and learning is both a cause and a manifestation of this, and we are unable to put our knowledge into question as perhaps valid but in a limited, specific way. Indeed, that is precisely why we *of necessity* must accustom ourselves to learning from others who are forced by their 'peripheral' situation to do just that.

And thus we arrive at an irony. Despite increasing possibilities of internationalising themselves, academics still in the main, as Gramsci pointed out some years ago, compose a social stratum which is 'narrowly national'[34] without recognising or acknowledging it. Given that all knowledge is an intervention in reality or informs such intervention, how much better it would be to incorporate the following insight.

> In reality, the internal relations of any nation are the result of a combination which is 'original' and (in a certain sense) unique: these relations must be understood and conceived in their originality and uniqueness if one wishes to dominate and direct them. To be sure, the line of development is towards internationalism, but the point of departure is national – and it is from this point of departure that one must begin. Yet the perspective is international and cannot be otherwise.[35]

Although Gramsci was intervening in a particular argument with regard to political strategy in the 1920s and 1930s, he might well have been describing the task confronting intellectuals today. For the danger now is that the illusion of internationalism or universalism – which comes as increasingly we have the opportunity to 'internationalise' ourselves and our work[36] – may make us even less sensitive to the national specificities of our discourses. The experience of 'incomprehension', once recognised, can help us to reflect back on our own specificities. We need to try to understand the complexities of societies other than our own. First, in order to achieve greater knowledge about ourselves. But the only way to do this is to get inside another experience deeply enough to cease reading it as exotic and to acknowledge it as valid, as authentic in its own right.

And second, this kind of understanding gives us a greater capacity to approach the differences and complexities inherent in our own societies. Within a given national terrain, if we want our work to serve the needs of a culturally, spatially, ethnically, racially varied community, divided into different classes and socio-economic strata, we must learn how to conceptualise the differentiated ways in which knowledge and policy issuing from a 'centre' relates to people coming to it from different places. A precondition for overturning the power relations constituted historically in any constellation of centre and periphery is to take the measure of our 'otherness', of our specificity. There is a functional reason, a *need* to see things through different eyes to understand ourselves as complex and multifaceted and to be sensitive to the inevitable partiality of our knowledge.

How then are we to enrich our discourse with meanings and knowledge from other traditions and yet retain contact and communicate with a more narrowly bounded audience? Work that breaks the boundaries of a debate and tries to move the discussion on risks losing contact altogether.[37] At the same time, if we want to increase the capacity of each of us to learn from the 'state(s) of the art' in different countries, on the one hand, and on the other to deprovincialise ourselves in the sense of going beyond the constrictions of our ethnic and national boundaries to learn from rather than arrogantly 'teach' those whom we conceptualise as marginal, we cannot but engage in a collective project which puts these objectives on the agenda.

WHY NOT TRY SOMETHING DIFFERENT?

We each play an *individual* role in such a project. We each combine material and reflect on it as unique individuals. If we are to succeed in carrying on, without illusions, we have to consider new ways of working and of understanding our role in addition to some of the more traditional ones. And we also have to find new resources, which have always been at hand but perhaps not appreciated, in order to help us to improve the quality of our knowledge and especially its authenticity. As individuals, we are each at the centre of a web of intellectual and cultural influences, practices, and institutions.[38] These are the conditions of our existence within which we, too, need to fight for a new creative space even if in a different context than Christa Wolf. If we authenticate the value of the uniqueness of that intersection with its creativity and sensibility, we will realise that we do not have to aspire to be clones of a presumed 'model' intellectual.

As we recognise the limits and the difficulty of the classic intellectual project, which is not to imply that it is of no value, why not validate other ways of working as well? We *need* to diversify our ways of working: to combine traditional, academic, disciplinary modes; to build on the best that they have to offer; to include a wider variety of sources – subjective insights, conversations, intuition; to provide new leads in order to refocus the kaleidoscope to reveal new patterns, to verify more abstract and generalised theoretical and empirical knowledge. Does it *feel* right? Does it apply to *my* life? If not, does it apply to others? Since we can never know everything or even achieve a universal overview, why not make use of the material we 'happen' to have at hand, not as representative or as a populist reduction of 'true' knowledge, but as raw material for analytical reflection, which provides 'food for thought' to be digested, to provide us with new sources of energy, and new insights which will help to enrich the intellectual agendas we set – and even make it more fun and exciting to tackle them? Intellectual work as making use of daily life, including our very own, enabling us to make a worthwhile, beautiful object out of the fragments, as art is still work, is still difficult, but it how much less alienating and schizophrenic it feels and how much more authentic the product.[39]

New ways of working can not only add to older traditions, but may help us to emerge from more than one cul de sac. What is being suggested is not the substitution of one single way of working for all others but a plurality of approaches which legitimises, amongst others, a creative, intuitive, subjective, but critical process which is open rather than closed. If we allow ourselves to consider a particular question by seeking whatever might aid our search for an answer – utilising insights and new understanding from different approaches, being open to the most diverse, casual and 'incidental' material, such as conversations, newspaper articles, novels, films, impressions, our own experiences, thinking and reflections – our thinking will be stimulated. Use of these new kinds of material is not a substitute for analytical thinking or hard work, but it will set off ideas, supply missing links and provide an intellectual stimulus that a narrower approach is unlikely to locate.

Obviously what you look for will already reflect a set of questions, institutions, feelings, interests, an intellectual structure, personal experience that reflect what is considered 'normal' in a particular national context. But using the raw material of everyday life to think theoretically and to think theoretically about the raw material of daily life, moving back and forth between the general and the particular is profoundly necessary.[40] The endeavour will no longer have its feet in the concrete of a 'discipline' although it will be grounded in another way, and it does not mean that it will not be 'disciplined' but that discipline will derive from a need for rigour in order to arrive at clear, if tentative, ideas about a chaotic world.[41] It will be on the edge, less secure or sure. Certain forms can be constraining but while giving them up can be frightening, it is also exhilarating: using what is immediate while keeping one's eyes on the horizon; listening to one's own mind and one's own feelings – not as *the* source let alone the sum total of knowledge, but as a critical check on the authenticity and scientific, yes, validity of academic work, and to bring new insights to bear on traditional work.

There are a range of objections to using one's own experiences and impressions for intellectual work. It is easy to sneer at books and newspaper articles which generalise and sometimes pontificate because of the author's immediate situation or point in the life cycle. And there are serious objections to work which simply reflects the everyday uncritically. The complexity and masked nature of social relations are never revealed to experience in an unproblematic way.[42] But none of these objections vitiate the aim to have a more grounded, sensitive, authentic knowledge, open to nuance, texture, colour, complexity, contradiction. The attempt to change academic practices is also an aspect of a project of transforming intellectual work which is a precondition for democratising the intellectual sources of policy and therefore for democratising society. Thinking about our work (our profession) and making links with how we and others live leads to the formation of questions about how this relates to the working and being of others. It is easy to assume that as specialist intellectuals we are on the top of a hierarchy. In fact, we are connected through a myriad of mediations to 'others', those non-professional intellectuals of daily life. Professional intellectuals in fact build on rudimentary skills which the vast majority of the population have and, however specialised they become, they can always learn from everyday practitioners.[43]

Adding to and improving our working practices can bring rewards. It can make our work more women-friendly and less isolated and alienating and help us to overcome unnecessary closure. There should be space for a way of working in the social sciences which approximates art and literature. And of course we do in fact tell stories, which is different from telling tales. Despite post-modernist criticism, which in other ways has been useful in opening up new ways of seeing, we cannot avoid a narrative of one sort or another, unless we abdicate any attempt to relate constructively to those problematic realities in which we and others live. Like Christa Wolf, we, too, engage in 'a process which continuously runs alongside life, helping to shape and interpret it'. As with her, *our* 'writing can be seen as a way of being more intensely involved in the world'.[44] To enrich our way of working, as we intervene in particular realities, using observation, not merely in a quantitative sense but qualitatively as a novelist would, reflecting on conversations, a play, a film, listening to feelings, opening ourselves to inspiration, can all be very productive. It allows us to pick up details and colour and to dig more deeply to unearth realities and complexities. The particular, the individual, the concrete can help us to produce *better* knowledge. As the writer Alexander Stille comments,

> If there is a virtue to the collection of individual stories, perhaps it is as an antidote to overbroad generalizations. The complexity of individual experience, with all its rough, solid three-dimensionality, can be a useful touchstone for the abstract, linear theories of history.[45]

The same applies to theories and analyses of contemporary society. Inevitably we will be forced to ask new questions and to offer new answers. We may begin to allow ourselves to employ different metaphors and alternative formulations, to employ epigrams, and to write notes, essays, reflections, using a much wider range of styles. Just as, in fact, many of the 'greats' have done. Our work may become more fun and what we write more readable. It might also become more adequate for investigating and gaining new understanding of the myriad textures of the multi-cultural, vibrant and contradictory societies which are the immediate context if not necessarily the object of most of our efforts.

NOTES

1 FACING THE FUTURE, EVALUATING THE PAST

1 Adam David Morton argues a similar point. See 'On Gramsci', *Politics*, Vol. 19, No. 1, February, 1999.

2 The phrase 'pessimism of the intellect, optimism of the will' on the masthead of the newspaper, *L'ordine nuovo*, which Gramsci edited in Turin after the First World War, and closely identified with him, was borrowed from the French writer, Romain Rolland.

3 See the long list of themes on the first page of the first notebook he wrote in prison. Antonio Gramsci, *Prison Notebooks*, Vol. I, New York: Columbia University Press, 1992, p. 99. In his excellent introduction, Joseph A. Buttigieg discusses Gramsci's early plans for the notebooks, op. cit., pp. 5–41.

4 See Joseph A. Buttigieg's discussion of Gramsci's method, op. cit., pp. 42–64.

5 One model for Gramsci, which might appear surprising, was the fictional character Father Brown, who put himself into the mind of the perpetrator of a crime and looked for the evidence which did not fit immediate preconceptions. See his reply to the notion put forth by a visiting American that detection is a science. G.K. Chesterton, *The Secret of Father Brown*, London: Penguin Books, 1974, pp. 12–13. To Gramsci, G.K. Chesterton's reactionary ideas were no barrier to profiting from useful insights. Even those whose politics are quite alien could provide keys to a better understanding. See the scattering of references to Chesterton in the indices in the main editions in English of Gramsci's work and in the critical Italian edition. Antonio Gramsci, *Selections from the Prison Notebooks*, London: Lawrence and Wishart, 1971; Antonio Gramsci, *Prison Notebooks*, Vol. I, op. cit., Antonio Gramsci, *Prison Notebooks*, Vol. II, New York: Columbia University Press, 1996; Antonio Gramsci, *Quaderni del carcere*, Vols I–IV, Turin: Einaudi, 1975.

6 This is illustrated by his notes on the intellectuals. See, for example, Antonio Gramsci, *Selections from the Prison Notebooks*, op. cit., pp. 14–25.

7 Perry Anderson describes the elusiveness of Gramsci's meanings as 'slippage'. 'The Antinomies of Antonio Gramsci', *New Left Review*, No. 100, Nov. 1976–Jan. 1977.

8 See the essay by Carlo Ginsburg, 'Clues', in Carlo Ginsburg, *Clues, Myths, and the Historical Method*, Baltimore: Johns Hopkins Press, 1989.

9 There are some parallels here with the efforts of Diderot and the philosophes in the *Encyclopédie* to reformulate political language, facing a similar need to avoid

the censor, and to communicate with a wider albeit elite public before the French Revolution. See Marisa Linton, Ch. 4, 'Making the Man of Virtue, 1755–1770' in *The Politics of Virtue in Seventeenth Century France*, unpublished manuscript. Gramsci makes frequent reference to this example of the need to change ideas as a prelude to transforming society. There are also certain parallels with Michel Foucault's use of inverted commas to unsettle assumptions about terms. See, for eaxample, his discussion of 'repression' (sic), in *The History of Sexuality*, Vol. I, New York: Vintage Books, p. 10.

10 See 'Introduction' and 'Women's New Social Role: Contradictions of the Welfare State' in Anne Showstack Sassoon (ed.), *Women and the State*, London: Routledge, 1992.

11 See Carole Pateman, *The Sexual Contract*, Cambridge: Polity Press, 1988.

12 See Ruth Lister, *Citizenship: Feminist Perspectives*, London: Macmillan, 1997 for a book which so successfully combines discussions of theoretical and policy issues.

13 Commission on Social Justice, *Social Justice*, London: Vintage, 1994. Although the Commission on Social Justice was set up in 1992 by the late John Smith, leader of the Labour Party, its membership included academics and other experts and people from voluntary, trade union and business organisations, from several political parties and without party affiliation. It was not meant to make party policy.

14 For an acute, and very funny, account of this period from the point of view of a Labour Party activist, see John O'Farrell, *Things Can Only Get Better. Eighteen Miserable Years in the Life of a Labour Supporter*, London: Doubleday, 1998.

15 But see Robert Jackson, 'Mr Blair's Italian Job' *The Spectator*, 12 December 1998. The author is a Conservative MP.

16 See Nicholas Timmins, 'The Death of Universalism', *Financial Times*, Wednesday 10 February, 1999.

17 This metaphor is referred to by Gramsci. See Antonio Gramsci, *Prison Notebooks*, Vol. I, op. cit., p. 323.

18 Antonio Gramsci, *Selections from the Prison Notebooks*, op. cit., p. 418.

19 Although there have been many changes in the ways in which schools are governed and are accountable to parents since this essay was first written, the themes discussed are still applicable.

20 See Liz Stanley (ed.), *Knowing Feminisms*, London: Sage, 1997.

2 THE CHALLENGE TO TRADITIONAL INTELLECTUALS

1 Antonio Gramsci, *Selections from the Prison Notebooks*, London: Lawrence and Wishart, p. 106 (hereafter *SPN*).

2 *SPN*, p. 144.

3 See Giuseppe Vacca, 'Intellectuals and the Marxist Theory of the State', in Anne Showstack Sassoon (ed.), *Approaches to Gramsci*, London: Writers and Readers Publishing Cooperative, 1982, p. 38. I would like to acknowledge an intellectual

debt to Giuseppe Vacca's work which set me on the path of this article, although I have taken a different route than his.

4 *SPN*, p. 9. In the original notebook the parenthesis follows directly.

5 This was confirmed to me in 1995 by several students at the Central European University in Prague who were from various parts of the former Soviet Union.

6 Ibid., p. 12.

7 *SPN*, p. 13.

8 Ibid., pp. 106–14. See also Anne Showstack Sassoon, *Gramsci's Politics*, London and Minneapolis: Hutchinson, 1987, Ch. 13, 'Passive Revolution: a Strategy for the Bourgeoisie in the War of Position'; Christine Buci-Glucksmann, 'State, Transition, and Passive Revolution', in Chantal Mouffe (ed.), *Gramsci and Marxist Theory*, London and Boston: Routledge, 1979.

9 For an excellent discussion of ideology defined in this way see Stuart Hall, 'The Problem of Ideology – Marxism Without Guarantees', in Betty Matthews (ed.), *Marx 100 Years On*, London: Lawrence and Wishart, 1983.

10 Quoted in Sergio Romano, *Giovane Gentile. La filosofia al potere*, Milan: Bompiani, 1984, p. 200.

11 Antonio Gramsci, *Quaderni del carcere*, Vols I–IV, Turin, 1975 (hereafter as *Q*), p. 689. This edition of Gramsci's writings is cited when there is no English translation yet available.

12 *Q*, p. 689.

13 *SPN*, p. 12. See also 'Gramsci's subversion of the language of politics' below.

14 Ibid., p. 13.

15 Loc. cit.

16 Ibid., p. 97.

17 Ibid., p. 12.

18 Ibid., pp. 10–11.

19 Ibid., p. 13 and elsewhere.

20 The specific target of his polemic is Michels. See Antonio Gramsci, *Prison Notebooks*, New York: Columbia University Press, 1992, pp. 318–26.

21 Ibid., p. 236.

22 *SPN*, p. 418. See also 'The politics of the organic intellectuals: passion, understanding, knowledge' below.

23 Romano, op cit., p. 204.

24 See Dawn Ades, Tim Benton, David Elliot and Ian Boyd Whyte, *Art and Power. Europe Under the Dictators 1930–45*, London: Hayward Gallery, 1995.

25 *SPN*, pp. 186–8, 196.

26 Lenin, 'What is to be Done', *Selected Works*, Vol. I, Moscow: Foreign Languages Publishing House, 1946, pp. 149–274.

27 Lenin, 'State and Revolution', *Selected Works*, Vol. II, Moscow: Foreign Languages Publishing House, 1947, pp. 209–10. Lenin's emphasis.

28 After the revolution, Lenin was soon aware of the dependency on experts. See for example 'The Immediate Tasks of the Soviet Government', *Selected Works*, Vol. II, op. cit., pp. 319–21. But the perspective was still as I have described above which goes back to 'What is to be Done' and 'State and Revolution'.

29 See 'Back to the future: the resurrection of civil society' below.

30 *SPN*, p. 238.

3 THE POLITICS OF THE ORGANIC INTELLECTUALS

1 See 'Beyond pessimism of the intellect: agendas for social justice and change' in this volume.
2 Antonio Gramsci, *Selections from the Prison Notebooks*, London: Lawrence and Wishart, 1971 (hereafter referred to as *SPN*), p. 418.
3 While the discussion of the party is of considerable historical interest, the theme of education has greater contemporary resonance and illuminates many of the wider issues we are discussing. On the party see Anne Showstack Sassoon, *Gramsci's Politics*, London and Minneapolis: Hutchinson and University of Minnesota Press, 1987, chs 7–10.
4 *SPN*, p. 10.
5 Ibid., p. 30.
6 Ibid., p. 10.
7 Ibid., pp. 10–11.
8 Ibid., p. 106.
9 Ibid., p. 26.
10 The humanistic school, he writes, was 'designed to develop in each human being an as yet undifferentiated general culture, the fundamental power to think and ability to find one's way in life', ibid., p. 26.
11 Ibid., p. 27.
12 Ibid., p. 26.
13 My discussion here presupposes Gramsci's notes on the organic intellectuals of the working class. See ibid., pp. 9–10 and below.
14 Ibid., p. 40.
15 Ibid., p. 27.
16 There was disquiet in elements of the fascist movement that it was not democratic enough. See 'Un partito che cambia la scuola' in Sergio Romano, *Giovane Gentile. La filosofia al potere*, Milan: Bompiani, 1984, p. 200. It was 'sold' by Mussolini as fascist but represented the attempt of this phase of the regime to build bridges to the liberals and the Catholics.
17 *SPN*, p. 40.
18 Loc. cit.
19 Ibid., pp. 40–1.
20 Ibid., p. 41.
21 Ibid., p. 27. My emphasis.
22 Ibid., p. 33. See also ibid., p. 9.
23 Ibid., p. 9.
24 Ibid., p. 41.
25 Ibid., p. 9.
26 Ibid., p. 15. This passage was added in the second draft of the note.
27 Loc. cit.
28 Ibid., p. 37. My emphasis.
29 See ibid., pp. 33–4.
30 The 'simple' was a traditional term. See Umberto Eco, *The Name of the Rose*, London: Harcourt Brace, 1984, pp. 204–5. The dialogue between William and

Adso is symptomatic of the importance the Catholic Church gave to the relationship between the people and specialist intellectuals and which Gramsci also discusses. Gramsci notes that intellectual or specialist is associated with the word 'chierico', i.e. clerk or cleric, while 'laico' is associated with profane, or non-specialist. See *SPN*, p. 7.

31 Ibid., p. 418.
32 Ibid., pp. 42–3.
33 loc. cit.
34 Ibid., p. 28.
35 Loc. cit.
36 Loc. cit.
37 *SPN*, p. 12.
38 Ibid., p. 13.
39 The following section is particularly influenced by Giuseppe Vacca, 'Intellectuals and the Marxist Theory of the State', in Anne Showstack Sassoon (ed.), *Approaches to Gramsci*, London Writers and Readers Publishing Corporative Society Ltd, 1982.
40 *SPN*, p. 5. My emphasis.
41 Ibid., p. 6. My emphasis. See also ibid., p. 10.
42 Ibid., pp. 5.
43 Ibid., pp. 5–6.
44 Ibid., p. 12.
45 Ibid., pp. 10–11. See also pp. 17–23 for a discussion of intellectual traditions in different countries.
46 Ibid., p. 10. See also *SPN*, p. 5.
47 Ibid., p. 10.
48 Ibid., p. 333.
49 Ibid., pp. 330–1. See also Ibid., p. 333.
50 Ibid., p. 334.
51 Loc. cit.
52 Loc. cit.
53 Gramsci's discussion of the relationship between the Catholic hierarchy and 'the simple' is a relevant illustration. Ibid., pp. 331–2.
54 See 'The challenge to traditional intellectuals: specialisation, organisation, leadership' in this volume.
55 *SPN*, p. 6.
56 Ibid., p. 335. See Vacca op. cit., pp. 46ff with regard to the USSR.
57 See Franco De Felice, 'Revolution and Production' in Anne Showstack Sassoon (ed.), *Approaches to Gramsci*, Ibid., and his *Serrati, Bordiga, Gramsci e il problema della rivoluzione in Italia*, Bari: De Donato, 1971.
58 See Mario Telò, 'The Factory Councils', in Sassoon (ed.), *Approaches*, op. cit.
59 My discussion in this section owes much to the extremely useful introduction and notes by Franco De Felice to Antonio Gramsci, *Quaderno 22, Americanismo e Fordismo*, Turin: Einaudi, 1978.
60 *SPN*, p. 317.
61 Loc. cit.
62 See Telò op. cit.

63 See Vacca, op. cit., pp. 64–5.

64 *SPN*, p. 317.

65 Loc. cit.

66 Loc. cit.

67 Franco De Felice, footnote 3, in Antonio Gramsci, *Quaderno 22*, op. cit., p. 114.

68 Ibid., p. 113.

69 *SPN*, p. 335.

70 *Q*, p. 1138.

71 Loc. cit.

72 *SPN*, p. 9.

73 Ibid., pp. 9–10.

74 Ibid., p. 10.

75 Gramsci writes that the

> problem of creating a new stratum of intellectuals consists, therefore, in the critical elaboration of the intellectual activity that exists in every everyone at a certain degree of development, modifying its relationship with the muscular-nervous effort towards a new equilibrium, and ensuring that the muscular-nervous effort itself, in so far as it is an element of a general practical activity, which is perpetually innovating the physical and social world, becomes the foundation of a new and integral conception of the world.
>
> (Ibid., p. 9)

76 Gramsci sums this up when he writes, 'from technique-as-work one proceeds to technique-as-science and to the humanistic conception of history, without which one remains "specialised" and does not abecome "directive" (specialised and political)'. Ibid., p. 10.

77 Ibid., p. 189.

78 Ibid., p. 418.

79 This is in fact possible because 'it is not a question of introducing from scratch a scientific form of thought into everyone's individual life but of renovating and making "critical" an already existing activity'. Ibid., pp. 330–1.

80 Ibid., pp. 168, 333. Gramsci examines the reasons people so often cling stubbornly to a common-sense view of the world when confronted by experiences and articulate arguments which contradict them by putting himself in their shoes. Ibid., pp. 338–40.

81 See Antonio Gramsci, *Selections from Political Writings 1921–1926*, London: Lawrence and Wishart, 1978, pp. 429–40.

82 See Stuart Hall, 'The Problem of Ideology – Marxism without Guarantees', in Betty Matthews (ed.), *Marx 100 Years On*, London: Lawrence and Wishart, 1983.

83 Ibid., p. 418.

4 GRAMSCI'S SUBVERSION OF THE LANGUAGE OF POLITICS

1 See, for example, Franco Lo Piparo, *Lingua, intellettuali, egemonia in Gramsci*, Rome: Laterza, 1979. Tullio De Mauro and L. Rosiello have written widely in the area.

2 For a useful summary of important facets of Italy's tormented history, see Alexander Stille, 'Eight Million Bayonets', *London Review of Books*, 1 January 1998, pp. 21–23. The high rates of illiteracy, despite formal schooling in Italian, were another reason for the continued use of dialects. Television, and military service, made major contributions to Italian becoming a functional language. Disaffection was most marked in the South, including Gramsci's birthplace, Sardinia. Many Italian novels and films portray the split between intellectuals and people and the curiosity which popular culture aroused. See, for example, the novel by Carlo Levi, *Christ Stopped at Eboli*, London: Ferrar, Straus, 1947, and the film directed by Francesco Rosi, for reflective accounts of an anti-fascist Northern intellectual exiled to a remote village in the South.

3 See Leonardo Salamini, 'Gramsci and the Marxist Sociology of Language' *The International Journal of Sociology of Language*, 32, 1981 or Utz Maas, 'Der Sprachwissenschaftler Gramsci', *Das Argument*, January/February 1988.

4 See, for example, Ernesto Laclau and Chantal Mouffe, *Hegemony and Socialist Theory*, London: Verso, 1985.

5 See 'The Challenge to traditional intellectuals: specialisation, organisation, leadership' in this volume.

6 Pasolini has written a sensitive piece on Gramsci's struggle with Italian as he moved from a Sardinian peasant milieu to industrial Turin. Pier Paolo Pasolini, 'Gramsci's Language,' in Anne Showstack Sassoon (ed.), *Approaches to Gramsci*, London: Writers and Readers Publishing Co-operative, 1982.

7 Antonio Gramsci, *Selections from the Prison Notebooks*, London: Lawrence and Wishart, 1971 (hereafter *SPN*). For example, see p. 13.

8 Antonio Gramsci, *Quaderni del carcere*, Turin: Einaudi, 1975 (hereafter *Q*), p. 1245; *SPN*, p. 377.

9 *SPN*, p. 137.

10 *SPN*, p. 168.

11 See the entry 'hegemony' in William Outhwaite and Tom Bottomore (eds), *The Blackwell Dictionary of Twentieth Century Social Thought*, Oxford: Blackwell, 1993 for a fuller discussion of the following points.

12 Stephen Gill and David Low, 'Global Hegemony and the Structural Power of Capital', *International Studies Quarterly*, summer, 1989, discuss the traditional use and argue that Gramsci's concept has greater explanatory power, as does Robert W. Cox, 'Gramsci, Hegemony and International Relations Theory: an Essay in Method', *Millenium*, No. 12, 1983. See also Robert W. Cox, *Production, Power and World Order: Social Forces in the Making of History*, New York: Columbia University Press, 1987; Stephen Gill (ed.), *Gramsci, Historical Materialism, and International Relations*, Cambridge: Cambridge University Press, 1993; and Stephen Gill and James H. Mittelman (eds.), *Innovation and Transformation in International Studies*, Cambridge: Cambridge University Press, 1997. Edward Said has used hegemony to indicate American international dominance through cultural means, see 'Identity, Negation and Violence', *New Left Review*, No. 171, September–October, 1988, p. 57.

13 See Perry Anderson, 'The Antinomies of Antonio Gramsci', *New Left Review*, No. 100, November 1976–January 1977; Christine Buci-Glucksmann, *Gramsci and the State*, London: Lawrence and Wishart, 1980, pp. 7–8.

14 *SPN*, p. 144.

15 *SPN*, pp. 12, 275.

16 *SPN*, pp. 12, 258, 262–3, 275. See also Anne Showstack Sassoon, *Gramsci's Politics*, 2nd edn, London: Unwin Hyman, 1987, pp. 109–19.

17 See my entry on civil society in Tom Bottomore (ed.), *A Dictionary of Marxist Thought*, Oxford: Blackwell Reference, 1983. A fuller and somewhat different albeit related discussion of civil society is found in 'Back to the future: the resurrection of civil society' in this volume.

18 In a paraphrase which recurs several times when he discusses passive revolution, Gramsci argues that the

> fundamental principles of political science [are]: (1) that no social formation disappears as long as the productive forces which have developed within it still find room for further forward movement; (2) that a society does not set itself tasks for whose solutions the necessary conditions have not already been incubated, etc.
>
> (*SPN*, p. 106)

19 *SPN*, pp. 8–9. The inverted commas are in the original.

20 When Gramsci writes that 'All men are intellectuals . . . but not all men have in society the function of intellectuals', he illustrates his point with the following example: '(Thus, because it can happen that everyone at some time fries a couple of eggs or sews up a tear in a jacket, we do not necessarily say that everyone is a cook or a tailor)', *SPN*, p. 9. This in a sense was the inspiration for the essay 'Dear parent . . .' in this volume.

21 *SPN*, pp. 188–9. See *SPN*, p. 187f and p. 188 for organic centralism.

22 *SPN*, pp. 188–90.

23 For just some of the relevant passages see Antonio Gramsci, *Prison Notebooks*, Vol. I, New York: Columbia Univeristy Press, 1992, pp. 323–4; *Q*, p. 1706; *SPN*, pp. 198, 214; and Anne Showstack Sassoon, *Gramsci's Politics*, op. cit., pp. 162–79 and 222–31. Note that the Columbia University Press edition will eventually reproduce all versions of Gramsci's notes, many of which were not available previously.

24 *Q*, p. 750.

25 *SPN*, p. 214.

26 ibid., p. 196.

27 *Q*, p. 1706.

28 ibid., p. 1706.

29 ibid., p. 1706.

30 *SPN*, p. 144.

31 Luisa Mangoni has an excellent discussion of how Gramsci developed his categories. See 'La genesi delle categorie storico-politiche nei Quaderni del carcere' , *Studi storici*, No. 3, 1987; G. Francioni provides insights into the order in which the notebooks were written in *L'officina gramsciana*, Naples: Bibliopolis, 1984.

32 See 'Introduction: the personal and the intellectual, fragments and order. International trends and national specificities', in Anne Showstack Sassoon (ed.), *Women and the State: the Shifting Boundaries of Public and Private*, London: Routledge, 1992.

33 See note 17.
34 See Mangoni, op. cit.
35 *SPN*, pp. 366, 377, 418.

5 EQUALITY AND DIFFERENCE

1 See the introduction and the essays in Anne Showstack Sassoon (ed.), *Women and the State. The Shifting Boundaries of Public and Private*, London: Routledge, 1992.

2 It is also a contentious issue academically. For example, Quentin Skinner's work which emphasises the importance of the historical context of the work of political philosophy has provoked controversy in the Anglo-Saxon academic world.

3 This was what the Italian idealist philosopher, Benedetto Croce, suggested should be done with marxism at the end of the last century.

4 As I argue above in 'Gramsci's subversion of the language of politics', this is what Gramsci does with a number of concepts such as intellectual, civil society, state, hegemony.

5 See Chiara Saraceno, 'La struttura di genere della cittadinanza', in *Democrazia e diritto*, No. 1, 1988.

6 See T.H. Marshall, 'Citizenship and Social Class', in *Sociology at the Crossroads*, London: Heinemann, 1963. The original lecture was an intervention in the debate about the post-war welfare state. Ruth Lister has made a major contribution to incorporating social rights into the discussion of citizenship. See Ruth Lister, *Citizenship: Feminist Perspectives*, London: Macmillan, 1997.

7 See 'Back to the future: the resurrection of civil society' in this volume for a full discussion of the points in the next few paragraphs.

8 Ibid.

9 Studying the voluntary sector, which is so hard to define, and which has had a very different history in different countries, can tell us much about contemporary change. Some implications for Britain and Hungary are considered in Anne Showstack Sassoon, in collaboration with Sue Conning, Vera Gáthy, Zsuzsa Széman, and Colleen Williams, 'Complexity, Contradictions, Creativity: Transitions in the Voluntary Sector', *Soundings*, No. 4, 1996.

10 See Joan W. Scott, 'Deconstructing Equality-versus- Difference: or, the Uses of Poststructuralist Theory for Feminism', in *Feminist Studies*, No. 1, 1988; and Ch. 1, 'Rereading the History of Feminism', in *Only Paradoxes to Offer. French Feminists and the Rights of Man*, Cambridge, Massachusetts and London: Harvard University Press, 1996. The gendered character of liberal thought is powerfully argued in Carole Pateman's forceful critique of the liberal concept of the individual as constructing the suppression of women, *The Sexual Contract*, Oxford: Polity, 1988.

11 I do not mean to ignore Foucault's argument or those of others about the constitution of relationships of power, of domination and subordination, through the establishment of modern state institutions and through the effects of social policy and the power of experts, or the influence, for example, in Britain of top level committees which justified the introduction of social reforms in terms, say,

of guaranteeing a supply of healthy men for the armed forces. See Pat Thane, *The Foundations of the Welfare State*, 2nd edn, London: Longman, 1996. I would simply stress the importance of a multidimensional analysis which avoids reducing the development of modern social policy to an expression of domination.

12 The highly sensitive nature of the relationship between equality and difference and the continuing power of sexual stereotyping to justify discriminatory practices was illustrated in the United States in a case brought by the Equal Employment Opportunity Commission against the retailer Sears, Roebuck. Sears successfully defended employing women in certain lower paid jobs by relying on the testimony of one historian against another that women have historically chosen certain kinds of work. See Scott, op. cit. and Alice Kessler-Harris, 'Equal Employment Opportunity Commission v. Sears, Roebuck and Company: a Personal Account', *Feminist Review*, No. 25, 1987. Alice Kessler-Harris was the historian who argued against the Sears position.

13 The post-structuralist and post-modernist literature on this is immense. For a good summary of some of the important arguments see Scott, 'Deconstructing Equality-versus-Difference', op. cit.

14 The feminist critique, of course, is not identical with and is not even always parallel to the insights coming from a discussion of race and ethnicity, and it would be important to investigate the differences. Amongst the by now large body of literature which challenges feminist work to go beyond ethnocentricity, an article which I found particularly stimulating is Chandra Mohanty, 'Under Western Eyes: Feminist Scholarship and Colonial Discourses', *Feminist Review*, No. 30, 1988.

15 The public/private dichotomy itself varies at any one time for different groups in the population. Chiara Saraceno points out that, whereas once those who did not have sufficient property or were of the wrong gender could not vote and therefore did not have a public role so that they were confined to a 'private' life, now the poor in many countries hardly enjoy a private sphere at all as the most intimate details of their lives are subject to public scrutiny. She extends some of Habermas's ideas in this regard. op. cit., p. 285.

16 I discuss the ideas in this section as well as issues relating to the welfare state at greater length in 'Women's New Social Role: Contradictions of the Welfare State', in Anne Showstack Sassoon (ed.), *Women and the State. The Shifting Boundaries of Public and Private*, op. cit.

17 Sweden produced a report on the implications of this perspective for social policy. See Marten Lagergren, *et. al.*, *Time to Care*, Oxford: Pergamon, 1984. The Nordic discussion has had a significant echo in Italy. See Laura Balbo and Helga Nowotny (eds.), *Time to Care in Tomorrow's Welfare Systems: the Nordic Experience and the Italian Case*, Vienna: European Centre for Social Welfare Training and Research, 1986. In both Italy and Spain the concepts of a politics of time and of the rights of daily life have influenced urban projects which aim to create more 'people-friendly' cities.

18 See the essay 'Beyond pessimism of the intellect: agendas for social justice and change' in this volume for my argument that many of these perspectives informed the Commission on Social Justice report, 1994, and Patricia Hewitt, *About Time*, London: Rivers Oram Press, 1993.

19 On the relationship between the concept of reason as it has developed historically and gender see Genevieve Lloyd, *The Man of Reason. 'Male' and 'Female' in Western Philosophy*, London: Methuen, 1984. See also Sandra Harding, *The Science Question in Feminism*, Milton Keynes: Open University Press, 1987. In France the work of Hélène Cixious and Luce Irigaray has been very important in this discussion. Irigaray has been influential in Italy. The Italian debates, which have been more political, have influenced the thinking in this piece. See Adriana Cavarero *et al.*, *Diotima. Il pensiero della differenza sessuale*, Milan: Libreria delle donne, 1987; the publications of the Libreria delle donne in Milan: 'Più donne che uomini', *Sottosopra*, January 1983; 'Sulla rappresentanza politica femminile', *Sottosopra*, June 1987; 'Un filo della felicità', *Sottosopra*, January 1989; Maria Luisa Boccia and Isabella Peretti (eds), *Il genere della rappresentanza*, supplement to *Democrazia e diritto*, No. 1, 1988. For an overview which gives an impression of the impact of the discussion on difference on a wide range of disciplines see Maria Cristina Marcuzzo and Anna Rossi Doria, *La ricerca delle donne. Studi femministi in Italia*, Turin: Rosenberg and Sellier, 1987.
20 Foucault of course provides an extensive critique of the effects of discourse in these processes. Criticism of what post-modernists call metanarratives or of the universalising claims of philosophy are not new, of course. In Britain they certainly go back to Hume and Burke. Much more recently the experience of Soviet communism, Nazism, and fascism, and the horrors of the Second World War and reflections on the limits of the claims of other forms of social engineering provided the backdrop for the work of Popper, Oakshott, and Berlin.

6 BACK TO THE FUTURE

1 For example Risto Alapuro, 'Civil Society in Russia?' in J. Iivonen (ed.), *The Nature of the Nation State in Europe*, Aldershot: Edward Elgar, 1993 and Vadim Volkov, '*Obshchestvennost*: Russia's Lost Concept of Civil Society', paper presented to the seminar 'Citizenship in Northern Europe', the Finnish Institute and the School of East European Studies, London, 20–1 September 1996 argue against F. Starr, 'Soviet Union: A Civil Society?', in *Foreign Policy*, No. 70, 1988 that civil society should not be extended to informal social or economic networks in the pre-Gorbachev Soviet Union. They suggest that these networks could be better understood as individual, particularistic coping strategies and now, in post-communist society, as illegal activities which in fact undermine the construction of a modern civil society under the rule of law.
2 Any intervention in an international debate is inevitably partial and positioned by language, training, and intellectual biography. Regretably I cannot take account of an important contribution in German to a better understanding of Gramsci's concept of civil society because of my lack of German; see Sabine Kebir, *Antonio Gramscis Zivilgesellschaft*, Hamburg: VSA-Verlag, 1991.
3 For example, Ernest Gellner, *The Conditions of Liberty: Civil Society and Its Rivals*, London: Allen Lane, 1994; Ernest Gellner, 'The Importance of Being Modular', in John Hall (ed.), *Civil Society*, Oxford: Polity, 1995; Michael Walzer,

'The Civil Society Argument', in Chantal Mouffe (ed.), *Dimensions of Radical Democracy*, London: Verso, 1992.

4 See John Keane, *Democracy and Civil Society*, London: Verso, 1988; John Keane, 'Introduction', *Civil Society and State*, London: Verso, 1988; John Hall, 'In Search of Civil Society', in Hall (ed.), *Civil Society*, op cit.

5 See, for example, Chris Hann, 'Philosophers' Models on the Carpathian Lowlands', in Hall (ed.), *Civil Society*, op. cit.; Nicos Mouzelis, 'Modernity, Late Development and Civil Society', in Hall (ed.), *Civil Society*, op. cit.; Philippe Schmitter, 'The Pros and Cons of Civil Society', seminar paper presented at Birkbeck College, University of London, 21 March, 1995; Peggy Watson, 'Gender Relations, Education, and Social Change in Poland', *Gender and Education*, Vol. 4, No. 1/2, 1992; Peggy Watson, '(Anti)feminism After Communism', in A. Oakley and J. Mitchell (eds), *Who's Afraid of Feminism? Seeing Through the Backlash*, London: Hamish Hamilton/Penguin, 1997; Peggy Watson, 'Civil Society and the Politicisation of Difference in Eastern Europe', in J. Scott and C. Kaplan (eds), *Transitions, Environments, Translations: The Meanings of Feminism in Contempoay Politics*, London and New York: Routledge, 1997.

6 See Attila Ágh, 'The "Triangle Model" of Society and Beyond', in Vera Gathy (ed.), *State and Civil Society: Relationships in Flux*, Budapest: Institute of Sociology, Hungarian Academy of Sciences, 1989; Attila Ágh, 'Citizenship and Civil Society in Central Europe', in Bart van Steenbergen (ed.), *The Condition of Citizenship*, London: Sage, 1994; Hann, op. cit.; Mouzelis, op. cit.; Watson, op. cit.

7 For example, Mouzelis, op. cit.; Philip Oxhorn, 'From Controlled Inclusion to Coerced Marginalization: The Struggle for Civil Society in Latin America', in Hall (ed.), *Civil Society*, op. cit.

8 Drude Dahlerup, 'Learning to Live with the State. State, Market, and Civil Society: Women's Need for State Intervention in East and West', *Women's Studies International Forum*, Vol. 17, Nos 2/3, 1994; Tuija Pulkkinen, 'Citizens, Nations, and Women. The Transition from Ancien Regime to Modernity and Beyond', paper delivered at the symposium 'Rethinking Women and Gender Relations in the Modern State', International Federation for Research in Women's History, Zentrum für Interdisziplinäre Forschung, University of Bielefeld, 3–6 April 1993. See also 'Equality and difference: the emergence of a new concept of citizenship' in this volume.

9 Watson, op. cit.

10 Z. A. Pelzcynski, 'Solidarity and the "Rebirth of Civil Society"', in Keane, *Civil Society and State*, op, cit.; Wlodzimierz Wesolowski, 'The Nature of Social Ties and the Future of Postcommunist Society: Poland after Solidarity', in Hall, *Civil Society*, op. cit.

11 Schmitter, op. cit.

12 Alapuro, op. cit., Volkov, op. cit.

13 Robert D. Putnam, *Making Democracy Work*, Princeton: Princeton University Press, 1993.

14 This is exemplified by Keane (ed.), *Civil Society and the State*, op, cit., especially 'Despotism and Democracy', and Keane, *Democracy and Civil Society*, op. cit.

15 See, for example, Perry Anderson, 'The Antinomies of Antonio Gramsci', *New Left Review*, No. 100, November–January 1976/7; Norberto Bobbio, 'Gramsci

and the Conception of Civil Society', in Mouffe (ed.), *Gramsci and Marxist Theory*, op. cit.; Jean L. Cohen and Andrew Arato, *Civil Society and Political Theory*, Cambridge, MA: Massachusetts Institute of Technology Press, 1992; Keane, 'Introduction', *Civil Society and State*, op cit.; Jacques Texier, 'Gramsci, Theoretician of the Superstructures', in Mouffe, *Gramsci and Marxist Theory*, op. cit.

16 A notable exception is Jean L. Cohen's recent work, see Jean L. Cohen, 'A Bid for Hegemony: The Contemporary American Discourse of Civil Society and Its Dilemmas', paper prepared for the conference 'Gramsci and the Twentieth Century', Cagliari, 15–18 April 1997.

17 For example, Victoria De Grazia, *How Facism Rule Women, Italy 1922–1945*, Berkeley: University of California Press, 1992.

18 This was graphically illustrated in the art of the period as shown in the exhibition 'Art and Power', Dawn Ades *et al., Art and Power, Europe under the Dictators 1930–1945*, London: Hayward Gallery, 1995.

19 See 'The challenge to traditional intellectuals: specialisation, organisation, leadership'; 'The politics of the organic intellectuals: passion, understanding, knowledge'; and 'Gramsci's Subversion of the Language of Politics' in this volume.

20 The one which is most noteworthy and which has influenced my own work is Giuseppe Vacca, *Pensare il mondo nuovo*, Cinisello Balsamo (Milano): Edizioni San Paolo, 1994.

21 Antonio Gramsci, *Selections fom the Prison Notebooks*, London: Lawrence and Wishart, 1971, p. 238.

22 Antonio Gramsci, *Selections from Political Writings (1921–1926)*, London: Lawrence and Wishart, 1978, pp. 426–32.

23 Antonio Gramsci, *Quaderni del carcere*, Vols I–IV, Turin: Einaudi, pp. 703. Reference is to the Italian edition when the note has not yet been published in English. The Columbia University Press edition, edited by Joseph A. Buttigieg, will eventually publish all notes as they appear, in their various drafts, in the original prison notebooks. The handwritten notebooks themselves are due to be available electronically.

24 Gramsci, *Selections from the Prison Notebooks*, p. 12.

25 Gramsci, *Quarderni del carcere*, p. 868; Gramsci, *Selections from the Prison Notebooks*, p. 260.

26 Ibid., p. 263.

27 Gramsci, *Quaderni del carcere*, pp. 2057–8.

28 One of Mussolini's achievements, in Gramsci's view, was to overcome the split between Church and state by promulgating the Concordat with the Vatican. This was an example of what Gramsci called a passive revolution in which large sectors of Italian society which had previously been excluded from the national project were now included.

29 Gramsci, *Quaderni del carcere*, pp. 1302–3; Antonio Gramsci, *Prison Notebooks*, Vol. I, New York: Columbia University Press, p. 7.

30 Keane, 'Introduction', *Civil Society and State*.

31 Gramsci, *Selections from the Prison Notebooks*, p. 170; Gramsci, *Quaderni del carcere*, pp. 752–6.

32 Gramsci, *Selections from the Prison Notebooks*, pp. 54, 264.

33 Ibid., p. 264.

34 Gramsci, *Quaderni del carcere*, p. 2058.

35 Ibid., p. 734.

36 Gramsci, *Selections from the Prison Notebooks*, p. 263.

37 Gramsci, *Quaderni del carcere*, p. 763.

38 Gramsci, *Selections from the Prison Notebooks*, p. 267.

39 Ibid., p. 283.

40 Ibid., p. 263.

41 Gramsci criticised an idealised view of a limited liberal state which some political forces in Italy had clung to from the Risorgimento on, pointing out that economic liberalism did not inevitably lead to refusing to take responsibility for a country's economic interests or modernisation, ibid., p. 160.

42 Ibid., p. 238.

43 Ibid., pp. 235–6, 239, 242–3.

44 Ibid., p. 268–9; *Gramsci, Quaderni del carcere*, pp. 1028–9.

45 Gramsci, *Selections from the Prison Notebooks*, pp. 268–9.

46 Ibid., p. 264.

47 Ibid., pp. 219, 221–2.

48 Ibid., pp. 132–3; Gramsci, *Quaderni del carcere*, p. 2108. See also 'The challenge to traditional intellectuals: specialisation, organisation, leadership' and 'The politics of the organic intellectuals: passion, understanding, knowledge' in this volume for more extended discussion of the points in this and the following paragraphs.

49 Gramsci, *Selections from the Prison Notebooks*, pp. 257–8.

50 Ibid., p. 263.

51 Gramsc, *Quaderni del carcere*, p. 1254.

52 Ibid., p. 734.

53 Gramsci, *Selections from the Prison Notebooks*, p. 12.

54 Ibid., pp. 160, 263–4, 403; Gramsci, *Quaderni del carcere*, p. 876. Although Gramsci carefully re-read and in parts re-worked and developed further various notes in prison, a process which is only evident in the 1975 Italian edition, and which is now becoming clear in the Columbia University Press edition, he never eliminated these contradictions, perhaps because of the apposite contradictions and complexities of the evolving state–society relationship. Perry Anderson simply reads what in fact are great insights as 'slippages', or antinomies, Anderson, op. cit.

55 This argument is developed more fully in Anne Showstack Sassoon, 'Complexity, Contradictions, Creativity: Transitions in the Voluntary Sector', *Soundings*, Issue 4, London: Lawrence and Wishart, 1996.

56 See, for example, Birte Siim, 'Engendering Democracy: Social Citizenship and Political Participation for Women in Scandinavia', *Social Politics*, Vol. 1, No. 3, Fall, 1994.

57 Examples might be the campaigns of family and friends to bring the perpetrators of the Lockerbie bombing to justice, to outlaw handguns in the UK which followed the shooting of young children and teachers at a school in Dunblane, Scotland, or by relatives of drug dependants in Italy to pressurise government to

control the drug trade. For this last see Gabriella Turnaturi, *Associati per amore*, Milan: Feltrinelli, 1991; Gabriella Turnaturi, 'Tra interessi e dignita', *Democrazia e diritto*, 1993.
58 Watson, '(Anti)feminism After Communism' and 'Civil Society and the Politicisation of Difference in Eastern Europe'.
59 Siim, op. cit.
60 Sassoon, op. cit.

7 BEYOND PESSIMISM OF THE INTELLECT

1 Will Hutton, 'Raising the Stakes', *The Guardian*, Wednesday 17 January 1996, p. G2.
2 Interview with Andrew Jasper and Sarah Baxter in *The Observer Review*, Sunday 10 September 1995, p. 2
3 See Antonio Gramsci, *Selections from Political Writings, 1910–20*, London: Lawrence and Wishart, 1977. The actual phrase came from the French writer Romain Rolland.
4 Gramsci refers to a piece written by Mussolini in the early 1920s, *Prelude to Machiavelli*. Antonio Gramsci. *Selections from the Prison Notebooks (SPN)*, London: Lawrence and Wishart, 1971, p. 276. See op. cit., pp. 125–43, p. 147, pp. 169–75, 247–52, 266–7, and 413–14 for further references. For a much fuller discussion see Benedetto Fontana, *Hegemony and Power. On the Relationship between Gramsci and Machiavelli*, Minneapolis: University of Minnesota Press, 1993.
5 Antonio Gramsci, *SPN*, op. cit., p. 171.
6 The classic statement is found in 'What is to be Done?', in *Selected Works*, Moscow: Foreign Language Publishing House, 1946.
7 He writes that one 'of the most important questions concerning the political party [is] the party's capacity to react against force of habit, against the tendency to become mummified and anachronistic. . . . Parties . . . are not always capable of adapting themselves to new tasks and to new epochs', Antonio Gramsci, *SPN*, op. cit., p. 211. I have a fuller discussion of these themes in Anne Showstack Sassoon, *Gramsci's Politics*, 2nd edn, London: Hutchinson, 1987.
8 See, for example, his criticism of the inability of the 'left' in the Italian Risorgimento to develop a programme reflecting popular demands. See Antonio Gramsci, *SPN*, op. cit., p. 61 and p. 168.
9 See Antonio Gramsci, *SPN*, op. cit., pp. 169–72. The question, he writes, 'is one . . . of seeing whether what "ought to be" is arbitrary or necessary; whether it is concrete will on the one hand or idle fancy, yearning, daydream on the other. The active politician is a creator, an initiator; but he [sic] neither creates from nothing nor does he move in the turbid void of his own desires and dreams. He bases himself on effective reality . . . to dominate and transcend it (or to contribute to this)', op. cit. p. 172.
10 See 'Americanism and Fordism' in Antonio Gramsci, *SPN*, op. cit., pp. 277–318.
11 See 'The challenge to traditional intellectuals: specialisation, organisation, leadership' and 'The politics of the organic intellectuals: passion, understanding,

knowledge' in this volume. For contemporary applications of some of these ideas see Ken Spours and Michael Young, 'Beyond Vocationalism', *British Journal of Education and Work*, Vol. 2, No. 2, 1988; and Michael Young, 'A Curriculum for the 21st Century: Towards a New Basis for Overcoming Academic/Vocational Divisions', *British Journal of Educational Studies*, Vol 40, No. 3, 1993.

12 See Antonio Gramsci, *SPN*, op. cit., pp. 237–8 and Anne Showstack Sassoon, *Gramsci's Politics*, op. cit., p. 93.

13 Radical is defined as 'Original, fundamental; reaching to the center or ultimate source; affecting the vital principle or principles; hence thoroughgoing; extreme.' *Webster's New Collegiate Dictionary*, Springfield, Massachusetts: Webster's, 1961.

14 Ross McKibbin, 'On the Defensive – Ross McKibbin Asks Who's Afraid of the Borrie Report, And Gets a Surprising Answer', *The London Review of Books*, 26 January 1995, p. 7.

15 Commission on Social Justice, *Social Justice (CSJ)*, London: Vintage, 1994.

16 *CSJ*, p. 16. See 'From realism to creativity: Gramsci, Blair, and us' in this volume. The Commission's terms of reference were:

> To consider the principles of social justice and their application to the economic well-being of individuals and the community; to examine the relationship between social justice and other goals, including economic competitiveness and prosperity; to probe the changes in social and economic life over the last fifty years, and the failure of public policy to reflect them adequately; and to survey the changes that are likely in the foreseeable future, and the demands that they will place on government; to analyze public policies, particularly in the fields of employment, taxation and social welfare, which could enable every individual to live free from want and to enjoy the fullest possible social and economic opportunities; and to examine the contribution which such policies could make to the creation of a fairer and more just society.
>
> (op. cit, p. 412)

17 *CSJ*, pp. 18–19. In his Singapore speech Blair argued,

> The implications of creating a Stakeholder Economy are profound. They mean a commitment by Government to tackle long term and structural unemployment. The development of an underclass of people, cut off from society's mainstream, living often in poverty, the black economy, crime and family instability is a moral and economic evil. Most Western economies suffer from it. It is wrong, and unnecessary, and incidentally, very costly. . . . The Stakeholder Economy has a Stakeholder Welfare system. By that I mean that the system will only flourish in its aims of promoting security and opportunity across the life-cycle if it holds the commitment of the whole population, rich and poor. This requires that everyone has a stake. The alternative is a residual system just for the poor. After the Second World War, the route to this sort of commitment was seen simply as universal cash benefits, most obviously child benefit and pensions. But today's demands require a more active conception of welfare based on services as well as cash, childcare as well as child benefit, training as well as unemployment benefit.

(Tony Blair, *New Britain. My Vision of a Young Country*, London: Fourth Estate, 1996, pp. 292–4). See also Tony Blair, 'A Stakeholder Society', *Fabian Review*, Vol.

108, No. 1, Feb. 1996. In a speech to Church and community workers on the tenth anniversary of the publication of the report, *Faith in the City*, published in *The Guardian*, Blair maintained that 'social justice is a necessity not a luxury. The most meaningful stake anyone can have in society is the ability to earn a living. So we propose education, employment and community initiatives for the young unemployed that would slash youth unemployment over a parliament. Benefit reforms would provide hope for the one-in-five workless households, trapped on benefit by a system designed for a labour market and family structure that no longer exists. A jobs, education and training programme for single parents would offer help to a group of people on a 16-year ticket to reliance on the state.' *The Guardian*, Monday 29 January 1996, p. 11. For a fuller version see Tony Blair, *New Britain*, op. cit., pp. 297–309. In Singapore, he argued that 'a life on benefit – dependant on the State – is not what most people want. They want independence, dignity, self-improvement, a chance to earn and get on.' op. cit.

18 *CSJ*, pp. 62–3.
19 Ibid., p. 64.
20 Ibid., p. 64.
21 Ibid., p. 3. For a summary of each 'revolution', see p. 64, p. 77, and p. 84.
22 Christopher Pierson, 'Doing Social Justice: the Case of the Borrie Commission', *Contemporary Political Studies*, Vol. 2, No. 2, 1995, p. 240. For just a few examples of critiques: G. A. Cohen, 'Back to Socialist Basics', *New Left Review*, No. 207, September/October 1994 (in response to the Commission on Social Justice discussion documents, 'The Justice Gap' and 'Social Justice in a Changing World' published prior to the report, London: Institute for Public Policy Research (IPPR), 1993); Editorial, 'Labour's Currant Bun', *New Statesman & Society*, 28 October 1994; Ian Aitkin, 'Borrie Ducks Commission to Explore', *New Statesman & Society*, 11 November 1994, p. 12; David Purdy, 'Commission Opts for Caution', *New Times*, 12 November 1994, pp. 6–7; Anthony Arblaster, 'Don't Follow the Tory Agenda', *Red Pepper*, December, 1994, p. 30; *Action for Health and Welfare*, Bulletin of the Welfare State Network, No. 2, 1994, pp.10–11; Megnad Desai, 'Borrie Is No Beveridge: Citizen's Income Now!', *Citizen's Income Bulletin*, No. 19, February, 1995; 'A Critique of the Report of the Commission on Social Justice', *Socialist Campaign Group News*, n.d.; Anne Kane, Ann Pettifor and Pam Tatlow, 'The Hijacking of Feminism', Labour Women's Action Committee, n.d.; John Pilger, 'Emily Wouldn't Like It', *New Statesman & Society*, 7 July 1995; (For responses to Pilger see Letters, *New Statesman & Society*, 21 July 1995, pp. 25–6.); Miriam David and Dulcie Groves, 'From Beveridge to Borrie and Beyond', *Journal of Social Policy*, Vol. 24, No. 2, 1995, pp. 161–2; Stuart White, 'Rethinking the Strategy of Equality: a Critical Appraisal of the Report of the Borrie Commission on Social Justice', paper for Institute for Public Policy Research 'Back to Basics' Seminar, 21 March 1995; Peter Townsend, 'Pessimism and Conformity: an Assessment of the Borrie Report on Social Justice', *New Left Review*, No. 213, Sept.–Oct., 1995. For a few examples of more positive discussion, excluding pieces by people who served on the Commission, see: Malcolm Wicks, 'A New Beveridge?', *New Statesman & Society*, 28 October 1994, pp. 18–21; Richard Thomas, 'Strong Welfare and Flexible Labour? Why Kenneth Clarke Is Wrong'; Christopher Pierson, 'From Words to Deeds: Labour

and the Just Society'; Fran Bennett, 'Ambition, Checked by Caution: the Commission on Social Justice Reviewed', all in *Renewal*, Vol. 3, No. 1, January, 1995, pp. 37–61; Shelagh Diplock, 'Recognition at Last. Women Should Not Allow the Borrie Report to Gather Dust on the Shelf', *Towards Equality*, The Fawcett Society, winter, 1995.

23 Will Hutton, *The State We're In*, London: Jonathan Cape, 1995.

24 See the letter from James McCormick and Carey Oppenheim in response to John Pilger's article, both cited in note 22 above.

25 See Antonio Gramsci, *SPN*, op. cit., p. 129, p. 168.

26 See Antonio Gramsci, *SPN*, op. cit., pp. 172–3.

27 See Townsend, op. cit. and Peter Townsend and Alan Walker, 'Revitalising National Insurance', *Fabian Review*, Vol. 107, No. 6, December, 1995.

28 I have to confess that I have personally done so in an earlier, youthful Trotskyest incarnation.

29 Anna Coote made some similar points in 'A Bit Too Much', in *The Independent*, 3 July 1995. 'In the fine print of his speeches, Blair is often a sophisticated, liberal social analyst. The sound-bites and the silences tell another story.'

30 On a broader note, Will Hutton has written that the report represents:

> (o)ne step nearer to genuine citizenship . . . a remarkable document, for throughout there is the point/counterpoint between the economic, social and political that must be at the heart of any reform programme. And if a *still* intellectually timid Labour Party could be persuaded to sign up wholeheartedly there would be a transformation of British political life – and a genuine threat to sleaze and social injustice at the same time.

Quoted in Ruth Lister, '"One step nearer to genuine citizenship": Reflections on the Commission on Social Justice Report', in *Soundings*, No. 2, 1996.

31 Ross McKibbin, op. cit., p. 6.

32 Loc. cit.

33 *CSJ*, p. 64.

34 This is well portrayed in the first two chapters of the report. Peter Townsend's criticism of a lack of attention to increasing poverty and social polarisation in the report is not justified. Nor is the kind of international strategy which he suggests is necessary by any means precluded by its perspective, op. cit.

35 The bestseller status of Will Hutton's book op. cit. and the success of Andrew Marr's *Ruling Britannia: the Failure and Future of British Democracy*, London: Michael Joseph, 1995 were indicative of the changing mood.

36 James McCormick and Carey Oppenheim, 'Options for Change', *New Statesman & Society*, 26 January 1996, pp. 18–21. They compare the *CSJ* with two other major reports: Joseph Rowntree Foundation, *Inquiry into Income and Wealth*, York: Joseph Rowntree Foundation, 1995 and Ralf Dahrendorf *et al.*, *Report on Wealth Creation and Social Cohesion in a Free Society*, London: Commission on Wealth Creation and Social Cohesion in a Free Society, 1995 which was initiated by the Liberal Democrat leader Paddy Ashdown. Another important contribution to the debate has come from Frank Field, *Making Welfare Work: Reconstructing Welfare for the Millenium*, London: Institute of Community Studies, 1995, although this stands out for the stress which is placed on the need to overcome the 'play the system' culture because of the existing incentives for

those on welfare to stay on welfare, and for taxpayers to feel they have an individual stake in pension and other funds, which it suggests should be in the hands of a non-state corporation. See a summary of his argument in Frank Field, 'Making Welfare Work – Assaulting Means Tests', *Fabian Review*, Vol. 107, No. 4, August, 1995. Malcolm Wicks has also argued that 'the Left cannot afford a lingering look back to 1979. For by the late 1970's Labour's welfare statism represented a faded and jaded project'; see 'A Modern, Democratic Welfare State', *Fabian Review*, Vol. 106, No. 6, December, 1994, p. 13 and Malcolm Wicks, *The Active Society: Defending Welfare*, Fabian Discussion Paper, No. 17.

37 It is the lack of depth of analysis to explain the reasons for the policy proposals they suggest which makes Peter Mandelson's and Roger Liddle's *The Blair Revolution – Can New Labour Deliver?*, London: Faber and Faber, 1996 much more part of the old Labour tradition than they might like to admit.

38 The way the report is organised gives a sense of its general perspective. In the section 'Strategies for the Future', the first chapter is 'Investment: Adding Value Through Lifelong Learning' which expands the notion of education well beyond schooling. 'Opportunity: Working for a Living' goes well beyond Beveridge's definition of full employment as full-time male employment with men earning a high enough wage to cover family needs (family wage) to consider the need for family-friendly employment practices, a minimum wage, etc. See for example, *CSJ*, p. 205. 'Security: Building an Intelligent Welfare State' argues for working with the grain of change to develop ways to combine work, benefits, caring, and education in new ways. See for example, *CSJ*, p. 223. 'Responsibility: Making a Good Society' concerns facilitating local initiatives for community regeneration, investment in children, and housing, whereas 'Taxation: Investing in Ourselves' makes the case for fair and acceptable taxation. None falls easily into the usual academic or government department categories. For illustrations of the report's down-to-earth tone see the page long letter from a lone parent in Belfast about her struggle to get a job and her description of how the benefit system undermines her once she finds one, *CSJ*, p. 238; narratives of different welfare to work strategies, *CSJ*, pp. 238, 256, 259; or 'Emma and the Learning Bank', *CSJ*, p. 146.

39 Of all the recent reports on reconstructing the welfare state and the economy only the Commission on Social Justice report places women's roles at the heart of its analysis. See James McCormick and Carey Oppenheim, 'Options for Change', op. cit., p. 18.

40 Anne Showstack Sassoon (ed.), *Women and the State*, London: Routledge, 1992. The book first came out in 1987.

41 In 'Women's New Social Role: Contradictions of the Welfare State', I talk about a male model of work which assumes that whoever is in fact employed, the premise around which paid work is organised is that another person has the main responsibility for household needs. In Anne Showstack Sassoon (ed.), *Women and the State*, op. cit. The term male-breadwinner model is, however, more widely used. See Hilary Land, 'The Family Wage', *Feminist Review*, No. 6, 1980.

42 I argue this more fully in 'Introduction: the Personal and the Intellectual, Fragments and Order, International Trends and National Specificities', and in my piece, 'Women's New Social Role: Contradictions of the Welfare State' in *Women and the State*, op. cit. Recent information reinforces this view. The *Financial*

Times, Tuesday 30 January, 1996, p. 2, reports that a European-wide survey shows that women

> with jobs make significant contributions to their household incomes. Fifty-nine per cent of employed women in the survey, covering France, Germany, Britain, Spain and Italy, provided half or more of the incomes of their households. Highest contributors were in France and Germany where more than one-in-three supply all the income, according to the survey by the Mori research organisation for Whirlpool, a US charity. British women were least likely to supply all the income. This may be associated with their relative concentration in low-paid, part-time work.

This refers to *Women: Setting New Priorities*, Whirlpool Foundation, 400 Riverview Drive, Suite 410, Benton Harbor, MI49022, USA.

43 *CSJ*, p. 3. Also Patricia Hewitt, *About Time. The Revolution in Work and Family Life*, London: IPPR/River Orams Press, 1993.

44 This concept derives from an essay by Yvonne Hirdman, 'The Gender System. Theoretical Reflections About Women's Social Oppression', *Kvinnovetenskaplig tidsskrift*, No. 3, 1988 (in Swedish). It attempts to take account of the social agreements which arise around the divisions of labour between men and women and between the state and family-households with regard to services, paid work, caring, and financial and other arrangements and which become part of a country's political and wider culture.

45 It is noteworthy that Townsend, op. cit., and Townsend and Walker, op. cit., despite recognising that poverty in old age is mainly a problem for women, treat these questions almost as asides. One of the contentious issues in the report is the suggestion that retirement should be equalised between men and women at 65. However, as with many of the policy proposals in the report, it must be taken into account that this is suggested within a perspective of facilitating periods of full-time and part-time work, if desired, of education and training, and of caring work over the life cycle without disruption of pension contributions.

46 See the letter from James McCormick and Carey Oppenheim to the *New Statesman & Society*, op. cit.

47 *CSJ*, p. 154. It should be noted that given that Britain had almost the worst child-care provision in Europe when this was written (see *CSJ*, pp. 122–3), one might reflect on how few car workers there are left.

48 *CSJ*, pp. 122–8.

49 *CSJ*, pp. 141–7. The report argues for the establishment of a learning bank for *all* to enable people to have the *right* over a lifetime to financial support for education and training, rather than devote government resources so overwhelmingly to the tuition costs of full-time students between 18 and 21 as at present.

50 See 'Equality and difference: the emergence of a new concept of citizenship' in this volume.

51 *CSJ*, pp. 28–9.

52 *CSJ*, p. 28.

53 As someone from Newcastle told the commission, 'Unemployment is not about why you lost the last job: it's about why you don't get the next one', *CSJ*, p. 154.

54 See, for example, OECD Center for Educational Research and Innovation, *Education at a Glance. OECD Indicators,* Paris: OECD, 1992; Robert Barrow,

'Human Capital and Economic Growth' in *Policies for Long-Run Economic Growth,* A Symposium Sponsored by the Federal Reserve Bank of Kansas City, Jackson Hole, Wyoming, 27–9 August, 1992; Ray Marshall and Marc Tucker, *Thinking for a Living. Education and the Wealth of Nations*, New York: Basic Books, 1992.

55 These arguments are echoed in Andrew Glyn and David Miliband (eds), *Paying for Inequality*, London: IPPR/Rivers Oram Press, 1994. See also David Miliband (ed.), *Reinventing the Left*, Cambridge: Polity Press, 1994.

56 *CSJ*, p. 223.

57 See Fran Bennett, op. cit. and James McCormick and Carey Oppenheim, op. cit.

58 Ruth Lister, op. cit., p. 7.

59 See *CSJ*, pp. 263–5.

60 See *CSJ*, pp. 17–22. See also the Commission's interim reports, *The Justice Gap*, and *Social Justice in a Changing World*, both London: IPPR, 1993. These latter two are criticised by G.A. Cohen, op. cit., while Stuart White, op. cit., provides a critique of ideas of social justice in the report itself. For other, earlier contributions to the discussion see Anna Coote (ed.), *The Welfare of Citizens. Developing New Social Rights*, London: Rivers Oram Press, 1992, and Raymond Plant, 'Social Justice, Labour and the New Right', Fabian Pamphlet 556, London: The Fabian Society, 1993.

61 On a different plane, which social and political philosophers should take account of, there is a clear recognition in the report of the need to invest in social capital and to involve local people to facilitate community regeneration, that is, to invest in creating those conditions which are needed to underpin citizenship rights and responsibilities. Ruth Lister comments that this last point has not received the attention it should, op. cit. See *CSJ*, Ch. 7 'Responsibility: Making a Good Society', pp. 306–73 which discusses social capital, support for children and families, and building strong communities through regeneration from the bottom up and reform of housing provision.

62 *CSJ*, p. 398.

8 FROM REALISM TO CREATIVITY

1 Jonathan Glancy, 'Who Would Live in a World Like This?', *Guardian*, 17 November, 1997, p. G11.

2 Tony Blair, 'Introduction: My Vision for Britain', in Giles Radice (ed.), *What Needs to Change. New Visions for Britain*, London: HarperCollins, 1996, pp. 3–4. These themes run through the election manifesto, *Because Britain Deserves Better* and Blair's 1997 conference speech. They are threads in speeches going back many years. See Tony Blair, *New Britain*, London: Fourth Estate, 1996.

3 Commission on Social Justice, *Social Justice. Strategies for National Renewal*, London: Vintage, 1994, p. 16.

4 Upon return from a visit to the Soviet Union in the early 1930s, the American radical journalist Lincoln Steffens claimed that he had, 'seen the future, and it works'. There was also, of course, the important, mainly Italian, cultural movement known as the Futurists.

5 See Dawn Ades *et. al.*, *Art and Power. Europe Under the Dictators. 1930–1945*, London: Hayward Gallery, 1995, the catalogue for the exhibit of art and architecture in Paris, Madrid, Berlin and Moscow in that period. This is not, of course, to deny the complex relationship with the past, and in particular with pre-industrial traditions of the different political forces, which is also made clear here. Some of these themes are discussed in 'Back to the future: the resurrection of civil society' in this volume.

6 Antonio Gramsci, *Selections from the Prison Notebooks*, London: Lawrence and Wishart, 1971, p. 172. It should be noted that the gender of the subject of verbs, e.g. 'he', is not necessarily specified in Italian as it is in English.

7 'I think it may be true that fortune is the ruler of half our actions, but that she allows the other half or thereabouts to be governed by us', Niccolò Machiavelli, Ch. XXV, 'How Much Fortune Can Do in Human Affairs and How It May Be Opposed', 'The Prince', from *The Prince and the Discourses*, New York: The Modern Library, 1950, p. 91. 'Men make their own history, but not of their own free will; not under circumstances they themselves have chosen but under the given and inherited circumstance with which they are directly confronted', Karl Marx, *The Eighteenth of Brumaire of Louis Bonaparte*, in *Surveys from Exile. Political Writings*, Volume 2, London: Penguin Books, 1973, p. 146.

8 Antonio Gramsci, op. cit., p. 129. It should be emphasised that only some of his writing on the political party is still relevant today and in any case requires lateral thinking if we are to appropriate his insights for a very different context.

9 See 'New Labour's gurus. The Apostles of Modernity' and 'New Labour, New Language', *The Economist*, 25 October 1997, pp. 36–9.

10 Gramsci, op. cit., p. 130.

11 Gramsci in fact uses traditional language and refers to 'party programme', op. cit., p. 129. However, see 'Gramsci's subversion of the language of politics' in this volume for a discussion of how he transforms much of the traditional terminology which he uses.

12 Gramsci, op. cit., p. 130.

13 Gramsci, op. cit., pp. 125ff.

14 Antonio Gramsci, op. cit., p. 129.

15 There is an enormous literature and debate about Gramsci's concept of hegemony. A brief introduction can be found in my entry, 'hegemony' in Tom Bottomore *et al.*, *A Dictionary of Marxist Thought*, Oxford: Blackwell, 1991, pp. 229–31.

16 Gramsci, op. cit., p. 172.

17 See, for example, Antonio Gramsci, op. cit., p. 418.

18 See, for example, Antonio Gramsci, op. cit., pp. 188–90; p. 211. See also Anne Showstack Sassoon, *Gramsci's Politics*, 2nd edn, London: Hutchinson, 1987, pp. 162ff; pp. 249–84.

19 Antonio Gramsci, op. cit., p. 268.

20 Antonio Gramsci, op. cit., p. 172.

21 Gramsci's notes on what he calls Americanism and Fordism are an intervention in these debates. Gramsci, op. cit., pp. 279–318.

22 Glancey, op. cit.

23 See 'Equality and difference: the emergence of a new concept of citizenship' and 'Back to the future: the resurrection of civil society' in this volume for fuller discussion of this point.

24 Gramsci, op. cit., pp. 279–318.

25 See Linda Weiss, 'Globalization and the Myth of the Powerless State', *New Left Review*, September/October, 1997; and Anne Showstack Sassoon, 'The Space for Politics: Globalization, Hegemony, and Passive Revolution', in Johannes Dragsbaek Schmidt and Jacques Hersh (eds), *Globalization and Social Change*, London: Routledge, forthcoming.

26 Antonio Gramsci, op. cit., p. 285. Also see p. 310–13. There is an interesting parallel with Gramsci's definition of the state as 'hegemony protected by the armour of coercion', op. cit., p. 263. Gramsci's concept of the state is a vast topic. For an introduction, see Anne Showstack Sassoon, *Gramsci's Politics*, 2nd edn, London and Minneapolis: Unwin Hyman and University of Minnesota Press, 1987.

27 See notes on 'Some Aspects of the Sexual Question', 'Feminism and "Masculinism"', and '"Animality" and Industrialism', Antonio Gramsci, op. cit., pp. 294–301. While some of his comments can be queried, his interest in these areas must have been reinforced by parallels with attempts in the Soviet Union and elsewhere to create 'new' men and women.

28 Antonio Gramsci, op. cit., p. 281.

29 Antonio Gramsci, op. cit., p. 317.

30 Antonio Gramsci, op. cit., p. 305.

31 Antonio Gramsci, op. cit., pp. 287–94.

32 Antonio Gramsci, op. cit., p. 292.

33 Antonio Gramsci, op. cit., p. 317. The full passage is worth considering:

> What is today called 'Americanism' is to a large extent an advance criticism of old strata which will in fact be crushed by any eventual new order and which are already in the grips of a wave of social panic, dissolution and despair. It is an unconscious attempt at reaction on the part of those who are impotent to rebuild and who are emphasising the negative aspects of the revolution. But it is not from the social groups 'condemned' by the new social order that reconstruction is to be expected, but from those on whom is imposed the burden of creating the material bases of the new order. It is they who 'must' find for themselves an 'original', and not 'Americanised', system of living, to turn into 'freedom' what today is 'necessity' . . . [B]oth the intellectual and moral reactions against the establishment of the new methods of production, and the superficial praises of Americanism, are due to the remains of old, disintegrating strata, and not to groups whose destiny is linked to the further development of the new method.

34 This is argued more fully in 'The politics of the organic intellectuals: passion, understanding, knowledge' in this volume.

35 See Antonio Gramsci, op. cit., pp. 106–20 and Anne Showstack Sassoon, Ch. 13, in *Gramsci's Politics*, op. cit. The terms come from conservative reactions to the French Revolution and its aftermath including, indirectly, the work of Edmund Burke. The notion that things had to change in order to stay the same has been

captured beautifully in Giuseppe di Lampedusa's novel, *The Leopard*, set during the Italian Risorgimento, which was made into a film by Visconti. Giuseppe di Lampedusa, *The Leopard*, London: Wm. Collins Sons & Company, 1960. The incorporation of left leaders by right governments and political forces after unification was known as 'transformism'. See Antonio Gramsci, op. cit., pp. 58, 97, 109, 128, 227.

36 Antonio Gramsci, op. cit., p. 114.

37 Antonio Gramsci, op. cit., pp. 106, 109.

38 Antonio Gramsci, op. cit., pp. 171–2.

39 Loc. cit.

40 Antonio Gramsci, op. cit., p. 173.

41 In fact, in an interview Blair gave to Martin Jacques for the *Sunday Times Magazine*, 17 July 1994, he said that at Oxford, 'I was very interested in political ideas. I was reading everything from Tawney and William Morris through to Gramsci and Isaac Deutscher.' Quoted in John Rentoul, *Tony Blair*, London: Little, Brown and Company, 1995, pp. 37–8.

42 The 1997 election manifesto is explicit about the need to 'renew faith in politics'. Tony Blair, 'Britain Will Be Better with New Labour', in *New Labour. Because Britain Deserves Better*, London: The Labour Party, 1997, p. 1.

43 Antonio Gramsci, op. cit., p. 133. A parallel is found in Gramsci's critique of the left in the Risorgimento for not having a concrete programme of government and not understanding the primacy of the crucial concrete policy issue of that time, an agrarian reform. This exacerbated another failing of the Italian left of the period, crude anti-clericalism, op. cit., pp. 62, 74, 78, 100–2.

44 Antonio Gramsci, op. cit., pp. 42–3. He also writes that in the first few years of school, 'in addition to imparting the first "instrumental" notions of schooling – reading, writing, sums, geography, history – ought in particular to deal with an aspect of education that is now neglected – i.e. with "rights and duties", with the first notions of the State and society as primordial elements of a new conception of the world which challenges the conceptions that are imparted by the various traditional social environments, i.e. those conceptions which can be termed folkloristic', op. cit., p. 30. I discuss these themes in 'The challenge to traditional intellectuals: specialisation, organisation, leadership' and 'The politics of the organic intellectuals: passion, understanding, knowledge' in this volume.

45 There is considerable consistency of vision in Blair's speeches before the election and extensive overlaps between him and other government ministers such as Gordon Brown, and also with the perspective of the Commission on Social Justice report. See Blair, op. cit.; Rentoul, op. cit.; Commission on Social Justice, op. cit. These ideas are further reflected in the election manifesto, speeches after the election by many figures in the government and also in a range of policies which are obviously, however, the product of many influences and requirements.

46 Michael Kenny, 'After the Deluge: Politics and Civil Society in the Wake of the New Right', *Soundings*, Issue 4, Autumn, 1996.

47 For a full discussion of the meaning of this term see Anne Showstack Sassoon, *Gramsci's Politics*, op. cit., pp. 119–25.

48 I discuss this more fully in 'Back to the future: the resurrection of civil society' in this volume.

49 Stuart Hall, 'Gramsci's Relevance for the Study of Race and Ethnicity', in David Morley and Kuan-Hsing Chen (eds), *Stuart Hall. Critical Dialogues in Cultural Studies*, London: Routledge, 1996. Hall stresses that, 'Gramsci was not a "general theorist" . . . . His "theoretical" writing was developed out of . . . [an] organic engagement with his own society and times and was always intended to serve, not an abstract academic purpose, but the aim of "informing political practice"', op. cit., p. 411. This essay is an excellent introduction to the nature of Gramsci's ideas as well as demonstrating his contemporary relevance.

50 Peter Hennessy, 'The Prospects for a Labour Government', in Giles Radice (ed.), *What Needs to Change*, op. cit., p. 289.

51 Antonio Gramsci, *Prison Notebooks*, Vol. I, New York: Columbia University Press, 1992, p. 323. Gramsci uses the metaphor of the conductor of an orchestra with regard to the legitimacy of divisions of labour within a democratic organisation of the party, but the point can be applied more broadly. Also see 'The challenge to traditional intellectuals: specialisation, organisation, leadership' and 'The politics of the organic intellectuals: passion, understanding, knowledge' in this volume. The Columbia University Press edition of Gramsci's work in prison presents all versions of all of Gramsci's notes, notebook by notebook. The introduction to the first volume by Joseph A. Buttigieg, translator and editor, provides an essential discussion of Gramsci's way of working and of key features of his thought.

9 RETHINKING SOCIALISM

1 See 'Subjective authenticity, cultural specificity, individual and collective projects' in this volume.

2 Although most of the context and many of the terms of Gramsci's discussion have been superseded, his writings on the party still have much to offer and influence in part what follows here. See Anne Showstack Sassoon, *Gramsci's Politics*, 2nd edn, London and Minneapolis: Unwin Hyman and University of Minnesota Press, 1987. Any similarity between the argument which follows and New Labour is purely coincidental, but it does explain why I have felt engaged positively with New Labour both in theory and in practice.

3 See Anne Phillips, *Engendering Democracy*, Oxford: Polity, 1991 for a thoughtful critique from a feminist perspective of the difficulties of political practice in small groups.

4 The extensive debate about how to define needs often fails to grasp the political nettle in an attempt to provide an baseline which can be defended. See L. Doyal and I. Gough, *A Theory of Human Need*, London: Macmillan, 1991 and Kate Soper's review article, 'A Theory of Human Needs', *New Left Review*, No. 197, January/February, 1993. Nancy Fraser has a good sense of the contested and constructed nature of needs. See 'Talking About Needs: Interpretive Contests and Political Conflicts in Welfare-State Societies', *Ethics*, Vol. 99, No. 2, January, 1989.

5 See 'Equality and difference: the emergence of a new concept of citizenship' in this volume for a fuller discussion of the points in the next two paragraphs.

6 Analyses of the changes being forced on the public sector and a critical re-evaluation of the assumptions of much modern management and organisational theory are rich sources for anyone trying to think through the theoretical implications of current developments. See for example, *New Forms of Public Administration, IDS Bulletin,* Vol 23, No. 4, October, 1992. 'Back to the future: the resurrection of civil society' in this volume has a fuller discussion on civil society.

7 See Dave Osborne and Ted Gaebler, *Reinventing Government,* Reading, Mass-achusetts: Addison-Wesley, 1992.

8 See Wendy Thomson, 'Realising Rights Through Local Service Contracts' in Anna Coote (ed.), *The Welfare of Citizens,* London: Rivers Oram Press, 1992 and Wendy Thomson, 'Local Experience of Managing Quality', in Ian Sanderson (ed.), *The Management of Quality in Local Government,* London, 1992.

9 See, for example, Nina Biehal, Mike Fisher, Peter Marsh, Eric Sainsbury, 'Rights and Social Work', in Anna Coote (ed.), op. cit.

10 There are many examples of such 'user led' services, such as one which is consistently threatened by under funding, the North London community mental health support service organised by a voluntary agency, the Family Welfare Association.

11 Many local authorities have made great strides in trying to ensure that services are run by people who reflect the ethnic mix of the local community and respond to specific needs in ways easily and comfortably accessible to different groups. In addition, although there is a long way to go, a number of voluntary agencies are beginning to take on board the lack of fit between how they work and what they offer, on the one hand, and the needs of ethnic minorities on the other.

12 See 'The challenge to traditional intellectuals: specialisation, organisation, leadership' and 'The politics of the organic intellectuals: passion, understanding, knowledge' in this volume. For a beautiful essay about Gramsci's creative way of working see Joseph A. Buttigieg, Introduction to Antonio Gramsci, *Prison Notebooks,* Vol. I, New York: Columbia University Press, 1992.

13 Of course all children have *two* parents, whether separated, or divorced, or never married, and another part of the picture has to do with developing strategies for enabling and ensuring that men fulfill their responsibilities as fathers.

14 See 'Equality and difference: the emergence of a new concept of citizenship' in this volume.

15 See Denise Riley's rich and complex discussion, *War in the Nursery,* London: Virago, 1983.

16 Of course many parents in other circumstances made even more constrained decisions, for example, in sending Jewish children to Britain from Nazi Germany and Austria. The psychological effects have often extended across several generations. See Diane Samuels' play *Kindertransport,* New York: Penguin, Putnam Inc., 1995.

17 In Prague, another friend, a Czech woman without children, commented to me that in the Czech Republic people would no sooner do without nurseries than without hospitals.

10 DEAR PARENT . . .

1 See 'The challenge to traditional intellectuals: specialisation, organisation, leadership' and 'The politics of the organic intellectuals: passion, understanding, leadership' in this volume.

2 Full-time schooling in the UK, which still has very little pre-school provision, begins at 5. Before that age, when the age of the youngest dependent child is 0–4, 54 per cent of women are economically active, that is, in work or seeking work, and of those in work, 65 per cent work part time; 5–10, 70 per cent are economically active, 68 per cent work part time; 11 and over, 80 per cent are economically active, 55 per cent part time. UK Labour Force Survey, spring 1996, Office for National Statistics. These features of women's economic activity reflect a long-term trend. A few years before this piece was written, the General Household Survey Preliminary Results for 1981, calculated somewhat differently, indicated that 30 per cent of women were in paid work at least part time even before their youngest child was at school, which rose to 62 per cent for the 5–9 age group, and 71 per cent over 10.

3 See 'From realism to creativity: Gramsci, Blair and us' in this volume.

4 This is one reason such reports were introduced.

5 This is discussed more fully in 'The challenge to traditional intellectuals: specialisation, organisation, leadership' and 'The politics of the organic intellectuals: passion, understanding, knowledge' in this volume.

6 For wider discussion of the roles of mothers, parents and family more generally in education see M.E. David, *The State, Family and Education*, London: Routledge and Kegan Paul, 1980; M.E. David, *Parents, Gender and Educational Reform*, Cambridge: Polity Press, 1993; M.E. David, 'Parental Wishes Versus Parental Choice: the 1944 Educational Act 50 Years On', *History of Education*, Vol. 24, No. 3, 1995; M.E. David, A. West and J. Ribbens, *Mother's Intuition? Choosing Secondary Schools*, London: Falmer Press, 1994.

11 SUBJECTIVE AUTHENTICITY, CULTURAL SPECIFICITY, INDIVIDUAL AND COLLECTIVE PROJECTS

1 Those trained in anthropology or psychoanalysis are probably amongst those most sensitive to a number of the themes discussed here. I would stress trained in a professional sense here. Recent academic uses of psychoanalytical theory has not in the main meant that self-reflection about one's own work is noticeable. For examples of a reflexive practice see, on the one hand, Christiane Olivier, *Jocasta's Children,* London: Routledge, 1989, and on the other, G.A. Cohen, 'Forces and Relations of Production', in *Marx: a Hundred Years On,* edited by Betty Matthews, London: Lawrence and Wishart, 1983 and 'The Future of a Disillusion', *New Left Review,* No. 190, November–December, 1991.

2 Christa Wolf, *The Fourth Dimension: Interviews with Christa Wolf*, London: Verso, 1987, p. 20. See also Elizabeth Mittman, 'Christa Wolf's Signature in and

on the Essay: Women, Science, and Authority', in Ruth-Ellen Boetcher Joeres and Elizabeth Mittman (eds), *The Politics of the Essay. Feminist Perspectives*, Bloomington and Indianapolis: Indiana University Press, 1993.

3 Op. cit., p. 21.

4 See the concise and extremely interesting introduction by Karin McPherson in Wolf, *op.cit.* See also Mittman, op. cit., pp. 98–9. She points out that the title in German is literally 'Reading and Writing' stressing the process itself, op. cit., p. 111.

5 Christa Wolf's novels, *The Quest for Christa T.*, London: Virago, 1982; *A Model Childhood*, London: Virago Press, 1983; *No Place on Earth*, London: Virago, 1983; and *Cassandra. A Novel and Four Essays*, London: Virago, 1984 demonstrate her approach. The essays in *Cassandra* which were originally lectures are particularly explicit. *Accident*, London: Virago, 1989 is a reflection on Chernobyl.

6 For just one example, see Anne Opie, 'Qualitative Research, Appropriation of the "Other" and Empowerment', *Feminist Review*, No. 40, spring, 1992.

7 See, for example, Liz Stanley (ed.), *Knowing Feminisms*, London: Sage, 1997. In the following discussion I am influenced by the Italian debates on difference. For a presentation in English of these debates see Paola Bono and Sandra Kemp (eds), *Italian Feminist Thought, A Reader*, Oxford: Basil Blackwell, 1991.

8 Just a few examples of what is by now an immense literature are Genevieve Lloyd, *The Man of Reason. 'Male' and 'Female' in Western Philosophy*, London: Methuen, 1984; Sandra Harding, *The Science Question in Feminism*, Milton Keynes: Open University Press, 1987; and Rosi Braidotti, *Patterns of Dissonance*, Oxford: Polity, 1991. The Italian debates are also very interesting. See Bono and Kemp, op. cit. In a different light, Kari Waerness has also challenged the notions of rationality which dominate social science discourse. See 'The Rationality of Caring', in Anne Showstack Sassoon (ed.), *Women and the State*, London: Routledge, 1992.

9 Dorothy E. Smith, *The Everyday World as Problematic. A Feminist Sociology*, Boston: Northeastern University Press, 1987. She continues the discussion in *The Conceptual Practices of Power. A Feminist Sociology of Knowledge*, Toronto: University of Toronto Press, 1990.

10 For a useful summary of Smith's ideas see Dorothy E. Smith, 'Feminist Reflections on Political Economy', *Studies in Political Economy,* No. 30, autumn, 1989; for a sympathetic but critical review, see Meg Luxton and Sue Findlay, 'Is the Everyday World the Problematic? Reflections on Smith's Method of Making Sense of Women's Experience', in the same issue.

11 See Gayatri Chakravorty Spivak, *In Other Worlds. Essays in Cultural Politics*, London: Routledge, 1988; and *The Post-Colonial Critic. Interviews, Strategies, Dialogues*, edited by Sarah Harasym, London: Routledge, 1990. (I have had a similar experience in an ironic way. Although I have lived the whole of my adult life in Britain, most of my work is oriented toward Europe, and I visit the United States only occasionally and mainly for family visits, because I grew up there and still have an American accent, others pigeon hole me, and I get asked all sorts of questions as if I were an expert on the US – on everything from the debate on 'political correctness' to American book contracts. It was only in the course of

writing this piece that I have realised why I am irritated at this – it reminds me that I am viewed as an outsider.) For a very different and very funny depiction of the contrasts between the academic worlds of the US and Britain, see David Lodge's novels, *Changing Places*, London: Penguin, 1976 and *Small World*, London: Penguin, 1985.

12 Spivak, *The Post-Colonial Critic*, op. cit., pp. 40–1.

13 See the introduction to *The Fourth Dimension*, op. cit., and Mittman, op. cit.

14 Wolf, *The Fourth Dimension*, op. cit., p. 22.

15 Loc. cit.

16 See Mittman, op .cit., pp. 98–9.

17 Wolf, op. cit., p.75.

18 An exception which is an excellent illustration of a successful grounding of a theoretical and analytical discussion in thoughtful and honest reflection on problems thrown up in her experience in the women's movement is Anne Phillips, *Engendering Democracy*, Oxford: Polity Press, 1991. Feminism has certainly created a space for this kind of combination as Smith and many others demonstrate. The question of who is reading is more elusive and dealt with more explicitly in literature. The role of the reader in 'constructing' or 'deconstructing' a piece of literature is a major theme both in literary criticism and in pieces of fiction where writers like Italo Calvino or Umberto Eco, to mention only two, can make the reader feel like a plaything.

19 In the context of discussing the essay as a form, Barbara Sichtermann points out the gendered dimensions of this fear. She writes, 'Whoever dares to enter the public sphere with nothing but a personal view of things depends on being heard by the public because he is who he is. Women generally do not have such firm faith in the extensiveness of their personal aura. . . . Generally speaking, when they speak up without institutional legitimization, women are not heard. When they take the floor in their own name, women are heard more seldom, more poorly, imprecisely, and fragmentarily than men, 'Woman Taking Speculation into Her Own Hands', in Ruth-Ellen B. Joeres and Elizabeth Mittman, op. cit., p. 90. See also Mittmann, op. cit.; and Tuzyline Jita Allen, 'A Voice of One's Own. Implications of Impersonality in the Essays of Virginia Woolf and Alice Walker', in Ruth-Ellen B. Joeres and Elizabeth Mittman, *op. cit.*

20 See 'The challenge to traditional intellectuals: specialisation, organisation, leadership' and 'The politics of the organic intellectual: passion, understanding, knowledge' in this volume.

21 And of course, Christa Wolf's insistence on a space for subjective authenticity was part of overcoming similarly reduced notions that artistic production was only valid as political intervention while 'science' was reified. See introduction to Wolf, op. cit. and Mittman, op. cit.

22 The classic challenge to this is found in C. Wright Mills, *The Sociological Imagination*, Oxford: Oxford University Press, 1959. It is no accident that the dominance of this approach was fundamentally if not fatally undermined in the 1960s as groups in American society whose voices were not adequately being heard took to the streets. See Peter Bachrach, *The Theory of Democratic Elitism*, London: University of London Press, 1969, for a defence of the value of political participation which was also a theme in Carole Pateman's early book, *Particip-*

ation and Democratic Theory, Cambridge: Cambridge University Press, 1970. Robert Dahl's revision of his previous ideas was an honest reflection on the adequacy of a democracy or a democratic theory posited on limited particip- ation. Robert Dahl, *A Preface to Economic Democracy*, Cambridge: Cambridge University Press, 1985.

23 See 'The challenge to traditional intellectuals: specialisation, organisation, leadership' and 'The politics of the organic intellectuals: passion, understanding, knowledge' in this volume.

24 This should be mapped country by country.

25 That is probably why work like that of Gayatri Chakravorty Spivak or others who have a place in academia but do not play the usual academic game is so shocking. There can be severe penalties for not doing so, like not getting a permanent job or promotion. What it could be argued is missing from much such work, on the other hand, is accessibility. It is no mean feat to achieve when you are breaking boundaries, but it is nonetheless necessary if the breakthrough is to be effective, mediated by others to a wider audience, and to result in a shift in understanding. However this in fact implies a certain concept of the relationship between intellectual production and the 'other' which may not be shared by Spivak or others.

26 This tradition is far from homogeneous, of course. Rousseau distrusted represent- ation and sought the authentic voice, the search for laws only applies to some thinkers, and Spinoza provides still another approach to connecting the inner and outer worlds.

27 See Barbara Sichtermann, op. cit., Mittman, op. cit., and Allan, op. cit. Such vulnerability can disappear, of course, if the author is well respected. An example of a reflective use of personal experience is found in Eric Hobsbawm's weaving of his own memories into his account of the twentieth century. Eric Hobsbawm, *Age of Extremes. The Short Twentieth Century. 1914–1991*, London: Michael Joseph, 1994.

28 Some of the most interesting discussions in this regard come from debates in human geography. Someone who has given me 'lateral' inspiration is Doreen Massey. See her piece, 'The Political Place of Locality Studies', in Doreen Massey, *Space, Place, and Gender*, Cambridge: Polity, 1994.

29 That it is not only a question of linguistic knowledge became apparent to me when I was teaching in Canada and saw how pieces written by French reading and speaking Anglophone intellectuals did not refer to Francophone literature because the debates are so separate.

30 Spivak, op. cit. See also Edward Said, *Orientalism*, London: Penguin, 1978; Edward Said, 'Narrative and Geography', *New Left Review*, No. 180, March/April, 1990.

31 No one seems to escape this. I wonder if Gayatri Spivak noticed the irony on the back cover of *The Post-Colonial Critic*, op. cit. where she is referred to as 'one of our [sic] best known cultural and literary theorists'. I could not help but wonder who the 'our' was referring to, the US, or English speaking readership world- wide, or? Nor is it specified that Trent University to which the editor, Sarah Harasym, is attached is in Canada, for 'provincials' in other continents who might not know.

32 This was brought home to me when I heard a paper by a Finnish feminist

researcher describing a women's studies conference in New York where third world women talked about and mainly to themselves in discussions about their realities, women of colour were told not to complain about the white shade of the main panel, women from Central and Eastern Europe were there to learn about Western feminism, with little notion that 'we' might learn about and from 'them', and the Finns did not feel they fit anywhere. The point is not to moralise but instead to ask what this represents and how to overcome it since the knowledge and messages lost make us all poorer. Chris Corrin describes a similar experience, Chris Corrin, 'Bordering on Change', in Liz Stanley (ed.), *Knowing Feminisms*, London: Sage, 1997, p. 88.

33 This is a concern of anyone who does transnational work with an empirical base.
34 Antonio Gramsci, *Selections from the Prison Notebooks*, London: Lawrence and Wishart, 1971, p. 241.
35 Ibid., p. 240.
36 In fact, although probably a greater number of people read more than one language now, I would guess that it is a smaller proportion of those in academia than previously, let alone compared to the time when Latin was a mode of communication amongst educated élites in Europe. In any case, as the Canadian example above shows, linguistic ability is a precondition but not a guarantee for de-provincialisation.
37 This, I think, was one of Gramsci's greatest worries, and one reason that his terminology is quite straightforward although many of his ideas are novel and complex and words are used in both traditional and very new ways. Of course, this in itself can also cause confusion. See 'Gramsci's subversion of the language of politics' in this volume.
38 This was expressed in slightly different terms by Gramsci when he explains the sense in which we are historically determined, 'i.e. man who has developed, and who lives, in certain conditions in a particular social complex or totality of social relations', op. cit., p. 244, and by Brecht, who wrote of 'a causal social nexus'. Quoted in Wolf, op. cit., p. 23. But if these 'masters' have something to say to me, it is because they 'make sense' of something I really feel, that is, that each of us is at *a centre*, as living, developing, organic beings, feeling the threads which connect us to so many others and which help to define us, in their unique combination, as finite.
39 Laura Balbo's metaphor of patchwork quilts is particularly appropriate here. See 'Crazy Quilts: Rethinking the Welfare State Debate from a Woman's Point of View', in Anne Showstack Sassoon (ed.), *Women and the State*, op. cit. In my introduction I discuss how one of the motivations for putting the collection together was to find material which reflected more authentically aspects of women's experience which the existing debate missed. See 'Introduction: the Personal and the Intellectual, International Trends and National Specificities', *ibid.*
40 If this approach has something of historical materialism about it, via Gramsci in my case, so be it.
41 Gramsci's writing on the democratic roots of discipline, although they are addressed to question of organisation, come to mind. See *Quaderni del carcere*, Turin: Einaudi, 1978, p. 1706.

42 See Dorothy E. Smith, *The Everyday World as Problematic*, op. cit., pp. 122–43. For a different discussion of the problems of referring to experience, especially with reference to making the 'other' visible, see Joan W. Scott, 'Experience', in Judith Butler and Joan W. Scott (eds), *Feminists Theorize the Political*, London: Routledge, 1992.
43 See 'The challenge to traditional intellectuals: specialisation, organisation, leadership' and 'The politics of the organic intellectuals: passion, understanding, knowledge' in this volume.
44 Wolf, *The Fourth Dimension*, op. cit., p. 21.
45 Alexander Stille, *Benevolence and Betrayal. Five Italian Jewish Families under Fascism*, London: Jonathan Cape, 1992, p. 16.

INDEX